CEYLON

THE LAND OF ETERNAL CHARM

CEYLON

THE LAND OF ETERNAL CHARM

ALI FOAD TOULBA

WITH FOREWORD BY

L. E. BLAZE

WITH 87 ILLUSTRATIONS

GYAN

Published by

GYAN

Gyan Publishing House
5, Ansari Road
Daryaganj, New Delhi-110002
Phone: 011-47034999, 9811692060
E-mail: books@gyanbooks.com

Distribution Network
gyanbooks.com
India, USA, Canada, UK, Australia, France

ISBN : 978-81-212-3207-4 (PB)
First Published, London, 1926

2nd Impression 2020

Printed at: Gyan Press, Delhi.

Ceylon
The Land of Eternal Charm
Author: Ali Foad Toulba

Dedicated, by Permission

to

H.E. DR. HASSAN NASHAT PASHA, LL.D.

Acting Chief of the Cabinet of H.M. the King of Egypt

FOREWORD

It is not easy for me to write a "Foreword" to the book of one whom I knew as a boy, and have since learnt to honour as a loyal and attached friend. But I have read this book in manuscript with intense interest, not only because it relates to the country in which I live, but because of the freshness and enthusiasm, as well as the marked ability with which the author describes the attractions of an Island which has charmed every visitor to its shores. Something of the author's enthusiasm will irresistibly convey itself to the reader of the book, and if a perusal of it results in the extension of friendly communication between the people of Egypt and the people of Ceylon, much good will be done.

The descriptions of Ceylon life and scenery are faithful, and if any visitor happens to form different impressions, that will be due to differences of temperament rather than to any question of fact. Ali Bey has taken the utmost pains to secure trustworthy information on the subjects about which he writes, and the conclusions to which he comes on various matters are worthy of the respect due to one who has seen and thought out things for himself, and admits his readers to the benefit of his personal experiences.

One cannot help noting in these pages, not only the love of Ceylon and its people, but also the passionate love of Egypt, and the earnest desire to serve Egypt. Nothing is more admirable in this book than that it reveals the author's patriotic zeal for his own King and Country. It is deeper than the love of School, more enduring than the love of Ceylon; and rightly so. We marked his patriotism when he was here, and honoured him for it. He has written this book with Egypt principally in his mind. We in Ceylon are grateful to him for his appreciation of this Island, and welcome every link which connects us with that ancient and mysterious land whose greatness we trust is beginning anew.

L. E. BLAZÉ.

Colombo, 8th September, 1925.

AUTHOR'S FOREWORD

Little did I dream, when I wrote the last chapter, *Au Revoir*, in March, 1922, praying the Almighty for a speedy repetition of my recent visit to Ceylon, that my prayer would be granted so soon!

So greatly, indeed, did I enjoy my trip of 1921 that, notwithstanding the lure of Wembley, and the manifold attractions of the Olympic Games at Paris, let alone the glamour of Europe as a whole, when it came, in my new married life, to the choice of a holiday abroad, the lure of Ceylon and the call of dear Kingswood proved even more irresistible. To this sweet land, therefore, we turned our footsteps; and right royally did this trip of 1924 bear out my fondest anticipations.

. . . . .

Notwithstanding that in April, 1922, the text of the present volume was ready for the press, not to mention how earnestly desirous and anxious I also was to see it published soon after my return, if only that it would thereby be fresher, circumstances over which one had no control, unfortunately delayed its publication to the present moment.

And, in the intervening period, having paid Ceylon a second visit, there might possibly appear to be some justification for making this work cover the experiences of both trips. Nevertheless, I have definitely decided to adhere to my original text, and thus present this book practically as I wrote it in the period between January and April, 1922. Nor have I found any reason to modify or qualify any portion of the original work in any way, except where I found it advisable or necessary to add a few notes now and then, in elucidation of certain points in regard to both visits, or to acknowledge kind acts rendered during my 1924 trip.

But in doing so, I venture to hope that, notwithstanding this fact, the book will suffer in no way by the inevitable delay, but that whatever little interest I may have succeeded in arousing in this modest work, will nevertheless be sustained.

Indeed, if anything, my second visit only enhanced my previous favourable impression of this beautiful land; and though, in view of my having visited a few additional places on this occasion, like Galle, for instance, there might have been some reason for adding to the original text, still, I have preferred in this edition to let well alone, so to say, pending such time as Providence favours me anew with the opportunity of a third visit, when I can undertake a more extensive tour of the Island, and thus visit places I missed on both the previous occasions, such as Bandarawela, Ramboddé, Badulla, Jaffna, Sigiri, Polannaruwa, Ratnapura, Hambantota, and so on, and then possibly bring out a more comprehensive and detailed description of the Island.

After all, it is commonly believed that the glamour of a first visit, and the lasting impression it leaves upon one's imagination, often prove more forcible and binding, and generally outweigh in vividness of recollection those of subsequent years. I have decided for these reasons likewise not to depart from the lines I originally penned in the full ecstasy of joy and exhilaration of delight on the realisation of a lifelong dream.

. . . . .

It is to my friend, and former colleague in the Royal Household, Mr. George Cattaui, a promising young poet, that I owe, in the main, the original idea of writing this book. When I returned from Ceylon in October 1921, and was recounting to him, with all the warmth and enthusiasm begot of an exceedingly enjoyable trip, the beauty, charm, and picturesqueness of that wonderful land, he repeatedly exhorted me to deliver a lecture about it before the Egyptian Royal Geographical Society.

But unprovided as I was with the material that could make a success of the attempt, inasmuch as I felt that I might prove unequal to the task, I felt disinclined at the time to entertain the proposal seriously.

But Mr. Cattaui's original suggestion, and his kindly interest in me seemed as if they were destined ultimately to set the ball rolling in the matter; for, when other friends of mine advised me to write some small account of my trip, thereby unconsciously kindling afresh the dying embers of this interest, I came to the conclusion that, after all, the game might be worth the candle, and so I finally yielded to the temptation. The outcome is the present volume.

. . . . .

Perhaps it would be well at the very outset to outline the scope and purpose of this work, and the nature of the somewhat difficult task entailed.

When I went to Ceylon in the summer of 1921 it was to enjoy a long overdue holiday to the best of my ability; and never once did it ever cross my mind that I would one day sit down to write an account of it. Even when one or two journalists seemed to be treading on what for the moment seemed to me to be forbidden ground, and were tentatively broaching the subject of the political situation in Egypt, I, divining their object, forestalled them in their intention, and made it quite plain to them that I was merely out on a quiet holiday, and could not, therefore, discuss the question, adding, however, that I sincerely hoped that a satisfactory settlement could be reached compatible with the dignity and interests of both England and Egypt.

Thus, during my stay, and in all my tours in the Island, not being haunted by the shadow of a book in the making, or the collation of notes for it—so essential to such an object—I wandered about with the free, easy, jaunty air of one who was bent on taking his pleasure gaily and joyfully.

But emboldened by the encouragement given me by my friends, with the additional incentive that I might thereby be doing Ceylon a good turn, however slight it may be, in acknowledgment of the most delightful holiday I had spent within its hospitable and entrancing shores, I decided to make the attempt.

But little did I dream at the outset of the laborious task that confronted me, or the length into which my originally intended brief account would ultimately run. Handicapped as I was, by a total absence of material and of first-hand notes and information gathered on the spot, I had to make the best of the situation, and draw upon memory's holy shrine and rely practically entirely upon what she could suggest to me.

However, having undertaken the task, I was eager to see it through to the end. There were times indeed when I found it more difficult than I expected; but with me it was now, not so much an account of my trip, as an acknowledgment and appreciation of Ceylon's beauty, and I was all the more determined not to be beaten.

. . . . .

In writing this book I have not been inspired by any idea of giving just a bare chronicle of facts, or a diary of events, nor with the object of hoping to write a book of travel in the real sense of the word, or of the more ambitious kind, which can aspire to a place by the side of such works on the Island as Cave's *The Book of Ceylon*, or even a tourist's vade-mecum. I have merely recorded things, and jotted down my impressions just as they have occurred to me each time I felt disposed to take up my pen. In other words, I have merely brought out in print what I might have conveyed in conversation, in a quite frank and natural way, unbound by convention, to any friend wishing to hear of my experiences in this lovely land.

Desirous, however, as I am to show Ceylon to the best advantage—which my own simple account cannot of course adequately fulfil—I have been obliged to supplement it by two or three lengthy quotations from Cave's admirable book, if only to drive home more forcibly than ever the attractions of the Island, and thus induce people of other lands to pay it a visit, as if they heard the magic "East a-callin'", and distant Lanka beckoning to them with all her unheard of wonders.

If, in doing so, I shall have succeeded in this simple way in appealing to the fancy of a wider public, and in bringing home to them the beauty and irresistible charm which I had the joy of experiencing to the full, and thus persuade them to obey with alacrity the call of the East, and see for themselves the wonders of this land, then my feeble efforts will not have been in vain, and I shall have the satisfaction of feeling that I had fulfilled in some sense, however faint it may be, the spirit of the saying, "Something attempted, something done."

. . . . .

One distinct advantage, however, did my 1924 trip bring me, for had the present work been published before, I should not have been able to include several of the illustrations I was fortunate enough to secure later on. For, with no intention during my first trip of writing this book, nor being an adept in the art of photography, I did not bother much about laying in a stock of snapshots and prints which could come in useful afterwards. But when I did finally make up my mind to write this book how sorely did I feel the lack of them, especially as in a book of travel illustrations serve to enhance its value, and render it more interesting.

I had no other expedient at the time but to fall back on the generosity of friends and well-known photographers to make good this want; and in this connection I avail myself of the present occasion to tender my warmest thanks to all who have assisted me in this respect, and notably Mr. H. F. Macmillan and Messrs. Platé & Co., for their kindness and courtesy in allowing me to reproduce many of their pictures in this book.

In 1924, however, I was more careful, for though I was but a novice in the art of photography, I believed that a few snapshots taken by me, and included in my book, would not be without their sentimental interest, if only that I could give the very views and objects I was so anxious to present, and which I could not procure elsewhere.

To give a few instances: try ever so hard, I could not come across any good views of Lady Blake's Road and the Rapids in the Mahawila Ganga (River) alongside it, all in one picture, which might give a fairly adequate idea of the beauty of this spot and route; so I had to include mine. Again, although Platé's have a fine picture of Colombo Harbour and the landing jetty, still I have inserted mine because in it there is more life and local colour, so to say. I have given the jetty on a passenger day, with all the bustle and animation consequent upon the presence of one or two big liners in the harbour on that day. The Dalada Maligawa of Kandy also inevitably finds a place in books on Ceylon but does not the Temple at the time of the Perahera, with all the crowds, present a more lifelike picture of this famous shrine? And with the Perahera on, could I omit such a golden opportunity of snapshotting the Maligawa Elephant in the very precincts of the Temple in the very act of its being got ready for the Day Perahera on the last day? Certainly not. And how gratified I am that, acting on the spur of the moment, I did dash to the Temple, force my way in through the crowds, and get a snapshot of this rare sight. Also, the Kandyan Chiefs we are accustomed to see figuring often in books on Ceylon. But with pardonable pride, does not an impromptu picture of them, in full ceremonial garb and array, in the Perahera itself, look more original and interesting than the usual stereotyped ones taken to order in a group? And what I have said of them applies likewise to the Temple Elephants bathing at Katugastota, for, as a rule, pictures of them are taken, as it were, to order, and their attitudes and poses are generally rehearsed beforehand, whereas although I did take one or two such photographs, still I was bent on snapshotting them in their natural attitudes unawares, and this I succeeded in doing one afternoon.

But I must stop. What I really wanted to explain is that I was anxious to get views of scenes and objects taken in natural attitudes and environment and setting as far as possible, so that they might look more lifelike and original.

I must, however, not fail to impress upon my readers the fact that though the pictures may go a long way to justify the extreme beauty of the Island—which I have mainly sought to emphasise by the inclusion of these illustrations—nevertheless, even then several of them still fall short of the reality, and it is only by seeing them personally in their natural surroundings, that they can be fully appreciated and admired.

. . . . .

The "Kingswood Week" being also one of the main inducements which took me to Ceylon in 1921, I have deemed it only fair and fitting that a full account of it should be included in this volume, if only to preserve a worthy record of a memorable occasion; for if I am not sure that this little work can enjoy a wide circulation, still I venture to hope that I can pardonably presume, with some degree of certainty, that several of my friends and acquaintances, not the least among them Kingswoodians, would each like to possess a copy, if only as a memento of their Egyptian friend who was glad and thankful to be amongst them such a short time ago.

Thus, if in these ensuing pages, to all who have extended to me their welcome, and helped to brighten my stay in Ceylon I have, in duty bound, found it incumbent to acknowledge such kindnesses, how should I not accredit to beloved Kingswood, Mr. Blazé, and all those associated with her the place of honour rightfully due to them in this book, when this dear school so heartily welcomes back to her fold her own sons, as they only too readily deem it their sacred duty, in their turn, to be loyal to so worthy an *alma mater?*

But no more, alas! will Kingswood's Grand Old Man control the destinies of the dear school he founded in 1891, and watched over with a rare devotion and paternal solicitude to grow into the fine and worthy institution which will stand as an imperishable monument to his credit and genius. He rightly or wrongly believed that a younger man, with all the energy and vigour of youth, should now be called upon to bear his heavy burden of responsibility, and has withdrawn from active participation in the work of the school.

It is gratifying to find that in her new Principal, the Rev. Robert Pearson, Kingswood is blessed with one who is deeply and enthusiastically interested in the school, and eager to abide faithfully and loyally by, and to maintain the noble traditions of Mr. Blazé. Nor can I, for my part, fail to record and express to him and the Kingswood Union my wife's and my deep appreciation of the generous sentiment that inspired them to induce me to preside at the Kingswood Prize-Giving of 1924, and to persuade my wife to distribute the prizes at the Kingswood Sports the following day.

And if now we ring down the curtain on a phase in Kingswood's history with the appointment of a new Principal, and her removal to palatial premises, thanks to the munificence of Sir John Randles, and the generosity of the Wesleyan Missionary Society, can we forget the man, to whom, above all, she is indebted for the proud position she holds to-day in the educational world? Certainly not. And in this connection I can do no better than quote the splendid tribute paid Mr. Blazé at the prize-giving of 1923 by so high a dignitary and distinguished a personage as the Honble.

Mr. Cecil Clementi, the Colonial Secretary of the Island:

"I understand from what has been said that this is the last occasion on which Mr. Blazé will appear as Principal at the annual prize-giving. It is a fact which we must all deplore, and which will mark, if it occurs, the end of an epoch in the life of the school; for Mr. Blazé has been identified with Kingswood since it first opened on the 4th of May, 1891, and he has seen its numbers grow from an annual average attendance of sixty-two in the first decade, to 142 in its second decade, and 240 in the present year. Mr. Blazé has also given the school its tone, and if you ask me to illustrate the tone of Kingswood, I cannot do so better than by reminding you of the fact that seventy-seven Gentlemen of Kingswood served in the Great War, and that of these eleven laid down their lives in the King's service. The school has, therefore, been tried in a fiery test, and it has deserved well of the Empire. If, therefore, it is not to be the good fortune of Mr. Blazé to build the new Kingswood with bricks and mortar; if he is not to see during the term of his office more than the foundation laid and the construction begun; if he stands to-day, as I may say, on Pisgah, and looks towards the promised school-house which his effort and enthusiasm have made possible, but which he is not to enter himself as Principal; nevertheless, I think he has already achieved something which he himself will value far more highly. *He has built the Kingswood not made with hands. He has moulded the character of a generation and more of Kingswood boys.* He has set a fine example, and left an enduring tradition to his pupils past and present, and to all who may hereafter enter Kingswood whether as masters or as boys. We are all one this afternoon in congratulating Mr. Blazé on his great work, and in wishing him a long, happy enjoyment of the rest which he has well earned."[1]

. . . . .

[1] *Our Boys: The Kingswood* Magazine, Vol. VII, No. 144.

One last word I should like to add. How many there are who, on travel bent, go to Europe, or come here to Egypt, from that great Continent and the New World, but as often as not how few, far too few indeed, compared to these thousands and tens of thousands, whether Europeans, Americans, or my own countrymen, ever go beyond the Suez Canal. It is true every country has its own attractions, not the least the mighty Occident, with its advanced civilisation, and its greater facilities of travel and manifold amenities of life. It cannot thus help being in the limelight. But in very few countries can one find such a combination and diversity of variegated charm and interest as in Ceylon, and I can safely affirm without fear of contradiction, like the enterprising firm which so cleverly advertises its tea as "Once tried, always used," that Ceylon, once visited, will ever prove an irresistible magnet.

Though it may need a more ambitious work than this modest volume to give a more comprehensive account of "The Pearl of the Eastern Seas," still, the reader who cares to go through the following pages, however inadequately they may have brought out the manifold attractions of beautiful Ceylon, cannot fail to test for himself to some extent the truth of my assertions, and realise the immense possibilities of this land as a tourist's paradise; and I only hope, as the years go by, there will be an even greater influx into it, not the least from the ranks of my own countrymen. Seeing is believing; and people have but to go and judge things for themselves, and how they will regret that they had not visited Ceylon before!

But it is to her own people more than anybody else that Ceylon should look for support in this direction. Shockingly indifferent, and culpably lacking in the enterprise which should spur them on to further endeavour to reveal to the world at large its picturesqueness and infinite charm, when other lands, far less attractive, still contrive to draw their thousands towards them, it is high time indeed that Ceylon cast off her torpor and awoke in grim earnest to the necessity of advertising her claims, and this cannot but redound to the benefit of both the tourist and the Island.

. . . . .

Most lovely as I had always known Ceylon to be, still in 1921, after an absence of twenty-four years, it seemed to me to be even more lovely. Was it that maturer years had developed a higher and keener sense of appreciation, or, as the saying goes, " Absence hath made the heart grow fonder," and in the ecstasy of the fulfilment of a lifelong dream I was lost in wonderment over its surpassing loveliness? In any case, approach it in what light I may, the fact remains that I did enjoy that trip as I had never enjoyed a holiday before.

But what diamond indeed, sparkling with all the lustre of its brilliance, or what picture painted by some master hand, could show to advantage if there were not the perfect setting to shed its additional charm to the already existing beauty?

In some such light, therefore, stood my friends to me in Ceylon. I certainly should have found it as enchanting as ever; but most assuredly I would not have enjoyed my trip so thoroughly as when I was blessed with the genial company of those kind friends who so generously extended to me the hand of welcome. It is one thing to feel lonely, and as if one were a stranger, and an entirely different thing to be fortunate enough to have the rare pleasure of being amongst friends, and wandering about as if one were in his own home.

It is these friends of Ceylon, therefore, who, by their warmth of feeling, and their hearty welcome, rendered my trip doubly enjoyable. To them, accordingly, I once more reiterate my lasting gratitude and deep appreciation of all their courtesy, kindness, and hospitality.

In thanking all, however, I cannot but, in duty bound, single out two for especial mention, namely, Mr. L. E. Blazé and Mr. A. R. Stonestreet, for all they have done for me by their invaluable suggestions and generous aid.

Indeed, indebted as I have always been to Mr. Blazé for all he has done for me throughout all these years, ever since I had the fortune and pleasure of being a pupil of his at Kingswood, down to this day, still, with what rare devotion and corresponding bigness of heart has he capped all his previous kindnesses by adding yet another to his long list by his most welcome Foreword. Need I say how deeply touched I have been by this distinct mark of his lasting solicitude for, and interest in, his old pupil?

Nor can I fail to as deeply appreciate, and as profoundly acknowledge with a grateful heart the way my dear friend Mr. Stonestreet, with such rare and brother-like devotion, volunteered and actually rendered me every assistance in the publication of this book by his generous intervention and good offices, none the least in reading through the proof-sheets. But for his invaluable and generous aid, I would certainly have been at sea, so to say, and quite at a loss how to see this matter through.

Thus, what promised at one time to be an obsession, eventually turned out to be a pleasant reality, thanks to both Mr. Blazé and Mr. Stonestreet; and with such a load lifted off my mind, giving room to a feeling of relief and gratification that at last my labours had yielded the fruit I was so anxious to see in tangible form, what words of thanks, what expressions of gratitude, can adequately affirm the imperishable debt both Mr. Blazé and Mr. Stonestreet have laid me under towards them for all time?

. . . . .

And, ere I close, may I make it quite plain that, in writing this book, I have always been imbued with the one and sole desire to approach my subject with as open and quite an unprejudiced mind as possible. Inspired, therefore, by such a spirit throughout, I have, accordingly, as I have already said, merely endeavoured to present a simple and readable account, in a frank and natural way.

If, therefore, I may seem to have erred at times on the side of outspokenness, still, let me hope, that none the less my readers will generously and magnanimously accept my remarks in the friendly spirit and good faith and sincerity in which they are given. And, in indulgently bearing with me, let me hope, however, that in this modest work they nevertheless recognise the product of a warm and sincere friend of Ceylon, who has drunk deeply of her beauty and her glories, and now seeks to place on record some feeble acknowledgment of, and lasting gratitude to, this most beautiful and fascinating land, as to her most warm-hearted and hospitable people.

ALI FOAD TOULBA.

Cairo, May 30th, 1925.

CONTENTS

LIST OF ILLUSTRATIONS

COLOURED PLATES

CEYLON

THE LAND OF ETERNAL CHARM

CHAPTER I

"THE PEARL OF THE EASTERN SEAS"

AT last the dream of a lifetime nears fulfilment, and Ceylon's sunny shores lie almost within my sight. No longer is it the airy vision of a troubled mind or the craving of a soul, but a delightful reality granted by a kindly Providence. For years I have waited patiently for this happy day, and now at last I reap the reward of a quarter of a century's expectation. Only those yearning for some dear object, who have known how to wait patiently, until Time rewards them with the realisation of the cherished dream, can now adequately appreciate my present rejoicing.

Hail! Ceylon! land of eternal charm, "Pearl of the Eastern Seas!" to your loved soil I now hasten, to your charming Kandyan Hills I once more return. Within thy hospitable shores may I find the relief these years of sorrow, these harsh tempestuous times have so long denied me. As a boy I left thee, as a man in the prime of manhood I now return. But where, alas! where are those friends, those parents dear, who once shared my happy home, my many joys? Gone are they, as are gone so many hopes, so many day-dreams, as gone shall each of us be in his turn along the destined eternal way. And Life cries out in all its inexorable, harsh, and pitiless mockery: " I am one long delusive dream! "

. . . . .

It is not always that I find someone born outside the limits of his mother country taking fondly to the land of his actual birth. But with me it has been otherwise, and Ceylon I have always loved. My interest in it is second only to my interest in my beloved Egypt.

Long desirous as I have been to visit it, still I realised that such a visit could only be practicable after I had gone through my studies. It happened, however, that though my yearning increased when I graduated in 1910 from the Royal School of Law, my dear mother would still prove a stumbling-block in the realisation of such a hope; and even now I recall the words with which she would often try to dissuade and admonish me.

" Ceylon! Why Ceylon, of all countries? " she would say reprovingly, with a touch of petulance. " Mention Europe; go to England; these are the places worthy of a visit, not Ceylon, the land of exile! "

" But, Mother," I would remonstrate, " we seemed to be quite happy there; and the people used to be so kind to us; and what a beautiful country Ceylon is."

" Ah! dear son," she would proceed, her petulance softening to a sad note, " you little realised our broken hearts, and the resignation with which we bowed to the hand of Destiny. Outwardly cheerful though at times we appeared to be, you should have seen the agony and homesickness which rent your father's heart as he pined for his loved Egypt. Yes, dear boy, Ceylon is a beautiful land; but you were of an age not to be able to appreciate sufficiently the bitterness of banishment. However beautiful a country may be, still it were enough to feel that you were a prisoner in it. And, after all, Egypt is our native land, not Ceylon. Can you wonder, therefore, if your father pined for his distant home? Enough, therefore, my son, enough of that land of exile."

In her lifetime, therefore, how could I have crossed the will of that dearly beloved mother for whom I would have sacrificed anything, already as I had, for the sake of her failing health, the once cherished dream of going to Eton and to Oxford?

" Render honour where honour is due." Overjoyed as I have been at the chance offered me to pay Ceylon that long overdue visit, can I forget to whom in the main I am indebted for it? Certainly not. To my Chief, Mohammed Tewfik Bey El-Sawy,[1] Director of the European Service of the Cabinet of H.M. The King, goes practically the whole credit of my having been able to enjoy such a delightful trip; and to him all my life I shall ever be most deeply grateful for the noble part he played in obtaining my long-awaited leave. Virtually I had obtained my furlough, but curiously, this time in my case, it was held in abeyance right up to the last moment of the eve of my departure for Port Said pending the favour of the sanction of H.M. The King, though, as a matter of fact, all these little formalities could have been effected long ago!

With what a nobleness of heart, therefore, and as rare a courage did Tewfik Bey, throwing red tape to the winds, and taking the bull by the horns, so to say, seeing how worried, careworn, and anxious I looked, most considerately, and on his own initiative, go forthwith himself to H.M. The King to crave the favour of His Majesty's sanction. And I shall never forget that beaming, radiant expression of intense joy and pleasure with which he broke the happy news of His Majesty's most gracious confirmation of my leave. Yes, I shall always most gratefully cherish this noble act of his; and may the Almighty ever bless my august Liege and Sovereign His Majesty The King, and Tewfik Bey El-Sawy for all the goodness they have done me in thus enabling me to realise this lifelong dream of mine.

[1] He has since retired on pension owing to ill-health, after having risen to be Private Secretary to H.M. The King, with the rank of Pasha conferred on him by His Majesty.

CHAPTER II

EN ROUTE FOR "THE SPICY ISLE"

LONG before I actually started for Ceylon I had set my heart on sailing by the R.M.S. *Mantua*, and returning by the R.M.S. *Naldera*, both of the P. & O. S. N. Co., for I had timed my embarkation to synchronise with the official departure of H.M. The King and his Court to Alexandria for the summer. Thus, as early as April, I had booked my passage, procured my passport, and had it viséd at the British Consulate, which, however, was not without its funny side, for the gentlemen there were at first not a little amused that I should elect to go to Ceylon for my holiday, unlike the rest of my countrymen, who usually go to Europe, until I told them of my connection with the island. Having thus finished with the more important details, I left the minor items usually bound up with impending departure abroad for the end.

Unfortunately, the big Coal Strike then prevailing in England quite upset the sailings of the various steamers, and they could not thus leave at the scheduled time, inasmuch as one never knew what port they would be compelled to drop out of their usual itinerary. As a matter of fact, I learnt on board eventually that the *Mantua* had actually to go to Germany to coal, and this naturally carried her out of her course, and correspondingly necessitated some modification in her sailing.

Thus, even as late as the 11th of June, when I inquired last for the exact time when she was due to leave Port Said, no definite answer was forthcoming, and the only thing my Agents could say with some degree of certainty was that the *Mantua* was due at any moment between the 13th and the 16th of June; and they therefore deemed it advisable for me to proceed to Port Said at once, and there catch the boat any time she arrived.

Thus, through no fault of theirs, but mainly owing to the Coal Strike which so dislocated everything for some time, I had to rush precipitately down to Port Said on the evening of the 12th, leaving several things undone, not the least being the settling of certain private affairs, and looking up certain books and newspapers, to lay in a stock of useful information of the sights and places of interest in Ceylon worth visiting. In the circumstances I, therefore, missed taking note of some of the beauty spots of Ceylon I had read of some time ago.

Interesting as I had found Port Said on previous occasions, this time, however, the feeling of suspense was killing, the more so that the 13th and the 14th passed off without the *Mantua* putting in her appearance, whereas I could have found these days most useful to attend to several things I had put off for the last moment. On the 15th, however, the local Agents of the P. & O. were able to announce that the liner was due the next day; and it came out later on, that the lack of definite information on the present occasion was due to the ship not calling at Marseilles, but coming on direct from Gibraltar.

At last in the forenoon of the 16th the fine, stately *Mantua* steams into port past the town's far-famed landmark of the magnificent statue of de Lesseps, and anchors almost in front of the Marina Palace Hotel. How my heart leapt with joy as from the verandah of my room in the hotel in question I watched this great liner slowly, majestically creeping to her anchorage.

But, even as I step on board my thoughts go back to the loved land I am now leaving, to wander far, far away in some other clime. I was going away, but none so close or so dear as a beloved parent was I leaving behind to miss me. To Ceylon's lovely shores I was going, but ah! my distracted country, that I could find you happier on my return. Egypt! my Egypt! come what may, still claim back your loyal son. Grant, O God Almighty, that I may return once more to this historic strand. If I die, let it be on Egypt's hoary soil, where I may lie beside my loved parents. And even as I stood on the promenade deck and surveyed the scene around, some feeling prompted me to send a parting farewell to those friends from whom I stole away unknown to them:

Farewell, dear friends, God bless you all,
  As He has blest my land;
I hie to far Serendib's call,
  That charming, wondrous strand.

Good-bye! God grant I live to see
  My Egypt once again;
Borne homewards o'er the distant sea,
  The land unsplit in twain.

. . . . .

At last at 6 p.m. sails the *Mantua* down the Suez Canal—that fierce bone of contention, and the bane or blessing of Egypt according as each may construe it. Through the high sandy banks on either side we thread our way, but uninteresting, parched, and repellent as they looked, still each was not without its own bloody tale. Ask them, and they will tell of anxious times in the Great War, of moments when Egypt entered into the fray and tasted of the din of strife, when almost to her very hearth grimly stalked the god of war.

A short while more and night closes on us. A quite novel experience to me as was this passage of the Canal—for I used always to land and embark formerly at Suez—how much more interesting and beautiful was the sight of the huge beam of the powerful searchlight that lit our way through the waters; and when the moon combined with man's handiwork to shed its silvery rays on the scene around one felt that life was really worth living.

. . . . .

[Photo by Platé, Ltd., Colombo

The Author: Mr. Ali Foad Toulba

Facing page 40]

[By courtesy of the P. & O. S. N. Co.

THE R.M.S. "MANTUA" IN STORMY WEATHER

Facing page 41]

Morning dawns, but I am up betimes. There on the deck the cool fresh morning breeze plays upon my temples. Afar loom the walls and the avenue-flanked streets of once prosperous Suez, now shorn of its pristine glory. No one there is astir as yet at this early hour but one sole companion—a venerable old lady, who greets me with such a soft and gentle "Good morning, Sir. What a lovely morning!" Here was my first acquaintance, and a most courteous and benign lady she proved; and I shall always remember with pleasure this good Mrs. C. W. Bell, and her daughter and son-in-law, Mr. and Mrs. R. Fraser Douglas, of Colombo, to whom she introduced me there when we landed, and thus enabled me to widen my circle of good friends.

Suez we then pass, and enter the Red Sea proper; but here it is like some great inland lake, not the open sea with the roar of waves, so calm and placid are the waters. We have now actually emerged out of the Suez Canal, and are sailing down the gulf that bears its name. The *Mantua* is now gently ploughing through the waters, and even as the huge 11,000 tonner softly cuts her way through, I settle down to take stock of my environment and adapt myself to my novel surroundings. In the novelty of the scene, however, and the new experience of a long sea voyage after so many years, I hardly take more than a passing interest in the barren mountain ranges on either side. Thus passes the first day.

The morrow dawns, and I feel more at home. There is no sight of land now. Even the *Karmala*, of the same Company, which had preceded us by an hour or two, *en route* for Bombay, we gradually overhaul, and little by little outdistance her until she is lost to view. The *Mantua* is now on the high seas sailing towards Ceylon. At last my trip is a reality, and not a mere dream of the night, as I had so often dreamt of in my sleep, only to find the morn bring bitter disappointment.

CHAPTER III

LIFE ON THE OCEAN WAVE

CONSIDERING the fact that I was undertaking my trip in summer, and at a time when the south-west Monsoon bursts in all its fury, still the voyage was not so unpleasant after all as one naturally feared. But this does not mean that we escaped scatheless. In the Red Sea, warm as it usually is, this time the heat was abnormally intense, and as we learned subsequently, we were at the tail end of the heat wave which had just swept over Europe. As a consequence, sleep in the cabins was out of the question; and our only alternative was to sleep on deck with such bedding as one could personally convey from below to ensure some comfort and repose in these cruel times when one had to pander to all the fads and foibles of syndicates, unions, guilds, and what not.

Again, once past Perim Island and Aden out into the Indian Ocean, we were in grim earnest, in for a taste of the Monsoon. But even then it was mere child's play compared to what I experienced in June, 1896, with my mother on our way out to Ceylon on board the *Preussen*, of the Norddeutscher Lloyd, and whether this was due to the smallness of the German boat which was of about only 6,000 tons displacement, as against the big, stout *Mantua*, which seemed to be heroically holding her own against the buffeting of the waves, or a relaxation in the temper of the elements I cannot definitely say. But the fact remains, as expressed by the Chief Engineer, a veteran "salt of the sea," who had been ploughing the waters these twenty-five years past, and whose testimony, therefore, was not to be despised, that we were lucky to be having such a mild monsoon.

The point where the climax is generally met with, and where most seasickness remedies seem to be of but little avail, is generally off the coast of Socotra, and I think the waters in these latitudes can safely bear comparison with their counterpart of the Atlantic as "The Bay of Biscay of the Indian Ocean." For, even though we may not, as a rule, experience extremely rough weather, still there are sure to be heavy seas running, which cause ships to roll a good deal; and as often as not one begins to ask oneself whether "Life on the Ocean Wave," so poetical to the ear, is really as pleasant and enthralling as one pictures it to be!

. . . . .

When the first Sunday service was held on board, and the passengers were streaming in their twos and threes to the dining-hall, I noticed that the bulk of the congregation were the transferred passengers from the *Benalla*, which had run aground somewhere in the English Channel. They were, for the most part, emigrants going out to Australia; and I could not help reflecting on this curious phenomenon of human psychology.

Why is it that often it is the poorer and lower classes who seem to be the more pious and more strictly devoted to the observance of their religious duties? Is it that poverty and need compel them to supplicate for greater bounties from the Almighty, or that prosperity and affluence make the people blest with them oblivious of their duty to their God, if not actually agnostic, in their giddy rush through life, as they are drawn into the vortex of its thousand pleasures and sins? Years seem sometimes to make converts of such misguided individuals and sinners late in life; but how many, if any, of the *jeunesse dorée* ever pause on the downward path? Truly God is all-merciful. Yet, though it is not every one who suffers in this world, still in the next shall each of us answer for his deeds.

Gone alas! are the good old days when men seemed to be unhardened by the materialism of the world of to-day, and the poor could oftener find some benefactor. The very things that were barred yesterday, seem to-day to be the passwords of popularity; but this is no reason why each should be weakly drawn into the maelstrom of sin, and fall a prey to cheap, transient popularity.

Where, indeed, can we now see that once familiar and touching sight, so moving and so inspiring, of the late Ahmed Rashed Pasha, with lantern in hand, and back bent with years, tottering to the Seyyida Zeinab Mosque in the grey hours of the dawn, to say his early morning prayers within its holy walls, as if he were another Florence Nightingale, ministering to his soul, even as the " Lady with the Lamp " of her day ministered to the needs of the Turkish wounded?

" Yes, this is the picture of the world of another day," some may say apologetically! But it is not the world that changes, it is man; for the world untouched by man would be the same unaltered world but for the changes wrought by him. And if we must change, then, for the love of God, let us change for the better, not rush down to our own destruction along the downhill path.

CHAPTER IV

GAMES AND AMUSEMENTS AFLOAT

ONE of the welcome amenities of travelling on British liners is that one is sure to be amply catered for in games and amusements, a feature, however, which the Germans, with their proverbial thoroughness and enterprise, were not loth or slow to recognise and adopt, as their fine ships of pre-war days bore ample evidence of. They even went one better by providing their passengers with music twice a day—the brass band in the forenoon, and the orchestra at dinner—and the British Navigation Companies on the Eastern Seas, at any rate the more important concerns, might well take a leaf out of the book of their erstwhile foes.

What a boon games are on board! They not only kill the tedium of a long voyage, and provide one with exercise to keep fit, but serve also to bring people of different nationalities into contact with one another under favourable conditions, and render possible mutual esteem and goodwill by breaking down the barriers of international prejudice that have kept them apart. Indeed, how many misunderstandings and fallacies and mendacious reports can one hope to remove under the influence of a friendly chat following a pleasant game, and thus help to show the other side, erroneously labouring under some delusion, the real nature of things.

If only my countrymen could have heard what several fellow-passengers thought of Egypt and her struggle for a place under the sun. To take one mild example, that of a benign old gentleman from India who, though unlike the majority of those haughty, overbearing Englishmen serving in the Great Peninsula, still, basing his knowledge of the country on the Egypt of the period of the "frontiers incidents" of 1893, when he happened to be here—as if the world, and Egypt likewise had not changed and developed meanwhile—considered self-government a very big and substantial advance on the past. Or, in what a preposterous, distorted manner others magnified the Alexandria Riots of May 1921! Indeed, how surprised they subsequently felt when I had given them the other side of the picture, and showed them Egypt in its true light. Thus, whilst several eventually felt disposed to display no little sympathy for our cause, there were others who still could not disguise how staggered they were by our claims for full independence, and my assertion: As friends and equals we welcome you; as allies we'll stand by you; but as a subject race, never.

Again, take Turkey. She was always to blame, as if the Armenians and Greeks and other kindred turbulent elements were as innocent as the new-born babe! Indeed, one American missionary, out on his way to India, *via* Ceylon, a quite genial and affable gentleman though he was, still could never help returning to this topic, but would always keep harping on the subject, as if the so-called "Unspeakable Turk" was deep in guilt right up to the hilt! How I wish he could have seen Mr. Marmaduke Pickthall's spirited and generous defence of the Turk, and his plea for this race, or that of some other fairminded and unprejudiced Englishman, to realise that the Ottoman Empire hardly merited to be painted in so black a hue as its traducers would present it in, for there are always two sides to a question. Or, is it because the late Lord Salisbury is alleged to have said that "England had backed the wrong horse" (meaning Turkey) at the Congress of Berlin, in 1878, therefore, nowadays, and for all time, political punters must needs act on the "tip" of so great an authority, and accordingly back "Fair Hellas," since the "Sick Man of Europe" hardly showed any signs of recovery, and might as well perish, little dreaming of " Mustapha Kemal ", that " dark horse " of the Sakarieh Meet ?[1] No; no true Egyptian will ever court foreign domination; but what Egyptian cannot help having a certain sympathy for the Turk, even as an American would look on an Englishman for instance?

But to return, for I have digressed pretty long from the main point. Deck quoits I found to be a quite enjoyable game, providing, as it also did, plenty of exercise; and if the great numbers participating in it were any true index, it appeared accordingly to be the most popular game on board. The usual sweepstakes on the boat's run were, of course, inevitable, and sometimes they provided no little excitement. Bull board and Bucket quoits also might have their votaries, but they were rather tame; no wonder therefore that they claimed their enthusiasts from the ranks of the fair sex. Deck tennis and Deck cricket are indeed two exhilarating and somewhat strenuous games; and it was in these that the Indian Princes of Porebunder, whilst on board the *Naldera*, showed to the best advantage, often holding their own against all comers in company with a hefty son of Erin, popular amongst us, as he bubbled with all the sparkling wit, grace, and charm of his race.

Now and then we used to have a dance, but the biggest affair was a Fancy Dress Ball just before reaching Aden in honour of some of the passengers employed in the Eastern Telegraphs who were disembarking on the morrow at this " Gibraltar of the Indian Ocean," and were therefore bent on making the most of the occasion before they were left to eat out some of the best years of their existence on this barren rock.

And how remarkable is this devotion to duty, this pioneering spirit of the British race! Be it to the remo-

[1] Curiously, since these lines were penned, Mustapha Kemal not only won this victory, but followed it up the next year with the even greater triumph of Afion Karahissar, and the victorious campaign which culminated in the capture of the Greek Commander-in-Chief, the expulsion of the Greeks from Ottoman territory, including Smyrna, " The Flower of the Levant," and the glorious Treaty of Lausanne.

test corners of the earth, or the most desolate regions, or far away from the beaten tracks of civilisation, still loyally they go, these hardy Britishers to the outposts of Empire. It is these qualities that have helped them to expand, develop, and maintain their mighty Empire. Great, therefore, as they have been in colonisation, they can prove as successful in the maintenance of this vast empire if they display a corresponding wisdom, astuteness, and statesmanship in consonance with the new spirit that has dawned on the world. And the great British nation that stands for all that is just and fair, can as ably rise to the occasion, and, in as statesmanlike a manner tackle the problems that beset its path.

Apropos of this dance I might mention a small incident. I noticed on the evening in question that the poop deck of the Second Class was being gaily decorated and hung with bunting, the flags of most nations gracing the enclosure. Amidst them all, alas! I missed the "Crescent and Stars" of my own country, and which man in a similar situation would not have taken such an oversight to heart. I did not like the matter to pass unnoticed; so I approached the purser on the point, and politely remarked, with the tone of one hurt, that considering they had Egyptains on board, and the rules of international courtesy called for observance, they might as well have included the Egyptian flag amongst the many that were doing service that night. He replied that perhaps it was merely an oversight, or the sailors might not be possessed of one. I, however, returned that I should nevertheless like to see the point verified, and would be extremely obliged if he would kindly investigate the matter.

So, realising that I was bent on seeing the matter through, and that I felt much hurt, but evidently not wishing to shoulder the responsibility alone, he approached the officers of the ship, who had just sat down to dinner, on the matter. Soon afterwards he returned with the air of one who seemed to have had a weight lifted off him, and stated that the officers recognised the

[*Photo by Platé, Ltd., Colombo*

THE GRAND ORIENTAL HOTEL AND VICTORIA ARCADE, COLOMBO

Facing page 48]

[Photo by the Author

COLOMBO HARBOUR AND LANDING JETTY

Facing page 49]

justness of my plea, and had accordingly instructed him to adjust the matter.

Though ultimately the purser, after speaking to the sailors, expressed his regret that they had informed him that they had no Egyptian flag on board at the time, still I need not say how delighted I was that, in principle, I had been afforded due satisfaction, and had succeeded in gaining something for my beloved country; glad also that those English gentlemen, true to the best traditions of their race, had played the game in sportsmanlike fashion.

Surely, if the words be true:

> "What should they know of England, who only
> England know?"

then, in a somewhat analogous sense, how little does a person realise how much he loves his country until he leaves its shores for some foreign land.

CHAPTER V

ARRIVAL AT COLOMBO

It was with a thrill that I observed on the evening of the 25th of June that a notice had been put up which ran somewhat to this effect, as far as I can recall from memory:

"Weather permitting, the S.S. *Mantua* is due to anchor in the Port of Colombo on the morning of the 27th at 8 a.m."

To most of the passengers this bald statement did not seem of much import, except in so far as it provided them with a chance of landing and "stretching their legs a bit," as they were wont to say facetiously, and go about sight-seeing in such a big, well-known, and flourishing port as Colombo. But to me this terse statement conveyed more. Was it true after all that at last I was about to realise the dream of years? And so, after a quarter of a century kind Providence was enabling me to revisit my natal land.

What perchance would Colombo be like, as also "Fair Holme," our old residence in the Cinnamon Gardens? Was Kandy, and its amphitheatre of hills of perennial green, as beautiful and charming as ever? And the old school, dear old Kingswood, and its Principal, would they recognise me? Of my former comrades, and our old friends, how many, perchance, would be there in this land of eternal charm, and would they still welcome me back in their midst with the warmth of bygone days? And so on and so forth, in this frame of mind my trend of thoughts kept wandering and conjuring up visions which in my ecstasy of joy I could not help calling up.

. . . . .

I sat up late into the night, and even past midnight, stirred as I was with excitement and the anticipation of impending events, and when I did retire to my cabin it was only out of sheer exhaustion, but only to lie down, for sleep was out of the question. The first streak of dawn saw me up betimes strolling on the promenade deck, and there out into the far distance beyond my eyes peered Ceylon-wards as if to penetrate the morning haze and annihilate the miles that still lay between me and those welcome shores.

A little later, and then, behold, there in the distance dimly outlined against the Eastern sky lay a thin black line; and there at last, after years of patient waiting, lay before me the "Promised Land"—a land as joyfully and eagerly I now greeted as the Israelites of old hailed their own "Promised Land."

Little by little we leave the billows of the wild Indian Ocean behind, slowly and slowly nearing the Colombo roadstead. At one moment the ship seems to be gently, majestically, cleaving the waters, at another it seems to be skimming along the bosom of some placid lake. Gradually the distant panorama unveils itself, when lo! there, beyond Ceylon's palm-fringed shore, there in the far background towering above the surrounding ridges, hazy and eërie, and almost enshrouded in the morning mist, looms the famous peak named after our first parent.

But hark! there is some stir now. The decks are not so deserted as when I first emerged forth, but actually bustling with animation. Why, there is even some slight commotion. What perchance might all this hum and buzz, all this shuffling of dresses and feet mean? A speck in the distance speaks for itself, growing bigger and bigger as we mutually near each other. Cameras and binoculars now get busy; a moment later, and lo!

there tossed and pitched like a little cockle-shell lies before us a Ceylon catamaran—one of those familiar out-rigger craft peculiar to these climes—frail and puny by the side of the stately, majestic *Mantua*, yet plucky and daring enough to brave the dangers of the deep!

No shipwrecked mariner ever welcomed with bated breath and beating heart some distant approaching sail, or Columbus hailed with joy the floating log that told its own tale, as did I rejoice at the sight of that frail barque. To me, in this moment of supreme joy, the familiar canoe came as if bringing in tangible form some message of greeting and goodwill to Ceylon's hospitable shores.

A little farther on, and the distant panorama unfurls itself, the objects afar assuming shape and becoming more distinct, and Colombo, the great emporium of the Eastern Seas, bathed in the morning sun, now gradually comes into view, its familiar flagstaff, and its skyscrapers which did not exist in my time, cleaving the sky, and its magnificent hostelry, the Grand Oriental Hotel, dimly visible in the distance.

The stentorian voice of a sturdy sailor, as he stands on a ledge with weighted rope in hand, now and then breaks through the raucous cries of the oncoming craft, shouting out the soundings—sure sign that we are nearing port. A few minutes more, and the grating, rattling sound of the huge heavy chains mingled with the hum and bustle of the Lascars tell their own tale; and, past the Light-house, the good ship *Mantua*, which bore me safely and joyfully over so many thousand miles, now gracefully rides at anchor in the Inner Harbour, two consorts, as it were, the *Plassey* and the *Kashmir*, by a beautiful coinci-dence, on either side, and the solid, massive, concrete-built south-west breakwater keeping at bay the waves that show no mercy.

The excitement of reaching port is better pictured than described. Who does not rejoice to have a chance of landing—the more so after a long and somewhat stormy voyage? Change is the spice of life. Thus, even though our voyage could not be termed dull and monotonous, still we could not help welcoming change.

. . . . .

At my cabin's entrance a representative of the Grand Oriental Hotel meets me. With a polite "Good morning, sir," he informs me that rooms have already been booked for me at his hotel, adding that Mr. Aldo Diacono and Mr. Blazé were on the deck waiting to see me. The tidings were only too welcome; my gladness knew no bounds. How could I not feel so overcome with joy when here to meet me were the very two gentlemen whom, of all men, I was most eagerly looking forward to meet. And so kind Providence had spared me the mortification of landing as if I were a stranger come to a strange land. A moment, and I am on deck. Face to face we meet; greetings warmly exchanged, and the rest my readers can well imagine.

A few handshakes all round; the Captain, as Commander of the vessel, warmly thanked, as also the purser, for all his kindness; one parting, grateful, but none the less sad glance at the fine, stately ship, and the steam launch bears me away Colombo-wards, the *Mantua* growing smaller and smaller as the distance between us grew bigger and bigger.

The next thing we are at the jetty, and I am on *terra firma*—virtually, if not literally. And so at last I had set foot on this enchanting shore; and not even my father, the late Toulba Pasha Ismet, as he stooped down on the sands of Suez, on his return from his long exile, and, picking up a handful, fondly kissed it in thanksgiving that he had lived to see his native land, could have had more joy than I then felt at having at last realised the dream of years.

CHAPTER VI

THE GRAND ORIENTAL HOTEL

NATURALLY the first thing on landing was to repair to the Grand Oriental Hotel and have a look at the rooms reserved for me. Thither, therefore, I wended my way. That I was able to run the gauntlet of the taxis, guides, hawkers, touts, loafers and what not I have only my lucky stars to thank, though perhaps the presence of Mr. Diacono might have been a contributing factor to my good fortune. There at the G.O.H., as the famous hostelry is popularly known, I found two rooms reserved for my faithful Mohammed and myself. There also I experienced the pleasant surprise of meeting Mr. Magid Sappideen, the Head Clerk of the Enquiry Office, who, I found, had personally known my father, as he had occasionally met me with my father when I was a little child; and I was delighted to renew the old ties of acquaintanceship.

Such as Mr. Sappideen, with such courtesy and such an obliging manner, is a real find for any hotel—and in the present instance he had grown to become a veritable institution of the G.O.H., and as faithfully bound up with its fortunes and as inseparable from it as ever. He had survived the whirligig of Time, and the buffets of ever changing managerships at this hotel, and the fact that through all these changes he had still been able to accommodate himself with all in turn, cannot but redound to his credit. Let us, therefore, wish him all good luck in his endeavours, and as hale and hearty and long an existence. But when, in the fulness of years, the hand of

Time begins to weigh heavily upon him, let us hope he will meet with as merited a reward as his devotion to duty calls for.

. . . . .

My room I found ideal, and practically the very one I wanted, answering as it did the requirements I stated in my letter, and the position as far as I could recall from a dim and distant past. Abutting on the corner where York Street meets with Church Street I had my *sanctum*, and from such a fine vantage-point I enjoyed a sweeping view of the harbour and the south–west breakwater in front, to my right below being busy York Street, and stretching beyond in the distance the dockyards and the Mutwal. One slight drawback however, this room had in that during the south–west Monsoon it was a bit warm, the cooler part being in the other wing; but I preferred to remain where I was, in spite of my being offered a splendid room on the other side, owing to the fine panorama I enjoyed, and the interesting scenes below.

To me this hotel proved a real home, and my chamber a real *sanctum sanctorum;* no wonder, therefore, that I took to it so affectionately, for, wandering where I would in this charming and exquisite land, still to this haven I would come back for repose and reflection. Queen's Hotel in Kandy was, in turn, just as pleasing and comfortable, though the quiet of the town made a long residence there sometimes a bit boring.

. . . . .

The manager was all civility and consideration, and no wonder, for he hailed from Switzerland, a land well supplied with fine hotels, as it furnishes other climes with most efficient managers; and many a friendly and pleasant chat I had with him, as I benefited by sundry hints and advice so useful to the unwary traveller. My sojourn in Colombo, however, witnessed a change of managers, Mr. Frank Winfield, with a big reputation from Singapore in hotel experience, coming over *vice* Mr. J. A. Witzig. The new manager, in his turn, proved just as obliging and courteous as his experienced predecessor.

A complaint I once lodged with him, though a mere trifle, but had been repeated several times, and was thus not devoid of a certain amount of annoyance, elicited the reply, " Oh! but it is the very small things that matter, and should be promptly attended to, else the reputation of the hotel might suffer in the end," is quite characteristic of him, and of the spirit with which he was imbued; and if all managers display such scrupulous care for even trifles, there would be less cause for complaint.

Again, it was pleasing to observe how once he called the " boys " of the Lounge—as waiters and other servants in Ceylon are called, reminiscent of the manner the French call their waiters *garçon*—and admonished them for the way they swarmed round the passengers entering the hotel portals, thereby causing them no little inconvenience by a display of over-zeal on the part of several of them, when one only would have sufficed. This state of things I often noticed; but then, it was not my business to interfere.

But the funny part of it is that they had barely left his room, just a few minutes before, when a batch of passengers were making for the Lounge in a bee-line, and in a body nearly the whole lot of the " boys ", who had just been given a taste of the manager's opinion, rushed at the unfortunate passengers, all gesticulating to catch the eye of the " boss " of the party, as it were, and each striving to outvie the other in his attentions! Habit is second nature; so it would be inhuman to expect them to change their spots in a few minutes.

. . . . .

These remarks remind me what a slight nuisance this is compared to that which a passenger actually experi-

[Photo by Platé, Ltd., Colombo

ROADSIDE SCENE ON THE WAY TO MOUNT LAVINIA

Facing page 56]

[Photo by the Author

MOUNT LAVINIA

Facing page 57]

ences on first landing. How often have I gazed on the trim, neat, spotlessly clean square just below, adjoining the jetty, and as often observed how the poor passengers landing in quest of pleasure unfortunately find their path barred by the unwelcome attentions and pestering clamour of Colombo's vanguard of tourist-baiters!

Happy is he, indeed, who has the good fortune to land when a stalwart British constable is on duty—as if burliness and quite massive proportions must go hand-in-hand to make a more impressive show of force and authority! The taxis, of course, would be there, but each smugly roosting in his corner; a few licensed guides also will be in evidence prowling about, but they will be meekly and quite politely proffering their services; but the loafers and touts, a whole army of them perhaps, and a veritable pest, will be nowhere—they must have melted into space! York Street, Church Street, and the adjacent by-paths seem to abound with so many nooks and crannies to which all these must have betaken themselves, or, with the ostensible air of being seriously bent on business, they would be in the adjoining arcades.

The cat was on the scene, and so the mice must have disappeared. But away moves the strutting custodian of the Law, and hey, presto! from a dozen hiding places, as it were, come Indolence's minions to prey upon the hapless passenger—as if every tourist, whether in Ceylon or Egypt, where the guides and the dragomans are just as much a pest and nuisance, or Italy, or France, or anywhere else, must needs be legitimate prey for the local "sharks" to batten upon!

A passenger lands in Colombo; he wants to have a look round. A sea voyage is, no doubt, pleasant enough. But even a surfeit of good things must in course of time react the other way. This craving for pleasure, amusement, distraction, change, is only human. But is the luckless traveller given a fair chance to achieve this desire? Certainly not, in the majority of cases. Some, bold enough, hardened in the bitter school of experience, and with a long record of travelling, might not find it difficult to brush aside these " sharks ", and even get the better of them. But, alas! they are only a minority. The majority hardly have time to reflect or plan their movements, still less to find their bearings, and as often as not, they are literally shoved, nay, bundled into some car and wheeled off to some unknown destination, succumbing to the rosy accounts of some wily obsequious guide as he unravels to them in a most seductive and captivating manner the unheard of wonders of some place of interest.

And the hubbub! Through the din and roar of a score of voices round some prospective prey one catches, now the cry of a taxi as he holds forth on the merits of his car and his moderate charges; at another moment the raucous shout of the would-be guide, to whom the wonders of Colombo lie revealed—as if he were gifted with some occult power, and to other members of the fraternity it is a closed book! Even the poor gharry, of the five or six remaining,[1] so forlorn and dejected—for is not the all-conquering motor car carrying everything before it?—feebly intervenes in the hope of some " fare ", not to be shut out in the general scramble. But no, we have not reached the end of our tether. The ubiquitous 'rickshaw, indiginous product, alas! of " The Gorgeous East," so picturesque in its novelty, yet so remote, in its Oriental setting, from the ethics of altruism that obtains in the mighty West, will he be left out in the cold? But there is an end to everything, and even the din and tumult of a hundred voices must subside; and when finally the passengers have all gone their way, each conveyance carrying its load, and others on Nature's sturdy feet gradually melting away into the distance, I sometimes ask myself whether even the Tower of Babel, with its diversity of tongues, could beat some of the scenes of pandemonium witnessed here!

But then one need not be too hard on these poor fellows

[1] When I re-visited Ceylon in 1924 even these few had disappeared, leaving the field to the triumphant motor car and its less pretentious 'rickshaw.

and run them down ruthlessly—at any rate in regard to those who are genuinely bent on earning an honest living. Let us console ourselves that we might have been in their place but for an accident of birth perhaps, and be as thankful that a bounteous and kind Providence has blessed us with a more favourable position socially. After all, they are merely striving to earn their livelihood —a mere pittance at times—and if their methods at times have not much to commend them, still, with sound judgment and a judicious exercise of control on the part of the authorities concerned the nuisances can be mitigated, if not entirely eradicated, inasmuch as a certain amount of restraint and forbearance on our own part will not make us feel these annoyances so greatly as they would otherwise seem.

. . . . .

The servants of the Grand Oriental Hotel were, as a rule, polite and dutiful, especially, like their class all over the world, when the prospect of a handsome tip loomed ahead—and at scenting such they were very cute, for the Sinhalese are a very intelligent, cunning, and sharp-witted race. Clean and smartly dressed as they also were, the dark green cuffs and collars imparted a certain welcome patch of colour to what might loosely be termed their livery. It is a credit to the hotel also how wonderfully clean it was kept, and the management and the whole staff are to be complimented, and as heartily thanked, for the consideration, courtesy, and readiness they were always disposed to exhibit for the comfort of their patrons and visitors.

One waiter in particular, called Chandan, calls for especial mention. As one watched this little dwarf, or " Little Tich ", as he was affectionately nicknamed, as he often rushed wobbling to the switches to turn on the electric lights or electric fans, which a paternal management had installed over practically every table, *vice* the obsolete punkahs, and how often as not, with some hook or lemonade-opener he strained himself on tip-toe to set the welcome fans moving, and how with alacrity he then hopped off to execute some order, often to the detriment of his mates, one could not help at times relishing such a sight, and welcoming any comic relief in the humdrum routine of hotel life. No wonder, therefore, that, as I was told, he was known far and wide, and even globe-trotters passing through Colombo never failed to look him up. So it would not be far wrong if we assumed him to be an institution of the Grand Oriental Hotel, if not a gold mine of advertisement.

But, of course, not all the servants were flawless—but then, which hotel in the world has not got its slackers? In the case under review, if any were prone to show any remissness it was generally the residents and patrons of the hotel who had to suffer at the expense of the passengers, when an unusual rush from a big steamer sometimes made a good number of them lose their heads.

. . . . .

And then again, there was the tipping nuisance—yes, there must always be the inevitable fly in the amber! As a matter of fact, tipping in Ceylon is a veritable scourge! A pest though it is at all times all the world over, here it was in evidence in an even more glaring degree. Certainly, one does take into account such matters, and provides for them liberally. But no person would like to throw away his money promiscuously for nothing; and when he pays a tip he likes to feel that there is some justification for so doing. And in this connection I can do no better than quote the words of a gentleman passing through Ceylon commenting on this nuisance.[1]

" A representative of the *Ceylon Observer* had some conversation with Mr. H. G. Milner, brother-in-law of Viscount Northcliffe, with whom he has made the long tour of the East. After numerous complimentary refer-

[1] The *Ceylon Observer* (Wkly. Ed.), No. 1, Jan. 11, 1922.

ences to the conditions prevailing in Ceylon whence he returns to his home in Queensland before journeying across Canada to join Lord Northcliffe in England, Mr. Milner said that there was one feature distinctly not a good advertisement for Ceylon to which he took exception, namely, the tipping nuisance. 'We have now travelled throughout the East except India, and nowhere have been so plagued as in Ceylon hotels by servants who do nothing for you and expect tips for looking on. Of course backsheesh, under whatever name, is too familiar a feature of Eastern life anywhere not to be expected in the ordinary scheme of things, but in Ceylon it is reduced to an art which is by no means "fine." Not even in Singapore have we been so plagued by coolies and servants who have done nothing whatever to justify a tip, and nevertheless pursue you in search of it. A servant comes into your hotel bedroom, shifts a piece of soap or something of the sort, stands expectantly at the door, and unless you bribe him forthwith to clear out he pursues you through the hotel, chases you up and down stairs, waylays your outgoings and incomings, spies all your ways and finally drives you to tip him in order to be rid of his pestering. Your coolies are much more of a nuisance than your mosquitoes, and there is no net to protect you from them. You pay off one and another immediately appears and holds out his hand. It is perfectly impossible to keep track of them because apparently the same servant never does the same bit of work twice, and there are hosts of bits of apparent work which they seem to invent. They do nothing, and it takes half-a-dozen of them to do it.

" 'I am, of course, not complaining in the least of the tipping system generally. Nobody has the least objection to rewarding special trouble taken on his behalf or even to paying (for it amounts to this) for work which the hotel proprietors are supposed already to have paid for and charged in your bill; but this incessant plaguing by people who have really done nothing at all is an infliction which those interested in the attraction of visitors would do well to check ' "

. . . . .

I think the dining-hall of the Grand Oriental Hotel is the finest of its kind in Ceylon. The walls and ceiling most tastefully embellished and painted, the tables most daintily laid out in the grand spacious hall, well aired as it is, and copiously supplied with light, one finds it a real treat, with a gentle breeze blowing, thanks to kindly electric fans overhead, to enjoy amidst such ideal surroundings its fine cuisine which provides the finishing touches to this dreamland of the tropics.

And at night, oh! the fairy scene, as it were, that lies unfurled before us! And if it is a Dance night, or the evening of a Race Meet how considerably is the effect enhanced. The hall glittering and resplendent as ever, bathed in the soft, well-regulated glare of burnished electroliers overhead; the diners merry and jovial as ever, as if faithful disciples of the Epicurean school of

" Eat, drink, and be merry, for to-morrow we die! "

The fair sex in dresses of the finest and costliest texture and becoming robes of Dame Fashion's latest creations; their sterner brethren, all care banned as if by agreement, in conventional dinner jacket or evening dress, as occasions demands, relieved here and there by a splash of colour of the striking uniform or mess kit of some dashing officer, or the still languishing drab khaki of our time; Nicholas, the Tamil head steward, in mess jacket which ill becomes him, if actually not too grotesque, in one section, ably supported by Fernando and Perera his faithful and polite Sinhalese coadjutors in the other half, but in sober garb; and a host of waiters in snow-white and dark green livery flitting in and out; an occasional clang of plate, fork, spoon or knife now rising above the soft, welcome strains of soothing music which floats from some ensconced, invisible gallery adding its crowning charm to this entrancing scene—such in brief might be a faint picture. Well, therefore, might the Grand Oriental Hotel point with pride to its magnificent hall, and Ceylon be grateful that such a noted hostelry so ably maintains its reputation and proves equal to all the demands of hospitality and excellence.

. . . . .

I wonder whether even Cairo, with its world-famed hotels, can boast of such an excellent billiard-room as that of the G.O.H., and I think I should not be wrong to presume that it is fully entitled to claim premier honours in the island, though the head marker of the Queen's Hotel at Kandy once felt inclined to make a bold but ineffectual effort to challenge its supremacy. In quality, as in quantity, it excelled in its six full-sized tables that lay in its large roomy hall at the G.O.H. at the service of lovers of the game. The tables were always as well kept and as scrupulously brushed as they were maintained in excellent condition, and cues lay there galore, well tipped and of every weight to suit any taste. The more credit, therefore, to its head marker, Perera, Champion professional of the island, and a veritable Knight of the Cue, but withal extremely modest and obliging, as were the other seven markers, all good players, and most polite, as they were useful at times in lending a hand to anybody in sore need of someone with whom to enjoy a game. It is considerate of the hotel to provide each individual table with its own marker, and a seventh to act as *locum tenens* when any of them happened to be off duty or absent through illness.

A pleasing effect also was given by the interesting and appropriate coloured drawings and cartoons hung up round the room depicting droll attitudes and poses of votaries of this delightful pastime; but one missed the famous picture, "The Biggest Break of all," connected with the siege of Kimberley, depicting a shell crashing through a billiard table.

What a welcome retreat to me this room proved at times when I could snatch some pleasure in the otherwise generally dull and boring nights of Colombo, and even now I sometimes gratefully recall the exciting games I used to have there.

[Photo by Platé, Ltd., Colombo

GALLE FACE

Facing page 64]

[Photo by the Author

THE DHOBY (WASHERMAN) AT WORK IN THE KANDY LAKE SPILL

Facing page 65]

CHAPTER VII

MOUNT LAVINIA

There is hardly a traveller who lands at Colombo who is not sure to be wheeled off on to Mount Lavinia. Pretty it is as, perched on a rocky promontory—reminiscent of Zizinia, near San Staffano, Egypt's premier seaside resort on the Ramleh line east of Alexandria—it commands a wide stretch of the ocean, and the lovely seascapes here from the towering cliff might well provide profitable material for the brush of some ardent artist.

The very road to it is a gem of rural scenery, and once past Galle Face Hotel and Colpetty, another of Colombo's residential quarters, one traverses a road teeming with local life and colour; and the passenger who has but little time to spare can, nevertheless, as he is driven thither, get a peep now and then of *boutiques* and bazaars and divers scenes and races in which this locality is so rich.

The outrigger canoes also, called catamarans, that abound along these shores, so peculiar and yet so picturesque, can we forget them and the abundance of " seer" they bring from far beyond—the fish *par excellence* of Ceylon, so delicious that it can bear comparison with any of the best in the world.

How unremittingly also does its well-known hotel, so beautifully perched on the promontory overlooking the ocean, cater to the needs and comfort of visitors, not the least the well-known Fish tiffins on Sundays, for which it has acquired a reputation, and a favourite resort it has grown into for the jaded townsman or some bird of passage weary after a day's strenuous sightseeing. For where, indeed, but at this lovely spot of beautiful Ceylon, with the cool, soft, ozone-laden breeze of even-tide playing on one's temples, can the afternoon pleasure-seeker enjoy his tea better, or sip his ice under more delightful conditions, than here on this verdure-clad sloping lawn of the scowling cliff, within sight of the waving fronds of the coconut palm, and even some distant liner perchance on the far horizon, and to the sound of sweet music, now and again drowned by the roar of the billows breaking on the shore below?

But how much more beautiful and popular might Mount Lavinia be if it were rendered more easily accessible from Colombo. Thus, would not a tramway service, in lieu of the present railway, be better suited for its needs and prove a welcome innovation, and thus help to solve the problem of congestion on this suburban line? Not only will those who live about Colpetty, Bambalapitiya, Dehiwala, Wellawatte and their neighbourhood certainly benefit by the accelerated service of the tramways, but the line itself would be something of a joyride to those in search of pleasure or on outing bent by the sea. Even two-decked tramcars might be profitably introduced, and Mount Lavinia, seeing the greater possibilities of increasing its popularity, might feel disposed to march with the times and add other attractions to the few already existing. It might, in fact, become another Brighton, or Eastbourne, or Margate, with all the concomitant amenities and side-shows so dear to the heart of the holiday-maker or pleasure-seeker.

Probably also, there will then be not only one "Thalassa"—the charming seaside residence of Sir Christoffels Obeysekere, where I had the honour and pleasure of meeting this venerable gentleman—but the whole route from the Metropolis along the sea would be one chain of pretty bungalows and villas, and another of Colombo's problems—the house famine—would thus be incidentally solved, and its æsthetic reputation enhanced.

Speaking of Mount Lavinia reminds me how short of sea-bathing establishments Colombo is! As a matter of fact, there exist only two in or near such a large and prosperous city: that of the Mount Lavinia Grand Hotel being somewhat too far away for many to profit by, especially with the present handicap of the railway, and the other—actually a swimming bath only, but none the less supplying a much felt want—within the precincts of the Galle Face Hotel, and therefore, restricted in use.

Whether it is that the people in Colombo are indifferent to the advantages and thrills of sea-bathing—for who does not relish an early morning "dip" in the silvery sea?—or some enterprising syndicate or casino believes it will not pay to run such a concern, I cannot definitely say. The fact, however, remains that people in Ceylon—at any rate those in Colombo—are not so alive to the pleasures of the deep, and do not seem to appreciate them adequately—as if they were confirmed land-lubbers, and the call of the sea had no spell in it!

CHAPTER VIII

GALLE FACE

Of Colombo's public promenades pride of place must certainly go to Galle Face, and I wonder if in the whole of the East there is any spot that can bear comparison with it, still less surpass it in its extreme beauty and exquisite charm.

Nowhere as along its wind-blown sea-wall and the sloping turf beyond does one meet with such a conglomeration of races and diversity of classes; and yet old and young, high and low, rich and poor, meet here on common ground—all seeking to inhale the invigorating ozone of Ceylon's spicy shores, or to find relaxation after a day's hard toil. And here beneath the canopy of Heaven, and upon the soil where every man is born free, and in the very eyes of the Almighty to Whom all are equal may all Colombo assemble to disport themselves, each in his own way, and according to his own means and taste, and then return homewards refreshed and thankful that a bounteous Providence and a paternal government had provided them with such an enchanting spot.

But pause, gentle reader, and hearken to what a writer of my boyhood said,[1] which to-day, with but slight variation to make allowance for the advent of the motor car, holds good as it did seventeen years ago. In beauty of expression, vividness of description, and warmth of feeling, it transcends anything that has been said about it, and can hardly be surpassed.

[1] "Sundown Parade," by A. E. Murrell, in the *Daily Mail* of June 17, 1905.

Sundown Parade,
Colombo,
May 19.

"Every place has its haunt where rank and beauty throng to grace the hour and testify that clothes are more than raiment. Go where you will, even to the remotest parts of the world, and wherever civilisation has left its trail there you will find a rendezvous of more or less repute.

"Not every spot, perforce, can boast a far-extending avenue of sylvan beauty, a broad undulating, hill-crowned course, bordered by side-walks bright with flowers, blossoming trees, and patches of radiant colour, or a street of stately marble buildings under the shadow of a battlemented, feudal castle, whose very walls are embalmed with the spirit of historic romance. Many a town proclaims the salubrity of its fashionable, but uninspiring, and wind-swept parade. Not a few cling to tradition, and revel sartorically in an old-world, narrow, twisting High-street blinded with lattice casements. Some rest content with even a dismantled pier-head, where week by week, saunters a gaily-dressed throng.

"But except to the highly susceptible, it matters not greatly whether the resort is situated in a garden of Arcady or holds lingering traces of the glory of the past. Fashion is the child of civilisation. Everyone delights to walk abroad, however mean the streets. Love of admiration, a longing to be in the vogue, desire to wrest the passing triumph of the moment, are not least among the precepts of the everyday rationalism of the denizens of Vanity Fair.

"Along the seashore of Ceylon's beautiful marine capital stretches a far-famed parade set amid a wealth of natural splendour. To the west lie the sunlit waters of the Indian Ocean, that oft impel the exile's gaze and invoke the golden dream of promise. Eastwards, broad grassy slopes rise to the road-paved ridge. Beyond, the golden gleaming spires of the city shoot upward into the blue expanse. Away south stretches the palm-strewn shore, with its fringe of deep green and glittering yellow sands.

"It is five o'clock on Sunday afternoon. A little early yet for the belles of fashion and dames of rank to sally forth, for the sea still flashes with golden light. For the time being, the parade, despite the natural beauty around, looks for all the world like a civilised patch of some sun-baked desert. But by and by, when the orange ball is slowly sinking into the sea and the waters are sapphire-blue, and the heavens filled with sky splendours, the scene will as swiftly change as if a magic wand had passed thereo'er.

"The countless carriages and turnouts that stood, attended by silent, sable syces, under the lofty archway, of the palatial hotels and white porticos of flower-embowered bungalows, and at the outer gates of the churches and temples, are now filled with breeze-seekers, rolling along to the avenue by the sea. For a while there comes the sound of gliding wheels. Then from the roads leading north and south, streams of handsome equipages pour forth on to the parade and swiftly form in long, unbroken ranks, until anon, from end to end, a mustered host is gathered.

"You look upon a scene strikingly rare, whose parallel could be seen nowhere save in a corner of Imperial Britain, or, in earlier days, in the streets of ancient Cæsarian Rome, where Greeks and Italians, Britons and Germans, Africans and people from India commingled, and all the tongues of the earth were heard. In it there appear denizens of the far regnant Isles, bright-eyed Sinhalese and Tamils, Malays from the Dutch East Indies, descendants from the wandering tribes of the Arabian deserts, Afghans from Northern India, and Parsees from Bombay. All throng together, symbolising the two civilisations—the old order and the new. The diverse habits and ways of thought: the East, tired and weary, yet aspiring to new ideas, hopes and faith; the West, fervent and exultant, flushed with the pride of the flower of the age, and imbued with the ardour of prescribed dominion and triumphant strength.

"Indeed, there is a world of interest, a fascinating study, in this sartorial gala, the power and sovereignty of empire, the accord of races once hostile for centuries, the spread of modern institutions, the dominion and bondage of fashion. Gazing thereon the Imperialist might dream of a realm extending to the four corners of the earth, the historian revive in the mind's eye the dawn of civilisation in Asia Minor, the woman of fashion find delight and weave her thousand fancies, the moralist inwardly mark the ceaseless changes of life, yet note once more that there is nothing new under the sun.

"On roll the carriages, as far as eye can reach, until they disappear in clouds of golden dust. Mounted above, or in the boot behind, sit the dark-skinned servants, motionless as statues, in uniforms of snowy white, girt at the waist with yellow and crimson. Below the thin white lines and above the red brown roads gleam streams of bright colour flecked with silver, the raiment of many colours of the richly-dressed and the simple garb of the white apparelled. Here you see an Oriental profoundly salaaming, there a Westerner graciously bowing. All speed their hour pursuing the scene, talking the gossip of the day, telling stories, and admiring the loveliest women in the procession.

"The sun is now sinking into the quiet sea, flooding the horizon with gorgeous hues and filling the whole atmosphere with a fiery glow that brings every feature into fleeting prominence. In the mantling purple light the whole scene seems invested with the glory of pageantry. The eye is dazzled by the wealth of colour and the galaxy of dark-haired beauty. He who sang many an Eastern tale in immortal song, mayhap oft dreamed of such scenes and of women so fair of form. What more inspiring than this gala, with its bevy of lustrous-eyed houris arrayed in exquisitely-coloured garments that shine like gems? You revel in the indefinable charm held by such a scene, the potent spell of extraordinary personal loveliness.

"One by one the carriages go by, smart broughams, dogcarts, victorias, and lordly landaus; quaint, gloomy palanquins, blinded with Venetian shutters; roofed gharries with tattered silk sun curtains, and jaunty 'rickshaws bright with shining metal. There moves by a modern chariot equipped with everything required for comfort, and drawn by a horse ornate with gleaming silver harness. Beside her companion handling the ribbons sits a woman of peerless beauty, her eyes bright as jewels, her graceful form draped in folding robes of many colours. Now passes a sumptuous carriage filled with people that look as if the blood of Alexander's invaders flowed in their veins. And now an old-world palanquin with half-drawn blinds that but faintly screen its burden of pretty women with marvellous smiling eyes turned full upon the scene to catch closer glimpses of the procession.

"Now comes a show of pagentry that emblazons the scene wherever it appears: the Governor in his state landau, attended by his retinue and brilliant, mounted escort, the servants of statuesque splendour, clad in gorgeous scarlet uniforms and huge turbans, the outriders equipped with lances and graced with pennons that shine in the gleaming light. Shortly after, the wondering gaze rests on a group of brave Parsees, all dressed alike in quaint frock-coats and curiously shaped conical hats that date from the dawn of civilisation. There is something to interest or admire wherever you look in these endless, gleaming lines of carriages that pass, return, and pass again while the sun is sinking into the sea, until finally 'The sun's rim dips, the stars rush out, At one stride comes the dark'."

[Photo by Platé, Ltd., Colombo

SCENE IN THE PETTAH, COLOMBO

Facing page 72]

[*Photo by Platé, Ltd., Colombo*

VICTORIA PARK, CINNAMON GARDENS, COLOMBO

Facing page 73]

CHAPTER IX

RAMBLES AND REFLECTIONS

How to Enjoy a Stroll

A guide or dragoman is a useful person to the tourist as a rule; but it depends upon what genus you light. He may prove a veritable find, or *vice versa*, a bore and a pest. But if a tourist can dispense with him, and see things for himself, finding his way about with the help of a guide book perchance, or in the company of a genial, cheery friend, or armed with some slight knowledge he may have accumulated about the place he is visiting, how much more would he enjoy his sightseeing.

It is in consonance with the last alternative that I occasionally started on my rambles in Colombo, sometimes in a 'rickshaw, at other times by the tramway, and not seldom with the sole use of a sturdy pair of legs. The motor-car or cab, of course, I used for longer distances; but the other means of locomotion I found more suitable to penetrate right into the heart of Colombo's busy scenes, and mix with the people as if I were one of them, not a stranger from a distant land. If the passenger also happens to know the ways of the people, and is blest with a smattering of the Sinhalese tongue, as was the case with me, which even the lapse of twenty-four years had not effaced, why, his stroll would be all the easier, as it would be more delightful.

Colombo Streets

A welcome help in the Colombo streets, a small and insignificant item in its way, but none the less useful, are the sign-posts at certain important points where various streets intersect one another, and how often did that indicating " Fort " put me on the right track without my troubling to ask some passer-by the way; and the Cairo Tanzim might well emulate the example of Colombo in this respect. It might, however, in turn suggest to Colombo the creation of " refuges " or " islands " or " shelters " in the middle of busy streets where the traffic is heaviest, to afford facilities to pedestrians when crossing from one side to the other, especially in these days of the motor car when their need is sure to be more strongly felt than ever.

To my friends in Cairo it might come as something of a surprise that the rule of the road in Ceylon is " left ", after the vogue of London, and not " right ", as here and in Paris; and even up to now I have not been able to award the palm to either definitely, for the partisans of each are as determined and loquacious on the merits of the one over the other.

And the very fact that Cairo takes after Paris in so many ways makes public *cafés* one of its notable features, like the great gay city by the banks of the Seine, whereas Colombo, which naturally takes after its own model by the Thames, is conspicuous by their absence.

The Dhoby

The prodigious (I am using it correctly here, not indiscriminately after the way Dominie Sampson does in Scott's *Guy Mannering*) bundles of some dhoby, as they are wheeled off in the familiar Ceylon thatched cart, did not attract my attention so much, for I knew the dhoby pretty well, and quite appreciated his neat washing, and his cheaper charges. But the way he mercilessly dashes our clothing on some slabs of rock, as conducive to the best cleaning, vitiates the benefit of the so-called moderate charges, and necessitates the laying in of a big stock of apparel to compensate for premature wear and tear.

But what actually amazed me was the practically prohibitive sum asked for pressing or ironing one's suit—not the white drill or tussore silk so extensively used in Ceylon, which the dhoby as a rule looks to, but the tweed or serge or flannel or cheviot or cashmere, as the case might be. Could my friends here believe their ears when I tell them that Rs.3 (four shillings) were actually asked for at the Grand Oriental Hotel, which here in Cairo could be very well done for a shilling? But when I remonstrated vehemently, the hotel laundryman said that I should consider myself lucky that I was not charged more, for another establishment charged Rs. 4 (a little over five shillings) for each! And when I mentioned this to my friends in Cairo they did not evince much surprise, for in Great Britain six shillings are usually charged, that is to say, even more than what the Ceylonese ask, though they believed Ceylon was a cheap country! And from what I tasted of the laundry charges on board the steamers, I can be only thankful that Egypt is still far better off than either Ceylon or England in this respect.

Anyhow, I did not submit without a struggle, and tactfully expostulated with the laundryman that being a resident of the hotel, and owing to the fact that I was offering several suits *en bloc* to be ironed, and not a solitary one, he might as well be more reasonable in his charges. He finally thawed, and cut them down to Rs. 2 per suit, which I think was not a bad bargain under the circumstances; and even Old Monkbarns and his sister Grizel, such past masters in the art of haggling as Sir Walter Scott shows in his *Antiquary*, might have given me credit in the present instance.

Johann Tetzil, Redivivus

One afternoon as I was standing by the starting point of the Grand Pass Tramway, prior to my taking the car to go on one of my rambles, I had a somewhat queer experience.

"Good afternoon, sir," a suave voice suddenly addresses me, as a gentleman with a leather bag in his hand accosts me.

"Good afternoon," I replied.

"Would you like to buy one of these tracts?" he next adds, whipping out one and offering it to me.

"What tracts?" I rejoin, somewhat surprised, and politely waving it aside, but not a little nettled at the bystanders gathering round, for the unrestrained inquisitiveness of the lower classes in Ceylon is only too flagrant to be lightly ignored!

"For only ten cents, sir, you might buy one of these religious tracts asking God to forgive you your sins, and the very act of being willing to buy one will be enough"—as if absolution were a marketable article!

"Oh!" said I, "but what made you think I was a sinner?" and in a flash—

> "How fleet is a glance of the mind!
> Compared with the speed of its flight,
> The tempest itself lags behind,
> And the swift-winged arrows of light—"[1]

my thoughts went back to that famous episode of the Reformation connected with the selling of Indulgences by one Johann Tetzil, and Martin Luther's courageous stand against the Pope, even with the dread excommunication staring him in the face.

"We are all sinners, sir, and one can never be too late to seek forgiveness."

"Then keep one for yourself," I concluded; "I, for my part, would rather appeal to God straightway myself

[1] *The Solitude of Alexander Selkirk*, by W. Cowper.

than seek the intervention of anybody else. Besides, excuse me, please, if I tell you that proselytising in this manner is not the best way, for you never know whom you may come across."

And with a parting "Good afternoon!" I took the tramcar that was about to start for Grand Pass, leaving the little knot of people who had witnessed this scene to make out what they liked from our little talk.

The Author would be a Philosopher.

How hard would life be were it not for its humours. "Laugh, and the world laughs with you; weep, and you weep alone," goes the common saying, and there is a great deal of truth in it. One need not always be a pessimist although his fortunes may have fallen very low. Even in the worst circumstances one can be something of a Mark Tapley, and his misfortunes will then not weigh so heavily on his mind. Let him be hopeful as far as possible for "something to turn up", as Mr. Micawber so sanguinely put it, for

> "Hope springs eternal in the human breast,
> Man never is, but always to be blest."

Grave and joyful all of us in turn are, even as the very skies are sometimes radiant with sunshine, at others threatening with their frown. For pleasure and joy to Ceylon I went; armed thus with such a bright outlook I would always sally forth. Even when I would seem to be pestered or annoyed, still I would try to make light of such petty nuisances, for life is so short, and still shorter my stay in Ceylon, that I could ill afford to embitter my existence any further, already grief-stricken as I was by the blow of my beloved mother's death.

Oh! Dickens! Dickens! could we but make life as bright and light as you would have it, few broken hearts would there be in this harsh, cruel world, and fewer wrinkles and furrows of Time's insidious, remorseless hand!

Ceylon Postcards

It is a pity that Ceylon, a land flowing, not with milk (*vide* the chapter on Nuwara Eliya) and honey, as the familiar phrase says, but with beauty and charm, should not have postcards worthy of her! Now and then one does light upon a pretty card, but such are few and far between. You go to Platé's, a firm of photographers in Ceylon, and excellent exponents of their art, and they will offer you some which are very commonplace, if not too dull and drab to do justice to Ceylon as a tourist's wonderland. When you complain of a lack of better ones, "Sesame" opens, and a veritable galaxy is unfurled before your gaze. But they are not postcards, but photographs in varying sizes done up as works of art, and fit perhaps only for the collection of some connoisseur, or to grace the walls of some favourite study or grand drawing-room.

But why should these not be reproduced in postcard form? I am sure they would command a ready and very remunerative sale at once. Most regretfully, the god Mammon seems to be the one powerful deity of these days, and, as a consequence, it is only natural that a business firm should have an eye on its financial side. But that is no reason why any firm should be too materialist, and in saying this, I should like to make it quite plain that I am speaking in general terms, and not for one moment whatever casting any reflection on any particular business concern in Ceylon. And Platé's, most considerate and obliging people as they are, still, don't they think that they owe something to the country they live and prosper in, and should accordingly in their turn —so well fitted and equipped as they are for the purpose—try to bring home to the people of the world the beauty of Ceylon in some popular and inexpensive way? But not only in this may they be taken to task, for even if people were disposed to buy some of these fine pictures, how the prices hop up! Why, even the frog can hardly keep pace with them!

Which brings me to another point. How the French can relish King Frog as a delicacy I cannot conceive; but then, the native of Marseilles says "Taste bouillabaisse", (not Naples, as the Italians say) "and die!" Whether this is owing to the unthinkable savoury nature of this so-called delectable dish, or owing to the weird denizens of the deep, with King Frog thrown in as the tit-bit, which go to compose it, by the side of which even the uncanny concoction of the Witches in *Macbeth* pale into insignificance, I cannot say! Still, I personally would not care to partake of this dish, and its equally unpalatable consort "Fessikh" of my own land, for their weight in gold. But this is by the way.

The Colombo Tramways

Cave's advice, as to the adaptability of the tram as a suitable conveyance, wherefrom to get a good view of some of Colombo's scenes of local life and colour, which he gave in his admirable publication, *The Book of Ceylon*,[1] I most readily seized upon, and right glad was I that I did so, for the results amply bore out the promise. But I would rather give his most vivid and entertaining description than make any attempt at such on my part here:

"A start is made for Grand Pass from the Fort terminus near the Grand Oriental Hotel. Most of the cars are fitted with outside seats in front, which are first class. Into one of these we step. The first scene is Main Street. The *Times* (daily newspaper) office is on our right, and the Colombo Iron Works on our left. We now leave the Fort and are carried along past tens of thousands of coal which proclaim their own story of the vast amount of shipping that comes this way. A minute later we are in the Pettah, the natives' London. The effect is kaleidoscopic. Moormen or Indo-Arab

[1] *The Book of Ceylon*, by H. W. Cave, pp. 47–52 (London: Cassell & Co.).

traders occupy Main Street with well-stocked stores containing every description of goods. The street widens at Kayman's Gate, so called after a Dutch officer.[1] Here will be noticed an old Dutch curfew bell which may have been used in the seventeenth century to toll the knell of parting day, but not as in Europe to warn the inhabitants to put out their fires. Here in the vicinity of the Town Hall we notice the great diversity of races represented: Sinhalese, Moors, Tamils, Parsees, Dutch, Portuguese, Malays and Afghans; the variety of costume worn by each race in accordance with caste or social position, from the simple loin cloth of the coolie to the gorgeous attire of the wealthy and high-caste gentlemen; the different complexions and form of toilet, the avocations carried on in the open street, are all interesting to the visitor who for the first time becomes a witness of the manners and customs of Oriental life. At every turn the eye is met by a fresh picture, and a new subject for study is presented to the mind. This mixed and motley crowd live their life and carry on their labours almost entirely in public. Neither doors, windows, nor shutters interfere with a complete view of the interior of their houses and stalls. The handicraftsman works serenely in his open shed, sometimes even in the open street; women are occupied in their most domestic affairs unveiled from the glance of the curious passer-by, and tiny children, clothed only in the rich tints of their own complexions, sport amongst the traffic. All this harmonises charmingly with the conditions of climate and the nature of the people. The heat renders clothing uncomfortable, and closed up dwellings unendurable. The tram ride is perhaps too rapid for the stranger to fully appreciate these novel scenes; but a glance at them through three miles of native streets is all that time affords. The terminus is reached at the River Kelaniya. We can spare a few minutes to look round at the scenes on the river bank and even to cross the river by the ferry, as the returning trams leave at intervals of five minutes. Or we can stroll

[1] This is said to be incorrect, for Kayman's Gate actually means crocodile gate;

along the Victoria Bridge which has replaced the old picturesque bridge-of-boats which once did the duty of connecting the northern road with Colombo. The native life and customs here will instruct and amuse us, and we shall regret that time does not admit of a more prolonged exploration. The return journey will enable us to enjoy more fully the points that almost escape our notice owing to the rapidity of the car.

"Having returned to our starting point we now take a seat in the car that moves off in the opposite direction. Proceeding up York Street, and turning by the Public Works Office we pass the Chamber of Commerce, the Survey Office, and the Fort Railway Station[1] of the Southern Railway. The lake scenery first claims our attention. Presently we pass the Royal College situated on high ground on the left. This is the principal Government educational institution, the nucleus of a future university.[2] A distant view of St. Joseph's Roman Catholic College across the lake is observed, a handsome building which we shall see later in the detail of closer inspection. A ferry connecting with a peninsula of the lake called Captain's Garden provides a pretty bit of scenery, and here we notice the operations of the washerman, the dark, dank dhoby who bleaches our soiled linen by the primitive method of beating it on slabs of rock. Upon leaving the lake the line passes the main Railway Station upon the right and the Technical School upon the left. The latter is an institution at present not very enthusiastically appreciated by the natives of the country for whose benefit a paternal Government has provided it. The object of its establishment is to provide training in civil engineering, surveying, telegraphy, electrical and mechanical engineering. The Ceylonese, however, do not take kindly to technical work, preferring rather the professions of clerks, lawyers and

[1] This station caters now, not only for the Southern Railway, but for Up-Country as well.

[2] Since these lines were written (1907) the Royal College has been transferred to the Cinnamon Gardens, and the Ceylon University even been founded.

doctors. It is hoped, however, that this attitude towards mechanics and art will soon disappear, and that the Technical School will serve the admirable purpose of supplying the Public Works, the Railway, the Irrigation and the Forestry departments of the Government with plenty of good men whose capacity will be as thorough, and whose enthusiasm in their profession will be as great and whole hearted, as that of the imported European.

"After passing the Technical School we proceed along Maradana Road for half a mile, when we pass over the railway at the Junction Station where trains leave for the coast line and the Kelani Valley as well as for Up-Country. Then we notice on our left the Police Headquarters and Parade Ground, and on the right the largest Mohammedan Mosque in Colombo. Other notable places are the Lady Havelock Hospital for women and children erected in 1896 by public subscription and named after Lady Havelock who was the leading spirit in its establishment; the headquarters of the medical department presided over by Sir Allan Perry;[1] the Roman Catholic Archbishop's house and Campbell Park, into which the visitor might stroll for a few minutes before taking a tram back.

"On the return journey we might look more particularly for quaint scenes in the bazaars through which we pass. Even the sign boards over the little open stall amuse us. 'A clever astrologer', words of no small import to the people of the neighbourhood whose horoscopes are cast at birth, and whose every subsequent step in life depends on, or at least, is influenced by the counsel of the astrologer. If a journey has to be taken the time of starting must be fixed by the astrologer. If a house is to be built the foundation stone must be laid in accordance with his advice. He decides the auspisious moment for everything, even for the first shave, whether it be of baby's head or young man's beard. The ordinary, no less than the important, events of life are determined

[1] This gentleman has since retired, leaving the Island for England soon afterwards.

The Lovely Kandy Lake, from Lady Horton's Road.

through the medium of astrology. However much of an imposture we may consider this art to be, there is no doubt of its immense influence upon the Sinhalese people, and that the less educated amongst them believe in it implicitly.

"The open character of the native shops is universal; they vary only in the classes of goods they have for sale. Here there are fruits, curry stuffs, dried fish, spices, market baskets and earthenware chatties. In another we notice baskets of fowls which are kept alive, and not as in the poulterers' shops in Europe. There we observe a native medical stall by the high-sounding title of "Medical Hall."[1] The tin-shop, with the tinsmith at work is ubiquitous. The bootmaker is patiently sticking to his last, manufacturing the latest creations in foot-wear upon the floor of his unfurnished den. In other shops are seen all manner of vegetables and fruits, native manufacturers in brass ware, the gay comboys or cloths worn by the people, and various useful articles made from the coconut and other palms. The Sinhalese man of sienna complexion, wearing his long hair gathered up into a knot surmounted by a comb of tortoiseshell, is attired in garb varying with caste, even the comb assuming different forms in accordance with social position. The Sinhalese women too, have a multitude of distinctions in dress and ornaments. All indulge more or less in jewellery, consisting of necklaces and bangles on both arms and ankles and rings on their fingers and toes. Many Tamil women wear but a single coloured cloth, which they gracefully entwine about their limbs, leaving the right side bare to the hip. The costumes of the native men are even more diverse. The Moormen[2] with shaven heads, crowned with curiously plaited brimless

[1] This reminds me of once noticing a very tiny, unpretentious building in Colombo answering to the equally high-sounding, and the world-famed "Eton College." I wonder what that famous Public School by the banks of the Thames opposite royal Windsor would think if it saw its presumptuous counterpart there in Colombo!

[2] The Moors have since discarded this unbecoming headgear, practically all of them now donning the familiar fez.

hats; the Parsees in still more curious headgear; the Tamils with religious symbols on their foreheads; the Afghans contrasting with the Tamils in superabundance of gaudy attire—such are the races, and such the dresses of the groups of people we see in the streets of Colombo."

. . . . .

The Colombo tramways, however, have two drawbacks. To start with, the accommodation of the first class in one type of car is supposed to be for four persons; but surely not every one of us is a " starveling ", or an " elf-skin " of a Prince Hal, as Falstaff has it, for the seats allotted to two would barely allow of a replica of this doughty knight to squeeze himself into the space, still less to accommodate two persons of fairly normal proportions! A reasonable ratio of comfort is what one naturally expects, not to sit jammed in like a pair of sardines, and it is odds when one wants to get up whether he will not force up his neighbour also to bear him company, as if they were a pair of indivisible " Siamese " twins, or like what happens when one picks out a biscuit from a well-filled tin the next comes out with it, so close and tightly are they packed.

Again, in the first class compartments an extra payment connotes extra comfort; so, why should the seats be hard board, and not upholstered in leather or oilcloth, or even with cane, which is so cheap in Ceylon? Indeed, the tramways will have to look to their laurels, else, with the advent of the motor car, and the motor buses which are bound to follow hard on its heels in the immediate future, the public might find it preferable to give their patronage to the newer modes of conveyance, unless the tramways can offer strong inducements to retain their goodwill.

Perhaps in the good days to come (ah! this time it is not the " good old days " we sigh after), when luxurious " two-deckers " perambulate on the Mount Lavinia and

Peradeniya Roads, then will such comfort be a reality; and one might even loll and lounge in them with the easy languor of Tennyson's *Lotos-Eaters*—unless, of course, aeroplanes are the " rage ", and the tramway exists only as a fossil beneath some glass case!

Colombo Motor Cars

It is curious how infectious criticism sometimes is. One shortcoming suggests another, until occasionally one easily succumbs. Why, in the name of Heaven, should Colombo be entirely handed over to the tender mercies of the motor car? Of course its triumphant march onwards is irresistible; but some room might generously be spared for the one-time omnipresent " cabby ". A car is useful for those in a hurry, or to cover long distances in a short time; but in sightseeing one does not always wish to hustle, as a good many Americans are universally known to do. Besides, slow or fast, there is always something mysterious—I almost said uncanny—about the meter, and I sometimes think it to be seized with the " jumps ", since it as often as not leaps forward unmercifully! And the tourist, of course, has other things to attend to, and the old-time gharry—within its limited means—in its day amply catered for his needs to the mutual satisfaction of both " jehu " and " fare ".

But *mutatis mutandis*, if the taxi must exist, and in these days of quick travel it is no longer a luxury, but has become an almost indispensable appendage to the ever-increasing claims of comfort—for when Dame Fashion sets the vogue her minions must blindly follow suit!—then, do away with the hiring cars and all their abuses; punctiliously examine the meters; provide adequate legislation for safeguarding the public against the folly and thoughtlessness of cruel road hogs; and, above all, regulate the fares and make the tariff more reasonable, so that travelling might be a real pleasure, not a luxury for a privileged few only!

Mr. "Boyagi"

Curiously, also, contrariwise, while there seems to be a glut of motor cars in Colombo, there is not a single shoe-black! The hotel's retainers do not excel in this direction as a rule, though whether from lack of polish withheld, as some excused themselves with, or, what is more likely, owing to a touch of the "doldrums", I cannot say definitely.

Ah! if only, instead of receiving with open arms so many undesirable *im*migrants, and aliens, Egypt could generously export a few superfluous *em*igrants of the boot-black fraternity and kindred species who spring up like mushrooms from nowhere!

Indeed, we should be only too cheerful and willing to render Ceylon any service in this line, and thus provide it with one of the diverting features of everyday life in Cairo in the neighbourhood of her big hotels, as when a devil-may-care, almost cheeky genus of "boots", with a deceptive, but would-be winsome twitter chirps, "I shiny yur bots, Sar, very good, very clean, very nice, Captain Mackenzie," and ere you realise what you are doing, he has actually grabbed your feet with a startling suddenness, and is polishing away for all he is worth!

And a wonderful linguist he would aspire to be, Mr. "Boyagi", no matter whether it is "pidgin" English, Cockney English, or "Bush" English, for was he not the darling of Tommy and the hosts of Australians who were here during the Great War, and were naturally only too eager to avail themselves of any little distraction they could come across from the grim realities of warfare?

And so, *sic transit gloria mundi*, our former familiar figure, the donkey-boy, a remarkably good linguist in his day, but more of a *rara avis* at the present time, must needs pass his mantle on to Mr. "Boyagi"! But one thing I can affirm without fear of contradiction: the Egyptian "boots", whether he plies his itinerant trade in the streets, or waits patiently for his customers in a handy little shop, which he grandiloquently calls a polishing parlour, is a past master of his art, and does impart an excellent shine to our footwear. Indeed, one would like to have had the opinion of Mr. Sam Weller in regard to his ingenious counterpart here by the banks of the Nile.

The Cinnamon Gardens

Which traveller passing through Colombo has not heard of the Cinnamon Gardens? But vainly goes he who hopes to catch from afar the pleasant aroma of this spice, which has even given to Ceylon one of its many beautiful names! Perhaps at one time there it might have reigned supreme, but *mutatis mutandis*, again! Gone is it, as vanished are so many things in this ever changing world, and the Cinnamon Gardens we now find existing as Colombo's chief residential and aristocratic quarter, its pretty bungalows beyond peer set in a veritable sylvan paradise.

Here I called on several of our old friends, and how glad I was to meet them after so many years. Alas, however, there were others who had since been called away to the great unknown, and how I missed them. In this quarter I also had the satisfaction of seeing our former residence, " Fair Holme ", next to " Inveresk ", the residence of our good friends, Dr. C. T. van Geyzel[1] and the Misses van Geyzel, and what pictures of delight, of a time when the world was too young for me to dream of care and worry, did its view call back; but the very vision of my youthful past brought back in turn the sad memory of those dear parents, beneath whose watchful gaze and tender, fond affection I tasted of such delight.

Happy indeed must be the various Clubs set in this sylvan paradise, as thankful, no doubt, their members that they can enjoy their games and pass their time amidst such ravishing surroundings. Nor has the

[1] Since writing this he also has passed away, and how I missed this kind, bluff, hearty gentleman during my visit to Ceylon in 1924.

general public and the children even been forgotten by a paternal Government, as the existence of the splendid Victoria Park lying about here proves. A rendezvous for all, but children in particular, has this popular park become, a welcome feature of it being the Band, heard also! so seldom in this great city; for music "that soothes the savage breast", and is so dear to the heart of all, is, curiously, conspicuous by its rareness in this Island! But sad to note, beautiful as the Victoria Park is, still certain parts of it showed palpable signs of neglect. Could not the Government, therefore, see to this point, if only that by doing so it would considerably enhance the æsthetic beauty of this lovely spot?

The Museum of course, I did not fail to visit, and I was kindly shown round the whole place by a clerk detailed off to help to explain the exhibits to me.

Why not a Zoo in Colombo?

The sight of a small bear in the grounds of the Museum at once aroused in me the thought why Colombo should not have its Regent's Park. Rich in its fauna is Ceylon, as it is in close proximity to several large countries abounding with denizens of the forest, as India, Malaya, Australia, and the Sudan. So, if Kandy has got its show-place in the Peradeniya Gardens, Nuwara Eliya its Hakgalla, Galle its Dutch Forts, and Anuradhapura its ruins, why should not Colombo have something worthy of its dignity as the Metropolis of the Island, and one of the greatest seaports of the East? And a Zoo might well answer in some sense, as it is sure to prove a quite popular pleasure ground for all, and of no small educational value to many. Thus our little bruin might set the ball rolling, and form the nucleus of the Zoo to come.

The Fruit Market

If a person stays some time in a town it is as likely as not that he will not be able to resist the temptation of a

[*Photo by Platé, Ltd., Colombo*

CUP DAY AT THE HAVELOCK RACECOURSE, COLOMBO

Facing page 88]

[Photo by Platé, Ltd., Colombo

CEYLON POLICE

Facing page 89]

peep at the local market. And shopping and marketing are at all times a pleasant pastime, or at any rate a time-killer, when " we've got the money too." Oh! shade of Jingo, how times have changed, and your song has paled by the side of *It's a long way to Tipperary*, or *Take me back to Blighty*.

Of course I did not expect the Ceylon market to deviate from the general run, so I cannot see, as I once read in the *Ceylon Observer*, how the gentleman who lamented the disillusionment that awaited him in contradistinction to the poetical picture his fertile brain had conjured up could have expected the fruits to be otherwise than as they were offered for sale! Did he really expect to find the fruits so stacked and exposed, as if they were so many sweets and chocolates in a confectioner's shop in a glass case, instead of fruits offered for sale in the usual way in the market? At any rate, whatever might have been his fond and highly-coloured picture, still there they lay the fruits in the Pettah Market at the simple beck and call of any kind, well-disposed passenger: luscious fruits in heaps and rows, delicious fruits stacked up in groups, and toothsome fruits hung up in clusters.

Again, here, in its natural guise could one come across that wondrous thing that goes by the grandiloquent name of " mutton ", but which in Ceylon is in reality only goat's flesh—at any rate so I was told! What about the Alfred Model Farm? Would it not be worth while importing a few good sheep from somewhere near, where there is a surplus of them, say, Australia or Arabia.

" Land Sharks "

But beware Mr. Passenger. These backwaters of Colombo are no less infested with " sharks " than those which lurk about its harbour! You can afford to be generous here, for a tourist must make allowance for such on his travels; but one can never be too liberal, for at no time one would like to feel that he had been " done ".

Ah! next time when I go to Colombo's markets I shall not wear a fez or a dark suit, but go in a topee and a white drill or tussore silk suit, and be careful when I talk to Mohammed in Arabic, if it be only in whispers, so that I may not let the cat out of the bag after all the precaution I shall have taken to conceal my identity as a stranger, and this time they won't catch me napping.

Thus, on my first visit to the Pettah Fruit Market, a Malay spotting me for a likely victim in the common bond of religion that bound us, helps me, unasked for, with one or two purchases, and then pours out a woeful tale of how he has been stranded, and out go two rupees to him (I was almost giving him Rs. 5, but it was a two-rupee note that slips into my fingers in my trousers pocket).

A few yards further, "Salam Aleikum." Ah! the magic words! Was there really somebody who knew Arabic here—for it is music to hear one's own tongue in a foreign land. "Alaikim Es-Salam," I gladly reply. But no. "Bakshish," and my hopes sink as I survey the impostor with mixed feelings, and in pity I hand him a rupee.

But even as I do so, on finding that his vocabulary is confined to the two expressions which serve as a clever decoy and palliative at the same time, I recall our linguist's counterpart in my own country who, though higher up in the social ladder, and should thus know better, nevertheless most cheekily persists in making a parade of his French with "Oui Monsieur," "Non, Monsieur," "Bon Jour," "Bon soir," "Oui, Mon cher," "Non, Mon cher,"—his whole stock-in-trade!

The very fact, however, that these two acts were encouraging others to follow suit make me beat a hasty retreat at once.

An Awkward Visitor

But the very mention of them reminds me of how once I had a very awkward half-an-hour. An Arab somehow or other managed to worm himself into the Lounge of the Grand Oriental Hotel, where I happened to be at the time having my afternoon tea. A long tale he unravels in classical Arabic, and it was all I could do to understand, very difficult as it usually is to speak it correctly. After beating about the bush a good deal, he comes to the real object of his visit. He has run short of the cash he brought with him from the Hedjaz, for Ceylon is such an expensive country, he emphasises, and the Mohammedans did not feel very much disposed to lend a helping hand.

"But that is very strange," I remark, "for they have always been very kind and generous, and in particular to strangers in need of help."

"Oh no. They are awfully stingy," he proceeds; but I am not a little stung by the libel he utters.

"But has nobody helped you, as they have always assisted others?" I next add, controlling myself.

"Oh! very few; and the highest sum I ever got was Rs. 50 only (*sic*) which Mr. Macan Markar gave me, and this, of course, could not last for good!" As if Mr. Macan Markar should have paid him Rs. 5,000, or even Rs. 500, and charity were obligatory!

A dead silence follows. Then Mr. Arab breaks the ice again.

"I beg to take your leave," or what in English is tantamount to "I am going."

"All right," but in my inner soul I say something stronger, for I could not bear the thought of such cheek and ingratitude.

"But are you not going to help me with something?" he next adds.

"But what can I give you when you despise such a handsome sum as Rs. 50 which Mr. Macan Markar gave you?"

"Oh! anything will do," he replies, somewhat crushed by my reply.

And even though I was somewhat nettled, still I could not help pitying the man to some extent, a stranger as he was in Ceylon; and forthwith as I go out to consult Mr. Magid Sapideen as to what amount might be suitable, Mr. Witzig, the manager, overhears me.

"The brutes, have they come again?" shouts Mr. Witzig. "Chuck him out, Magid, quick," and turning to me, he says, "Mr. Toulba, take my advice, never encourage these people, however kindly you may feel disposed to be, for you will never know when to stop, and they will keep pestering you, and come again and again."

But even as Mr. Magid Sapideen goes to see the man I accompany him, for I don't want to see him treated harshly; and being told by Mr. Sapideen that a few rupees will do, I quietly slip a ten-rupee note into the hands of Mr. Arab, and retire with some ostensible excuse, whispering, however, into the ear of Mr. Sapideen not to be too hard on the man, but to quietly see him off without hurting him.

This, however, was but a mere flea-bite compared to the way in which people tried to take advantage of Seyyid Talib Pasha's distinguished position, as I was told, to pester him with their importunities, so that finally he had to bar the gate of his house at Kandy, and hang up a notice to the effect that no admittance was allowed without permission, and the caller and the object of his visit being first announced to him.

Galle Face—The Promenade Par Excellence

Sometimes I would make use of an afternoon to combine both a drive and a walk, and to enjoy both the beautiful rustic scenery and the welcome, invigorating sea breeze. In other words, I would go for a drive through the Cinnamon Gardens and Victoria Park, and finish with a walk on Galle Face promenade after coming *via* Bambalapitiya and Colpetty, and a very enjoyable outing it would prove.

It was on one of these rambles that I had the pleasure of making the acquaintance of Mr. J. S. Perera, the Proctor, and a member of a well-known Ceylonese family, thanks to the introduction of Dr. C. T. van Geyzel; and in the light of subsequent events I can never be too grateful to him for all his kindness towards me, inasmuch as I appreciated his genial friendship from the very beginning. And the memory of the lovely and magnificent Galle Face sea-front will ever be most fondly cherished by me, and how many a pleasant afternoon did I spend on this most delightful spot of Colombo.

An Anecdote of the "Emden"

Associated with Galle Face, or rather the splendid hotel that graces its southern extremity is a wonderful anecdote that reads like a page from romance; but the very singular and remarkable point about it is that it is true in every detail, as has been affirmed to me; and I now narrate it in case it might prove of some interest to my readers, and in particular to those of Ceylon who might not have heard of it previously.

The story goes that in 1914, about the beginning of the Great War, at the time that the *Emden* was still at large and carrying on her depredations, a Dutch steamer was stopped on the high seas by this German warship. The *Emden's* Commander warned the other ship not to use its wireless on pain of immediate destruction. He then boarded it, giving the other Captain to understand that he was going to take command of the Dutch ship, after disguising himself and posing as its real Captain, and steer her into Colombo. Meanwhile the Dutch Skipper, the First Officer, and some other senior members of the crew would be detained on board the *Emden* as hostages, pending his safe return with the Dutch boat after it had coaled, watered, and provisioned. There could be no question of resistance, of course, against the warship's powerful armament, and the Dutch Captain had no alternative but to submit to these imperious terms.

Complacently Captain Muller steers his temporary charge into Colombo, undetected and unsuspected, and as smugly the Dutch boat rides at anchor in the harbour as if it were any ordinary merchantman. Here into the very jaws of the lion had this modern sea-rover come, and little did anybody dream that here in their very grasp lay the elusive will-o'-the-wisp Captain of the *Emden* they would have paid anything to catch!

To Galle Face Hotel he goes and enjoys a hearty tiffin. And being ashore he must, of course, do a little sight-seeing, if only to stretch his legs a bit, and seek some ostensibly innocent diversion after the tedium and hard routine of a humdrum sea voyage. But what expensive sightseeing it eventually proves to the British, yes, sight-seeing wherein with the experience of a past master of his art he manages to locate Colombo's defences, of fortifications, batteries, and the like, and spot the calibre of the heavy artillery, and accumulate as much useful information as he can in so short a time. And all this right under the nose of an unsuspecting British public, and in such a clever and unobtrusive manner as not to arouse the shadow of a doubt whatever on their part! For once the German Eagle had bearded the British Lion in his den!

What was the amazement and consternation of Colombo a short while later when, after the Dutch steamer that sailed in so innocently weighed anchor and departed, Ceylon's Metropolis received a wireless message from the *Emden's* Commander thanking Colombo for all its hospitality, and the pleasant time he had ashore at the Galle Face Hotel and elsewhere in the guise of a friendly Dutch Captain, in view of which he would spare Colombo for the time being, and only bombard it with his last shell, since war is war!

Of course we all are aware how the *Emden* soon after went to her doom off the Cocos Islands at the hands of H.M.S. *Sydney*, and how her chivalrous and gallant Commander (for as such he was recognised by even his foes the British, owing to the humane way he treated his victims) was captured, and thus did not live to see his threat carried out.

Nevertheless, how wonderful does this daring escapade of his read, and how aptly can we again apply to it the well-known saying "Truth is stranger than Fiction." In any case, *Se non è véro è ben trovato*, as the Italians say.

A New Definition of a "Gentleman"

To the many debatable definitions of the much-discussed word "gentleman", which even such an erudite body as the French Academy, though recently incorporating it in their language, have yet, in their turn, failed to solve convincingly, I might add another attempt in this direction.

Even if the Sinhalese conception of it—and the fact that I am giving it as defined by the less educated of their community, makes it all the more striking—brings us no nearer our goal, still the naïve, apt, and pithy way they have sought to give expression to their conception of a gentleman, is instructive and creditable.

Thus it will prove not a little interesting to my readers to note how amongst the less educated of this community the term "high caste" is associated with gentility and refinement.

"That gentleman, Sar," I have sometimes heard it said, "is very good. He very kind, *verry* polite, very nice gentleman. He high caste!" And those who know what the caste system is in India and Ceylon, and all that it connotes, cannot but be impressed and flattered should such a compliment be paid him.

Whereas, taking the other side of the picture, if a person is found wanting, he is not, for one moment, spared the lash of the critic's tongue. "That man, Sar," he would say (and note, it is "man" here, not "gentleman") "he no gentleman; he very bad; *verry* rough; nobody like him. He must be low caste." And to be of "low caste" in these countries was at one time tantamount to being an outcast from decent society. What greater indictment could one therefore shudder at!

" Natives "

Why is it indeed, that notwithstanding the many changes of modern times for the better, and the correspondingly higher standard of education and living in the Orient; and notwithstanding also a supposedly more broadminded and liberal outlook on life than obtained hitherto, in Egypt, but in an even greater degree farther East of Suez, inhabitants of the various countries of these latitudes will still be slightingly designated as " natives ", and not by the real appellation of the nationality of their respective countries? And this, above all, by the British who, apart from their one blemish in this respect of their unreasonable superciliousness and inexplicable indifference to the feelings of others are, as a rule, the most popular of all Europeans owing to the widespread belief amongst Orientals of their more liberal and tolerant spirit in religious matters, and their greater love of fair play.

Indeed, it is high time that this epithet, so apparently harmless when ordinarily used in its proper meaning, but which nevertheless acquires such an obnoxious and repulsive flavour in the derogatory and offensive manner it is hurled at us to assail our ears and our *amour-propre*, should decidedly vanish for good from the vocabulary of tactless and repugnant international expressions. The East is no longer the so-called supine, lethargic, docile East, Westerners have delighted in blissful complacency to picture it so often. No more will the new spirit that animates the Orient brook this hackneyed and time-worn shibboleth, and the sooner the Occident awoke to this fact and recognised it, the better.

If anybody, it is the British above all, with their bigger world-wide empire, their greater facilities of meeting Orientals, and their greater chances of studying them

[Photo by the Author

THE ATABA EL-KHADRA, CAIRO—SCENE OF A PICKPOCKET'S DARING EXPLOIT

Facing page 96]

[Photo by the Author

THE SILVER CAR OF THE VEL FESTIVAL OF THE TAMILS

Facing page 97]

more, and knowing their circumstances better, who should be the least prone to the use of this objectionable epithet; and popular as they are, as I have just pointed out, and endowed with so many sterling qualities, it is a pity indeed that they should not have sooner knocked off the ungainly shackles that have for so long chained them needlessly to this ugly term.

And the following lines, of an incident in the Kandy Municipal Council, so cleverly committed to verse by Mr. C. Drieberg in his charming volume, *Flotsam: Verses Grave and Gay*, a copy of which he kindly presented me with as a parting souvenir at Peradeniya Station, where he turned up to see me off and say good-bye, will indicate the temper and frame of mind that now rules in the Orient, and the indignant manner in which this Ceylonese Municipal Councillor denounced the use of this offensive epithet:

> "Then rose a doughty leader,
> A champion of his race,
> 'I will not have this noxious word
> Thrown ever in my face,
> It's "natives" here, and "natives" there
> As tho' we were a lot
> Of bally oysters (without pearls)
> Recruited from Bentot!'"[1]

We know what we mean when we speak of a person as a native of Cornwall, for instance, or a native of Devon, and so on. But in England a son of the soil is an Englishman, or a Briton, but not a "native"; and every stranger from across the Channel a foreigner, or more generally an alien, as he is even sometimes slightingly called. But here in the East, we are all "natives", and every foreigner a high-sounding, pompous European or American, even though some may be from the very dregs of humanity!

[1] Bentota is a small village to the South of Colombo along the coast. It is well known for its oysters; and its pretty scenery attracts many newly-married couples for a quiet and enjoyable afternoon.

Following, however, the tenor of the reasoning of the preceding paragraph, and with all due deference to tact and decency, could not Indian, Ceylonese, or Egyptian, and so on, be more considerably and generously used? For, apart from the fact that to be described as such would sound harmless, we are entitled to be designated as such, even as the inhabitants of the Occident are named according to their respective countries, not to mention the fact that, with the traditional courtesy of the East we always designate strangers by their proper nationality, and not as aliens! Indeed, this distinctive appellation of nationality is as much our birthright as our country is our heritage, and it is worth while that the West should endeavour to be as courteous to the East, as the East is habitually to the West.

As a matter of fact, how many a degraded white-skinned type of humanity do we meet, just as we meet many a noble-hearted but dark-skinned citizen of any State. Were there more courtesy, more mutual trust and respect, then there would be less bitterness, less antagonism, and incidentally less of world turmoil, and less of unexpected trouble. A man is a man, and a gentleman a gentleman, for what he is worth, and how he comports himself. Neither the white skin nor the colour of the Occident is a hallmark of excellence and superiority.

CHAPTER X

SPORTS AND AMUSEMENTS IN CEYLON

WITH how many things is Ceylon blest. Thus, for example, to the photographer it is a veritable paradise; to the motorist an Arcadia; to the tourist a wonderland; to the civil servant from neighbouring lands a haven of rest, and so on. But has it occurred to us that to the sportsman also it is an ideal playground?

"All work and no play makes Jack a dull boy," is a platitude we have learnt from our boyhood; but nowhere as in the East are the depressing heat and the enervating atmosphere more felt and the need for cool, pleasant recreation grounds more desirable. To cope with such needs, therefore, no sports and pastimes can be ever too numerous, and especially when there is such a paucity of other amusements, such as theatres, music-halls, and the like.

But to be able to enjoy one's favourite game amidst an ideal environment is what one often seeks for, and in that Ceylon again most readily comes to our aid. Nor have the various communities been slow to avail themselves of such fine opportunities, and each of them has its own club, and they arrange matches and fixtures between themselves, and play each other in a very cordial spirit of rivalry. Even Australian cricketers on their way to England or back, make it a rule to play a match in Colombo with an Eleven representative of Ceylon.

Tennis, golf, football (both Association and Rugby), hockey, boating, rowing, all have their votaries; but it is cricket that seems to have the greatest hold on the public of Ceylon, even as "Soccer" has developed into our national game here. There are even some in Ceylon who in their Cambridge days must have known, or at least heard of, Egypt's "Ranji" of football in the person of my friend and old schoolfellow of Nasrieh days, Mr. Hussein Hegazi, the old Cambridge "Blue", or "Heggy", as he was affectionately nicknamed by the London public, in the days he used to play for Dulwich Hamlet, before going up to Cambridge, and one of the greatest exponents of this game he has continued to this day. Though Ceylon has not produced its Ranjitsinhjis, still it has its Gunasekeres, its Saravana Muttus, its van Geyzels, who have all distinguished themselves, not only at their 'Varsities and gained their "Blues", but have even represented some of the First Class Counties of England in the game of King Willow.

Speaking of cricket reminds me of the influence of heredity, and how young van Geyzel at Cambridge, a chip of the old block, has taken after his father, Dr. C. T. van Geyzel. But who would have thought that the dear, warm-hearted old gentleman, the portly, bluff Dr. van Geyzel, was once the agile, nimble cricketer of the first order in his day? Ask the "umbrella" tree at the old Royal College, and what memories it will bring back!

. . . . .

There is another pastime which I cannot omit to mention. Racing has been called the "sport of kings", and in so far as it suggests the bottomless purse of a king it is true in a sense, for the king was something of a deity once, and his word was law, though in these democratic days of restricted and constitutional monarchies one does hear of plebeian plutocrats and multi-millionaires, who are no less a trouble than the royal autocrats and tyrants of the past.

If in Egypt racing is a craze, in Ceylon it is a veritable mania; and when a meeting is at hand, why, every second or third person you meet in Colombo seems to turn to

THE BULLOCK'S HEART

From "A Handbook of Tropical Gardening and Planting" (Colombo: Cave & Co.). *By courtesy of the Author, Mr. H. F. Macmillan*

THE SOURSOP

From "A Handbook of Tropical Gardening and Planting" (Colombo: Cave & Co.). *By courtesy of the Author, Mr. H. F. Macmillan*

Facing page 100]

By courtesy of Mr. H. F. Macmillan

THE JAK

THE PAPAW

From "A Handbook of Tropical Gardening and Planting" (Colombo: Cave & Co.). *By courtesy of the Author, Mr. H. F. Macmillan*

Facing page 101]

the topic at once; and even the shops, getting their cue from the craze of the moment, seem in turn also to go racing-mad, every bit of their goods being advertised and held up as the last word in smartness for the races—as if racing were the culminating point, the very acme of our existence!

A little punt here and there will do no harm, inasmuch as it will provide the necessary stimulus to excitement. But every picture has its bright and its sordid sides, and it is the wary and the sensible who can steer clear of the temptations that beset their path, or extricate themselves from the meshes that have ensnared them ere they sink deeper and deeper into the tangles that are fast drawing their coils over them if they are not careful. And how many are there who, once started on this dangerous path, have not sunk deeper and deeper in their frantic efforts to retrieve their fallen fortunes.

But even with all that may be said against racing, still it is not without its thrills—its comedies and its tragedies, as it were.

Can we forget that real story of about two years ago, which reads like a page from romance, when a would-be big punter dashes into the Racecourse, rushes up to the pari-mutuel windows, and lays a "tenner" (Rs. 150) on a particular horse just before the race begins? But it is not long ere he finds out his mistake, but it is too late, for the horses are already off. And even as he sits disconsolate, bemoaning his lot—for, whereas he thought he was backing a hot favourite in the First Race, the ticket he has just bought, as a matter of fact, gives him only a rank outsider in the Second Race, without the ghost of a chance whatever—wonder of wonders, what should happen but that the Fates smile on him, and his outsider passes the post first, paying him the handsome, almost incredible return (for he was absolutely dazed for some moments to realise the fact) of sixty to one! And so through a sheer mistake, but with a kind turn of the Wheel of Fortune this lucky man clears £600 (Rs. 9,000) in a sweep!

But now take the reverse. A friend of mine only last year was out to back six winners in the biggest race meeting of the season by the accumulating method (*paroli*), the chief race being the Champion Stakes of £1,000 for thoroughbreds. Of his selections, four who stood fairly good chances came in first, and the winnings showed a quite comfortable sum running into three figures from an odd pound! Even the horse he picked as the sixth winner materialised in due course. But in the race which was to give him his fifth winner, his choice, *Peep o' Dawn*, a hot favourite, as he was a "dead cert" to many, is nowhere at the finish, and thus lets him down wretchedly. One can quite imagine my friend's disgust.

Or again, the little known story of Lord Chaplin I read of in the *Daily Mail* when he was raised to the Peerage in 1916. As far as I can now recall, in a certain Derby the favourite was a horse belonging to a young peer who had staked his all in one big gamble on his horse to retrieve his fallen fortunes. But what is more, he was married to that beautiful young lady who, curiously, on the very eve of her wedding with Lord Chaplin (then Mr. Henry Chaplin), jilted him, giving him the slip so dramatically in a shop with two entrances, where they were shopping at the time in preparation for the morrow's wedding, the papers on the next morning announcing her marriage to the young lord alluded to! In the same Derby also Lord Chaplin had his own horse, the famous *Hermit*, running as well, but with very slender prospects of victory, as the public believed. But as if the Fates must interfere and provide some great sensation at the climax as a solace for unrequited love, it is Lord Chaplin's outsider that ultimately wins the day. Here indeed was revenge with a vengeance; and ever since that memorable afternoon Lord Chaplin[1] was accorded the honour of moving the adjournment of the House of Commons on Derby Day.

[1] But no more will this popular and familiar figure grace the Derby by his welcome presence, for Lord Chaplin passed away in 1923.

The Derby of 1913 also created something of a sensation, its sequel being no less dramatic. *Craganour*, the favourite, has proved true to expectations, and comes in first; but even as the lucky winner of the Calcutta Sweepstake who has drawn him is receiving the congratulations of his friends, and is, perhaps, even conjuring up some rosy pictures in his imagination of how he is going to utilise his windfall, there goes a cable just a short while after right across the world announcing the disqualification of *Craganour* for bumping, *vice Aboyeur*, a hundred to one chance, which had finished just behind. And such a staggering blow is indeed the cruellest cut of all: to find a fortune actually within one's grasp, and then to lose it almost immediately after through no fault of your own, as if it had been whisked out of one's hand by some malevolent, wicked fairy's magic wand, or, in other words, as if the thermometer had marked 100° cent. of a person's good fortune, and then as suddenly dropped to 0° cent. of ill-luck!

But I must stop, for I am no racing chronicler. I cannot, however, turn from this subject without touchign on Colombo's fine Havelock Racecourse. It can even bear comparison excellently with Egypt's various racecourses, a richer and bigger country though mine is. But there was a time when the races in Colombo used to be held at Galle Face, and even now I have a faint memory of seeing them in 1893, when I was with my father at the Galle Face Hotel on a change to the seaside from Kandy; and it must have been a happier public who could watch the races gratis, as if they were the guests of the Ceylon Turf Club, without having to pay the charges they are now asked!

On Race days all Colombo seems to turn out there, and as often as not the rain will come down most cruelly and unpolitely, as some facetiously put it, though happily this year (1921) we were spared the kind attentions of Jupiter Pluvius.

I shall always have the satisfaction of remembering my outing on Cup Day in the August meet of 1921, supplying me as it did with the chance of witnessing the creation of a "record" when *Mordennis* won the Governor's Cup—the Derby of Ceylon—for the fourth time running, a thing hitherto unprecedented in the racing annals of Ceylon. A noticeable feature of this meet also was when Mr. E. L. F. De Soysa went up and patted this famous horse; and many hearts must certainly have gone out in sympathy to this gentleman, from whose hands it had passed only so recently into the possession of Mr. Goculdas, one of India's great financial magnates, that he just missed the crowning satisfaction of realising a life-long dream with such a splendid horse as had served him so loyally and magnificently.

Another thing that will also live in my memory in regard to this meet is a short conversation I had with Mr. R. E. S. De Soysa, one of the leading members of the Ceylon Turf, and a brother of the former owner of *Mordennis*. The very fact that I came from Egypt seemed to be a sufficient basis for a conversation about my country.

After talking about my visit, and how I liked it, and how I was shaping at the Races, he even kindly giving me a "tip" in regard to his own horse, *Chapel Green*, which I only too gladly availed myself of to my own benefit. Eventually, the conversation veered towards Egypt.

"And so you are after self-government," says Mr. De Soysa.

"Self-government?" I ask in a tone of some surprise.

"Yes, self-government."

"No, Mr. De Soysa, it is not self-government, but full independence, the status of a sovereign state, that we are after," next comes my reply.

"Independence?" he then ejaculates, as if in his turn surprised; then laughing in a manner which jarred upon me, he adds: "You should consider yourselves lucky if you get full self-government."

"You wait and see," next unconsciously springs to my mouth the famous words of Mr. Asquith;[1] "and I hope

[1] This great English statesman has been raised to the Peerage with the title of Earl of Oxford and Asquith.

[By courtesy of Mr. H. F. Macmillan

THE SAPODILLA

Facing page 104]

THE AVOCADO PEAR

From "A Handbook of Tropical Gardening and Planting" (Colombo: Cave & Co.). *By courtesy of the Author, Mr. H. F. Macmillan.*

Facing page 105]

I shall be able to remind you of it one day," I added. And with that the next race starts, and his horse *Chapel Green* comes in second, and pays a cosy little sum, for I had backed it for a place.

But then, I should not blame Mr. De Soysa, for there are many who have spoken like him, and who still thought in his way, for the armchair critic, or one who bases his information on what he merely reads in the Press, sometimes not a little perverted and garbled, cannot always gauge the true state of affairs. Why, even Egyptians who have been away since the beginning of the Great War, and returned only recently, can hardly believe their eyes, so great and wonderful has been the transformation that Time has wrought on Egypt within so short a time!

Most likely Mr. De Soysa has now quite probably forgotten all about our interesting little talk, but perhaps it would be not a little interesting to know his opinion in the light of recent developments in regard to Egypt's new status as an independent, sovereign state. Still, though there may be yet much to be achieved, none the less I cannot but be thankful to the Almighty that my dream has come true so soon in more senses than one. May I yet live to see that day in the near future when I can have the great pleasure of toasting the health of "The Allied Sovereigns" (Of England and Egypt), and likewise have the pleasure of the company of Mr. De Soysa himself, and merrily recall our little former conversation.

. . . . . .

One of the most important events of "August Week", or rather more correctly, "August Fortnight", is the annual State Ball at Queen's House, the Colombo residence of H.E. the Governor of the Island. As a matter of fact, it is *the* most important social event of the year, proving as it does the *clou* of the Season.

Though I was most graciously invited to it by T.E. the Governor, Sir William Manning, and Lady Manning, and deeply as I appreciated this courteous act of theirs, for which I again avail myself of the present opportunity to record my gratitude publicly, still, most unfortunately, I was unable to attend. And though I could not help it, still how I regret even now the chance I missed of meeting the *élite* of Ceylon at the greatest social event of the year.

. . . . .

I might conclude this chapter by deploring the lack of adequate amusement at night in Ceylon in the shape of theatres and music-halls. But then, even if buildings themselves existed, they would be practically useless if there is not the material to grace their boards. Now and then one does hear of a touring troupe calling at Colombo for a short while, but such visits are few and far between; and England is such a long distance off that not many would care to travel so far from their homes unless they have the strongest inducements for doing so. This naturally raises the question: Why not encourage and develop local talent?

Why the drama or variety show should not catch on in Ceylon I cannot understand. Again, how little of music[1] does one get in Ceylon! As a matter of fact, it is practically *nil*, and apart from the Band of the Ceylon Light Infantry, one hardly ever hears any music—still less an orchestra. And this branch also should be stimulated.

If only the Ceylonese could see London, or Paris, or Vienna, or every big town in Germany, why, he would simply wonder; and even Cairo, which is rather poorly catered for in music when we compare it to the big European cities just mentioned, is a city flowing with music when we place it by the side of Colombo.

[1] Thanks to the enterprise of Mr. W. J. Byrne, the genial and popular Manager of the Queen's Hotel, Kandy, weekly violin recitals were arranged for at this popular hostelry through the courtesy of Mrs. W. G. St. Clair, and what a welcome treat they proved, as I had occasion to enjoy during my visit to Ceylon in 1924. If only the other big hotels could follow suit, what a boon this innovation would prove.

The cinematograph[1] itself is not sufficient, nor any amount of dances, such as the Grand Oriental Hotel and the Galle Face Hotel thoughtfully provide, and it is high time that Ceylon got to business in this respect. For, if a tourist in the daytime does admire its beautiful scenery and picturesque sights, how bored and dull he often feels at night—as I often had reason to feel.

With the prospect of a National Theatre, however, looming ahead, one might perhaps hope there is a turn for the better soon. Even cosy tea rooms and a pretty garden, with a fine orchestra thrown in, all amidst ideal surroundings, but in an accessible situation, will prove a great draw and a welcome innovation. Indeed, if a Ceylonese comes and sees our Groppis, our Saults, our Lemonias, our Athineoses, and the excellent confectionery, cakes, ices, and drinks supplied there, all to the sound of sweet music of fine orchestras, he would wonder why Ceylon does not follow suit.

[1] From what I experienced of the cinematograph in Ceylon, during my 1924 visit, though I found the programmes as a rule good, still the structure and accommodation of the so-called picture palaces—hardly in keeping with their grandiose description—leave a good deal to be desired, and can be considerably improved. And this matter should be seriously taken in hand by any enterprising syndicate without the cinematograph being any the worse for it—on the contrary the artistic and æsthetic reputation of Colombo would incidentally be enhanced thereby.

CHAPTER XI

THE CEYLON POLICE

I WONDER whether the Ceylon policeman has ever heard of that Gilbertian expression " A policeman's lot is not a happy one," and if so, whether he concurs in it. As far as appearances go it seems that he disagrees with it, else why should his offspring be ever so anxious to follow in the footsteps of their father, and take so enthusiastically after his vocation. The very sight of a young " Bobby " in embryo, as with cap tilted at a rakish angle, and a self-assumed martial air he struts about, causes no little amusement, as it nevertheless gives a certain feeling of satisfaction with the zeal and enthusiasm displayed by our young hopeful.

The Ceylon policeman, often a Malay, is a credit to the island. Well-built and wiry, like the neighbouring Gurkha, but trim and well shod, unlike his sandalled, turbanned, grotesque counterpart of Bombay, whose very umbrella, huge and ponderous, reminds one of Sairey Gamp's, or that of Don Basilio in Rossini's masterpiece *Le Barbier de Seville*, thus producing a quite comic effect, rather than a dignified manifestation of the majesty of the law, one finds it a pleasure to see how with our-stretched arm the Ceylon *shawish* cleverly manipulates the crushing traffic at some dangerous point, as his great paragon does by the banks of the Thames.

But, of course, London's famous " Bobby ", " The Emperor of the traffic ", stands on a pedestal all by him self in his glory, for where in the world can you find his equal? Still the Ceylon policeman runs him close, and

THE MANGOSTEEN

From "A Handbook of Tropical Gardening and Planting" (Colombo: Cave & Co.). *By courtesy of the Author, Mr. H. F. Macmillan*

Facing page 108]

[By courtesy of Mr. H. F. Macmillan

THE RAMBUTAN

Facing page 109

might even be considered a very worthy pupil. It is also a clever thought of the Police Authorities of Ceylon to have conceived the idea of having his arm at night in a white mock sleeve to control the traffic in the dark more effectively, though they might have gone one better and substituted this for a light white overcoat of fine texture, something like that of an umpire's, as is in vogue in Cairo.

It seems as if it were but yesterday, so fast does time fly, that a good proportion of them went barefooted, whether out of personal preference, or the parsimony of a niggardly Government, I cannot vouch for; but the fact remains that such an incongruity used to cause no little merriment to the Egyptian Pashas in Ceylon, as far as I can recall. At any rate, this is now a thing of the past.

The Ceylon policeman, however, like his species all over the world, is not always beyond reproach. But then man is fallible. Thus I remember how now and then some "Bobby" on duty in front of the jetty hardly troubled to exert himself sufficiently to mitigate the annoyances landing passengers sometimes suffered; and, as a consequence, their comfort and peace rose and fell according as the strict sense of duty of the "Bobby" fluctuated!

One experience, however, which I shall never forget, calls for my present remarks. I once beckoned to a cab, very few as they already were. But double the fare as I usually paid them—so cheap they were, as also the jinrickshaws, in comparison to the exorbitant charges of the motor cars—still, there was a steamer just arrived in port, and the passengers no doubt could be fleeced to the tune of treble or even quadruple the original fare; so, why give me a "lift" (whom they had come to look on as somewhat of a resident), when such a promising windfall lay so near at hand.

The first cab drove away on some pretext, with a parting shot at a second who was just coming round the corner. As I was walking up to it, the "cabby" warned by his first confrère, shouts out to one of the loafers, who jumps in as if he had engaged the cab and was a real "fare", and no amount of expostulation with the "cabby" avails. These tactics anger me, and to the policeman on duty at the spot I go and explain matters; but with a simple shrug of the shoulders he says he can do nothing! This enrages me even more, for I cannot dream of such a flagrant breach of duty, if not good manners, and of such culpable callousness on the part of one who was expected in such circumstances to uphold the full majesty of the Law and deal with offenders.

Fortunately, a British constable hove in sight after the first cab had just passed again right under my nose, but whose number I did not fail to take this time, seeing that it was empty, and to him I related the whole matter, and the subterfuge the second cab had employed. He told me that he was quite conversant with such dirty tricks on the part of cabmen, and that even if there was an unusual rush of passengers, this was no reason why others should suffer any discomfort, and forthwith he took down the number of the offending cab, and promised to charge him, I thereupon engaging a motor car and going my way.

I have related this little incident just to show how the proverbial fly in the ointment might often spoil the whole.

. . . . .

Whether the comparative non-existence of pickpockets in Ceylon is due to the vigilance of the police, or a very wary public, or a repudiation of the gentle art of the nimble finger, I cannot say, but anyhow, thank Heaven, I was spared the unwelcome attentions of any pilferer during my stay in Ceylon.

Indeed, when the papers reported that one—mind you gentle reader, *only one*—had been arrested redhanded during the great Vel Festival of the Tamils within the precintcs of their Temple at Bambalapitiya, I could not help laughing! I had been there on the last night but one, and as inevitably garlanded and "disced" by the red daub on my forehead by a leading Chetty, and the crush and crowd were simply bewildering. As usual on such occasions one had to rub shoulders with all sorts and conditions of people, and actually cut one's way through. But still in this vast concourse to catch *only one* pickpocket, a mere drop in the ocean, as it were, where there might have been at least a score, O fie on you, ye Ceylonese! Come and take lessons in the gentle art of "pickpocketry", and learn the wonderful tricks and ruses of our Fagins, our Artful Dodgers, and so on—unless, of course, you are all a band of saints.

Can you believe it, gentle reader, only the other day the Cairo City Police circulated broadcast some twenty photos of the most notorious pickpockets, and had them hung up in the various Police Stations, as a service to a long-suffering public; and the irony of it is that while a dozen people stood in front of them before the Mousky Police Station, situated in one of the busiest and most crowded parts of Cairo at Ataba El-Khadra, carefully scrutinising the faces of these geniuses of unenviable reputation, what should happen but that three of them would find that they were minus their portfolios! And what a picture of indignation and wrath they looked as they stepped in forthwith to report the theft which had taken place here right under the very nose of the Police, cursing the photos, and perhaps the Governorate into the bargain that it had, uncalled for, provided them with a picture gallery gratis on the public highway!

But "truth is stranger than fiction", and under its garb how many wonderful things take place in this world which even the wildest imagination would have deemed improbable.

CHAPTER XII

SHOPPING IN COLOMBO

In my rambles round Colombo I used sometimes to combine business with pleasure. Shopping at all times is a favourite pastime—if I can use such a term, even loosely, for ladies will always shop, whether they really have anything to buy or not—provided, however, one is blessed with a seemingly bottomless purse. So many are the big shops in the Fort that I sometimes wonder how they all carry on. In my time not so many seemed to exist, or rather to present such an important and prosperous appearance—or is it that my premature grey hairs and advancing years have tampered with my memory? As far as I can recollect, Cave's and the Apothecaries were the two largest establishments in Colombo, as Miller's was in Kandy.

But now a veritable galaxy of them exists in the Metropolis, and what with Cargill's—which seems to have outgrown all the others—Cave's, Miller's, Sime's, Smith Campbell's, the Apothecaries, Whiteaway Laidlaw's, Walker's, the Colombo Stores, and so on, to mention at random only some of the leading establishments, one can hardly be at a loss to find anything he wants, from the proverbial thimble to the motor-car *de luxe*—or is it the aeroplane in the near future?

But, curiously, when I once wanted a good dressing set to have overlaid with tortoiseshell, to take as a present to Cairo, I could find none except some in silver, and when I did come across any in wood, they were in folding portable leather cases with straps, whereas I wanted a

THE DURIAN

From "A Handbook of Tropical Gardening and Planting" (Colombo: Caye & Co.). *By courtesy of the Author, Mr. H. F. Macmillan*

[Photo by the Author

A MINIATURE CASCADE ON THE PERADENIYA-GALAHA ROAD

Facing page 113]

nice case itself, with the interior in silk or satin tastefully laid out so as to enhance even more the prettiness of the articles held.

Another advantage these shops have is that they are all near one another, so that what you may not find in the one you are pretty sure to come across next door. But no! quite contrary to my expectations, the prices were not a bit cheap compared to those of Cairo, and Cairo is the profiteer's paradise, where all have been trying to make hay—even with reasonable allowance for unusual conditions—while the sun of high prices still shone, and the public, well, why, they may suffer for all they knew!

It looks, if I am not wrong, as if there is no place in the world as here in Egypt where the shops and places of amusement are so callously indifferent to the claims of the public, as the wealthy are so glaringly and culpably oblivious of the needs of the poor, and the general principles of domestic economy, so long as they are blessed with the money to wallow in! And the rise of prices here and there, what do they matter? Surely they are not going to suffer any discomfort for the sake of a few extra piastres! And, naturally, the law of supply and demand rules, and so long as the wealthy or the *nouveaux riches* are willing to pay the prices asked, no matter how high they are, so long will the shopkeepers keep their prices up.

Ceylon during my visit was in the throes of a tea and rubber slump. No wonder, therefore, that the financial depression was so wide-spread as to seem to affect all —indeed to such an extent that I saw notices and advertisements to the effect that this shop had cut down its prices by ten per cent., and that one by twenty per cent., and so on, each and all seeming to vie with one another in the amount of its reduction, so keen was the competition to capture customers and give a fillip to trade.

One well-known firm very ingeniously went to the extent of making such a clever yet startling announcement as this:

"Walk in with your old boots, and walk out with a new pair; only the difference between both will be charged!"

But to this hung a tag. A new pair, of course, would be given for the old pair which you left there; but, gentle sir, remember there is the magnificent reduction of Rs. 5 off the price of the new pair of boots, and the heedless would-be maker of a bargain begins to see things! For I wonder which gentleman would have had the courage to walk in with such a tattered, battered, and worn-out pair which was not worth Rs. 5, and which might have graced the feet of some faithful servant! But then, the very original way the announcement was worded arrested one's attention in a very striking manner. And advertisement is the soul of business these days, as much as life is often a struggle of wits, though, alas! now and then one is forced to acknowledge the grim brutality of the Arabic proverb which might be loosely translated as: "An inch of luck is worth more than an acre of cleverness!"

Another revelation also was that although I thought prices were fixed, still whenever I evinced any disinclination, or the charges seemed a bit stiff, the shop people climbed down a bit and showed their readiness to make some reduction—which goes to prove how acutely they felt the general financial depression. Credit also seemed to be much in vogue in Ceylon, for whenever I purchased anything, I was generally asked whether it might be put to my account, but when I naturally said that I was paying cash down, I would, as a rule, find that ten per cent. was taken off the price asked—which certainly proved welcome.

. . . . .

But there is another genus of shops. A passenger should always be on the look-out not to fall into the clutches of a local "shark"—at any rate, whenever he is dealing with any of them he should keep his eyes wide open and try to bargain to the best of his ability, say, with a reduction of sixty per cent. at least to start with on the upward climb. I can speak from experience, for I have been bitten twice—by whom I need not mention. Suffice it to say I once bought a piece of the best China silk to make into suits, and at the practically high rate of Rs. 8.50 per yard (single width). When I got to the hotel some subtle mysterious feeling made me desire to have another look at it, and also to make sure of the measurement, which the shopkeeper told me was 15½ yards, after having seemed to have measured it in front of me very carefully without my paying any particular attention to him whilst he was doing so. What was my indignation when I found it to be only 13 yards?

Again, on another occasion I ordered a couple of fine carved ebony sticks surmounted by handles of ivory of an elephant's head. On the morning following delivery —for I received them the previous night—I examined them carefully, for "once bitten, twice shy," and the incident of the China silk had made me more cautious. What was my amazement and rage when I found both of them with cracks, one very slightly so as to be hardly discernible, which I was told was inevitable in ebony, but the other so defective as to be absolutely unworthy of a present! Together, therefore, with a friend of mine who knew them I went in the afternoon to the shop to see about the stick, and the people there were profuse in their regrets, and very obsequiously undertook to replace the defective stick by a good one.

What was my disgust, however, later on to hear this same friend tell me that when he once went to the shop to hurry up the stick owing to my approaching departure, I being at the time in Kandy, he overheard one of the shop people tell another that they did not think they could get another stick, but they would fill in the cracks of the original one with paste, and have it so "doctored" as to pass for a new one; so he warned me to be on my guard when they sent me the stick. And the worst part of it is that they actually had the cheek to send me the very same stick, as my friend had forewarned me, somewhat cleverly "cooked" to the unwary eye, but which, Mohammed, to whom I had related the incident, very cunningly spotted and showed the man who brought it before handing it to me, and the man in question seeing that his employer's trick had been detected, and finding that the game was up, simply scampered off without waiting to face me

These two incidents were sufficient to give me a very bad impression about some shops, and served ever after constantly to put me on my guard. I would, therefore, warn passengers and tourists never to be misled by the coaxings and honeyed words of importunate shopkeepers, but if they do enter a shop to buy anything, let them do so with their eyes wide open, and see to their purchases themselves, and leave nothing to chance, nor place implicit trust in the shop people.

One has, in particular, to be very careful in the selection of gems and jewellery, for which Ceylon is famous, especially in these days of the "cultured" pearl. There are a good many shops which are no doubt honest in their dealings, and can transact business with you quite fairly; but still it would be better to get the advice of some friend, or failing that, to consult the hotel management.

I for one had to make some purchases in this line, and somehow or other the jewellers got wind of my desire to buy one or two pear-shaped pearls for tiepins. Several actually approached me on the subject. But why go far when here in my very hotel was the well-known establishment of Messrs. Macan Markar.[1] Moreover, everyone had recommended them to me as reliable people, though somewhat stiff in their charges. But then, I would rather have something a bit dear, but which was

[1] Kind as I found the Macan Marker Family in 1921, they proved even doubly so in 1924, and I certainly cannot turn away from this chapter without recording once more my wife's and my lasting gratitude for all they did for us, and their hospitality towards us at Galle we shall always dwell upon with the pleasantest of recollections. Need I add how overjoyed I was to hear, after my return home, the happy news that the head of the family, the Honourable Mr. H. Mohammed Macan Markar had been elected to the Ceylon Legislative Council as First Mohammedan Member by a preponderant majority ?

[Photo by the Author

THE KELANIYA TEMPLE, NEAR COLOMBO

Facing page 116]

[By courtesy of Mrs. I. M. Del Tufo

ON THE KELANI GANGA—AN IDYLL OF RURAL CEYLON

Facing page 117]

really good stuff, than the reverse. Besides, they had a branch in Cairo at Shepheard's Hotel; so, there was some sentimental inducement to close in with them in my purchases. And I can only avail the present opportunity to record my fullest satisfaction in my transactions with them, inasmuch as they showed every consideration possible, whether in their dealings, or the reasonableness of their prices, or the excellence of their goods.

Another gentleman, Mr. Louis Siedle, whom many recommended, turned out to be an old friend of my father, and he remembered the time that the Egyptian exiles landed there. He also proved most obliging and considerate, and afforded me every satisfaction, all the things I ordered of him being marked by their fine finish, good workmanship, and moderate charges, especially the gold-edged tortoiseshell cigarette cases and mouthpieces.

These two firms I can safely and warmly recommend to all passing through Ceylon, and their close proximity to the jetty will come particularly useful to those in a hurry, with very little time to spare.

CHAPTER XIII

SOME CEYLON FRUITS

When I finally made up my mind to go to Ceylon, I had to choose between summer and winter for the projected trip. Winter had its advantages. It is supposed to be cooler out there, though in Ceylon one hardly meets with a change of seasons in the real sense of the word, it being actually influenced by the two periodical Monsoons; and thus one part of the island is considered cooler than the other according to the rainfall in that quarter, and *vice versa*. Moreover, the sea passage is usually calm during this period. But then, *per contra*, the customary period allowed in Egypt to go on furlough is summer. True, the south-west Monsoon would be in all its fury, and would probably give us a bad time in the Indian Ocean; but then, there were the big liners of nowadays to counteract this disadvantage to no small extent.

To me in particular the summer fitted in very nicely with my visit, and I had arranged and timed it to synchronise with practically all the things I wanted to see during my trip. The "Kingswood Week" was due in August, subsequently postponed to September; the Perahera also would be held in August; and so also the biggest Race Meetings of the year, especially that for the Governor's Cup, the Derby of Ceylon. But there was one thing in addition that turned the scales more heavily. I wanted to enjoy once more to the full Ceylon's most delicious fruits, especially the mangosteen, and summer was the time for them, May—September being the period when one is practically sure to come across most of them. And in summer accordingly I went.

. . . . .

It is funny that the very fruits which are such luxuries in Egypt are the very ones we can get fairly cheap in Ceylon. Can my friends here believe that a fine specimen of the famous *Menshawi* MANGO—as the well-known Jaffna mango of Ceylon is locally known—can be bought for only three or four cents at the most in Ceylon (2 or 3 milliemes or farthings), and not for a shilling, as here in Egypt? Mohammed even ate of them during the few weeks they were in season there what even the richest pasha here would not have enjoyed and cared to pay for in as many years! The pity is that I failed to come across any of the famous *rupee* mango,[1] the finest specimen in the market of this luscious fruit, for, apart from the fact that we were rather late for the height of the mango season, which is supposed to be in May, the crop itself was somewhat of a failure this year.

Perhaps it might interest my readers to hear that some of the mango trees fruit twice in Ceylon! As a matter of fact, when I was at the Queen's Hotel at the beginning of July, the few last mangoes on the trees just in front of my room facing the Bund were being gathered; whilst about the middle of September, when I was up at Kandy for " Kingswood Week ", the very same trees were covered with the blossoms of the second or minor crop, some even having turned to small mangoes!

What applies to the mango in price and agreeableness applies identically to the delicious CUSTARD-APPLE[2] and BULLOCK'S HEART which were coming into season just before we left, and which I was thus not able to enjoy

[1] In my 1924 trip, however, thanks to the kindness of friends, who presented me with a few of this rare variety, I was able to enjoy this sweet fruit, and quite amply did its flavour bear out its high reputation. So large indeed is this mango that some have even nicknamed it " baby's head."

[2] Curiously, during 1924, however, we were able now and again to partake of this delicious fruit; but it puzzled me no little why this time we were able to come across it during June and July, when in 1921 none were procurable during these months.

thoroughly. Another genus of it, however, the SOUR-SOP I now and then had, but though it is not up to the standard of its sisters as a fruit, still it can be made into a nice ice-cream.

Allied to the custard-apple is the famous CHERIMOYER, which together with the queenly mangosteen, are reputed to be *the* sweetest and most delicious fruits in the world. In Ceylon itself it is a rarity, and not procurable in the market, one having to rely mainly on the generosity and kindness of friends for any supply. Its rarity in Colombo is perhaps due to its being an up-country fruit, thriving chiefly in the districts near Bandarawela. The pity is that during this trip I missed this noted fruit.[1]

And the PINEAPPLE which everyone relishes so much—what a vast difference between the tinned article that comes from the Straits Settlements, and that eaten *au naturel*. But, of course, one must make sure of getting a good *Kew* or *Mauritius* variety which is well ripe, and this for only 40 or 50 cents (from six to nine pence), and of a size that would easily fill two or three of the tins one gets from the local grocer! There are, however, the common ones also, but though they can be obtained for even less, their quality is inferior.

BANANAS, called PLAINTAINS in Ceylon, of which one is a treat, two a luxury, and three, well, ambrosia! If only my friends here knew how I used to leave quite a plateful untouched after having had my fill of it! And a whole bunch of it of several okes,[2] for only two rupees, and not merely one kilogramme for the same sum—as is often charged here! No wonder that the passengers took them on board in huge bunches, like some curiosity, to enjoy its delightful flavour during the voyage, as I often noticed from the hotel.

[1] Thanks to Mr. H. F. Macmillan, the Superintendent of the Royal Botanic Gardens, Peradeniya, who so kindly sent me three cherimoyers, I was able during my 1924 trip to get to know this really delicious fruit, and right royally did we enjoy it, finding it, as had been rightly asserted, to be superior to the custard-apple even. But the palm I shall always give to the mangosteen—the queen of fruits.

[2] An oke is equivalent to 2¾ lbs.

[*Photo by the Author*

THE WONDERFUL ASSAM RUBBER TREES IN THE PERADENIYA GARDENS

Facing page 120]

[*Photo by Platé, Ltd., Colombo*

Plucking Coconuts

Facing page 121]

But then, although it is the modest *honuruwala* variety (ironically called "the right honourable") that one generally comes across in the market, it is the rarer *kolikuttu*, and the even rarer and superior *suwandale*, that are the leading varieties which one should partake of to really enjoy this delectable fruit.

And the PAPAW—not the insipid, hard, tasteless, local genus, and that for a rupee each, but a really sweet, succulent fruit, that usually melts in one's mouth more sweetly than the most toothsome ice, with even Groppi's well-known ices such as *Comtesse Marie*, or *Sfogliatella*, or *Cassata*, into the bargain, and this for a paltry fifteen or twenty cents (about threepence). And when iced, or served with crushed ice on top, what a fruit indeed, and how doubly sweet and delicious!

If, moreover, its medicinal properties of *papaine* were more widely known, how much more extensively would it be cultivated and its quality improved, and it become accordingly a delight to the most fastidious palate. Let one but have it in the early morning every day, as I used to when early morning tea was brought in, and how useful he will find it for his health. And after the heaviest meal what a powerful digestive it is, owing to the pepsin it contains; and indigestion, the bane of so many, why, it would then exist only as a memory. And all this for a paltry fifteen or twenty cents, as I have said. Is it conceivable?

People who have known the COCONUT with its hard kernel, wonder when I tell them of the KING COCONUT, or THEMALY, as varieties of it are known in Sinhalese,—not KURUMBA, as it is mistakenly called, which is in reality merely a tender young coconut. If they could but taste its tender, creamy kernel, and drink its sweet, wholesome, refreshing juice at the same time, why, they will find a real drink of the gods, without the necessary adjunct of whisky, which some suggest, and this for only ten cents (about twopence), or even less. And if to this I may add that some even believe the *themaly* to be a preventive to uric acid and gout, then how all the more eager will many be to partake of this delectable fruit. If only the three plants I brought with me from Ceylon would buck up, instead of languishing between life and death,[1] why, I should be only too pleased to have proved something of a benefactor to my friends here, apart from enabling them to taste of the sweetness of sweet Ceylon.

And the JAK, a veritable giant of the forest, rising as it does, to over a hundred feet high, what a sight it presents to the stranger as its wonderful big fruit, weighing sometimes a hundred pounds, hang in short stalks from the stem of this giant of the jungle. And if Ceylon has no chestnuts, why, here was a fairly good substitute of the jak's seeds roasted after the pulp surrounding them has been eaten! Jak wood also is one of the finest for cabinet making and furniture, and some even think it quite akin to mahogany in quality.

The very mention of chestnuts naturally reminds me of the CASHEW-NUT—the nut *par excellence*, not only of Ceylon, but of the whole world. Indeed, such at any rate is my opinion, and I notice many readers who have had experience of various kinds even endorsing my view though some believe that the Brazilian-nut might run it close. I, for one, would rather have a pound of cashew-nuts than ten of pistachio-nuts, agreeable though the latter also is.

The RAMBUTAN I eagerly looked forward to renewing my associations with. But one should partake of really good and ripe specimens to value them at their true rate, else the sourness of some may tend to make those tasting them for the first time not take a liking to them. A very pretty fruit indeed is the rambutan, and as it hangs afar in red hairy clusters of soft spines, one wishes its edible part was always as welcome as its alluring exterior.

The MORA not many Europeans seem to know; but still it is one of my favourites, and I was only too glad it was in season when I was in Ceylon. Egyptians who find such pleasure in *lib* (dried and salted water-melon seeds, of which they eat the kernel) might surely find the

[1] Alas! these three plants also have since shared the fate of the mangosteens.

mora just as acceptable, its dry, dull outer rind, the colour of the skin of the potato, and about the size of a marble, belying the sweet, white, creamy pulp inside round the abnormally large black seed!

The SAPODILLA I tasted for the first time in my life; but it is a fruit one rarely gets in the markets. It depends upon whether you come across a good one or not, for, whereas the fine ripe one will be a real delight, the other might make you hold a different opinion owing to its acrid nature.

The AVOCADO PEAR also I got to know for the first time in my life during this trip, and though at first one cannot see how such a great fuss has been made over it, still, when eaten in the right way, after coming across a really good ripe one, a person may enjoy it to some extent. In Ceylon, when eaten with jaggery, it is really delicious. Those who would detract it, however, say that they find nothing attractive about this fruit, unless that it falsely gives the impression of one having lighted on a fine big pear of the ordinary variety.

The ORANGE of Ceylon has nothing to recommend it—if anything, its so-called sweetest specimen is still sourer than the sourest Egyptian orange, and Egyptian oranges are, as a rule, quite sweet. The MANDARIN also, like the orange in Ceylon, is rather yellowish-green in colour, and not like our sweet golden orbs. However, it goes one better than its cousin the orange, it being fairly passable, though one lacks the juiciness of the pulp of our Egyptian variety.

GUAVAS I missed in Ceylon, though many trees were in evidence—not that I was eager to buy them, for they are very plentiful in Egypt now, and as cheap. But still one would like to have tasted a few, if only to see how they compared with those in Egypt. The pity is that abundant as they are in Egypt, still there is hardly anybody who benefits by such a circumstance to make of it one of the most delicious of jellies.

But the queen of fruits in Ceylon is the noted MANGOSTEEN, and I even wonder whether there is any other fruit in the world which can beat it. Side by side with it I am bringing the DURIAN, as the worst and nastiest fruit one can ever come across, though one confirmed durian-eater, Mr. Alfred Russell Wallace, actually said: "In fact, to eat the Durian is a new sensation, worth a voyage to the East to experience."

Just as a person will sometimes keep the best of a thing for the end, as the tit-bit, so have I retained the mangosteen for the close of this chapter, starting with its closest rivals, the mango, the custard-apple, and the cherimoyer; and the wonder is that so few have heard of this, "the most luscious fruit in the world, partaking of the flavour of the strawberry and the grape," as Mr. H. F. Macmillan the Superintendent of the Royal Botanic Gardens at Peradeniya, describes it.

The mangosteen[1] is the *fruit de luxe* of Ceylon, and is supposed to be the most expensive because you cannot buy a dozen for less than seventy-five cents, or a rupee at the very most—as if a penny for each is such a tremendously high sum for such excellent fruit! Nevertheless, at the hotels they are not included in the menu, but are supplied at an additional charge. *This indeed is the fruit worth a voyage to the East*, and I bet a hundred to one, that no person will ever feel disappointed with it, or regard it with mixed feelings, as is the case with the durian, which seems to have two parties in regard to it, each equally determined in its claims.

And now to turn to my friend, or rather my enemy the durian. Though its most offensive smell is enough to turn it down as a most objectionable fruit, still there are those, like Mr. F. L. Daniel, who eat it with a real relish and gusto, and to pique others, might even smack

[1] Ah! when I think of the four mangosteen plants I brought all the way from Ceylon, and which were in such excellent condition until I landed at Port Said, when ruthless and indiscriminate red tape, which seem never to have heard of the mangosteen, and could not distinguish between it and the mango, insisted that my plants were mangoes—in regard to the import of which there are some severe restrictions—and thus brought its baleful influence to work on the mangosteens in such a senseless manner, I simply wish I had never brought them, rather than to have seen them withered and scorched, and two actually pulled out of their pots, as I found on their reaching me a couple of days after my arrival at Cairo.

[*Photo by Platé, Ltd., Colombo*

A Freak Coconut Tree

Facing page 124]

[By courtesy of Mr. H. F. Macmillan

TALIPOT PALMS IN FLOWER IN THE PERADENIYA GARDENS

Facing page 125]

their lips, as if they would say, "Ah! you don't know how delicious it is; if you could only cultivate the taste!" As if this were a new culture for the gourmet to cultivate! But what is worse, as if the smell was not enough, the taste must needs make it even more repulsive; and I wonder whether a more sickening fruit one can ever come across! Indeed, the person who so aptly described it as "a custard passed through a gas pipe" deserves a medal.

I tasted the durian for the first and last time at *Nova Casa*, Borella, where I was lunching that day with Mr. F. L. Daniel, and what an experience it was! I should certainly thank Mr. Daniel for not having sent it to the hotel, else I cannot say how the hotel people might have stood its awful odour. But once at the Queen's Hotel I remember, on catching its malodorous smell, and expressing my disgust and wonder how anybody could relish such a fruit, the gentleman who seemed to have been enjoying it overheard me as he was passing, and smilingly remarked: "Oh! you just try it, and then you will change your opinion," little dreaming that I was already fed up with it, and would not eat it for its weight in gold! Indeed, the durian has come to be a standing joke in Ceylon, just as much as the *belle-mère* is made the butt of fun in Paris, or the famous Scot's "Bang went saxpence!" is in London.

Perhaps there are several other fruits which I have overlooked or missed; but then, I have merely described those which I actually came across during my visit, and are, moreover, supposed to be some of the best in the island. I must not fail, however, to add that in the districts near Nuwara Eliya and Bandarawela though one misses the Tropical fruits I have already mentioned, one finds there those which are more adaptable to colder regions, such as the plum, the pear, the peach, the apricot, the strawberry, the gooseberry, the apple, the cherimoyer, the granadilla, the passion fruit (more appreciated as an ice than a fruit eaten *au naturel*), the tree tomato (usually made into a jelly), and so on.

But the wonder is that so few people abroad seem to have heard, or at any rate, seem to have tasted of some of Ceylon's best fruits, and are thus able to appreciate more adequately the praise of those who have come to know and enjoy them personally.

CHAPTER XIV

THE BEAUTIFUL MOUNTAIN RAILWAY TO KANDY

CEYLON is provided with many fine public buildings, such as the General Post Office, the Public Works, the Survey Department Office, the General Hospital, the Victoria Memorial Eye Hospital, to name only a few at random; but when one sees Bombay's splendid Victoria Terminus, or even Cairo's magnificent Bab El-Hadid Station, one hopes in the days to come a grander edifice will grace Ceylon's Metropolis than her present ugly Railway Station at Maradana. Apropos of this, let us hope also that its Town Hall[1] in the Pettah, passable as it is at present, will be improved upon at some future date.

The old form of compartments in some of the trains in Ceylon are, needless to say, obsolete and quite out of place in these days of luxurious travel; but happily they are dying out, and being replaced by more up-to-date carriages.

But in one respect the Ceylon Government Railways have the advantage over our railways here. Apart from the cheapness of the fares, the fact that passengers are allowed a certain amount of luggage being conveyed gratis, namely, 112-lbs for the First Class, 84-lbs. for the Second Class, and 56-lbs. for the Third Class, comes as a welcome surprise and a real boon. But the wonder is

[1] Happily, I have not had long to wait, for there in the Cinnamon Gardens I noticed during my 1924 trip the scaffolding of what promises to be a magnificent Town Hall worthy of such a big and noted city as Colombo. May it be that when I re-visit Ceylon a few years hence it is a splendid Railway Station that likewise graces my view.

that even Third Class passengers should come in for such consideration when the claims of these unfortunate people are ignored for the most part in many lands, notably in the Orient; and the Ceylon authorities are certainly to be complimented on such consideration. But could they not add another feather to their cap by having the carriages for these people a little more commodious, or, at any rate, impart to them just some little semblance, however slight it may be, of the comfort of travel?

And in this connection I might remark that when I was at Kandy Station, when the Cadets of the various Schools were starting off for Diyatalawa for the annual Camp, I noticed that they were accommodated in Third Class carriages! I should have thought the claims of education were sacred enough to merit better and more generous treatment. Not that I criticise the action of the Ceylon Government Railways so much for putting them in Third Class carriages—which in itself is objectionable enough as a matter of principle in regard to the status of the pupils—as for the fact that they were crowded into such inconvenient compartments, and that not of their asking, on such a long journey! Such action certainly calls for strong condemnation, and I should have expected the schools themselves to have taken the move in the matter.

. . . . .

If Ceylon had been the goal of my hopes these many years past, Kandy was the culminating point. Here in this beautiful town I spent my last years in Ceylon, and of it more than anywhere else could I recall those haunting memories of a dear and happy past. Could I, therefore, not look forward most eagerly to visiting it soon after my arrival in Ceylon? It was with a thrill accordingly that I jumped into the train, my heart beating and throbbing with the anxiety of expectancy and the joy of the approaching fulfilment of a cherished dream.

. . . . .

[Photo by Platé, Ltd., Colombo

"SENSATION" POINT ON THE COLOMBO-KANDY RAILWAY OVERLOOKING THE DEKANDA VALLEY

Facing page 128]

[Photo by Platé, Ltd., Colombo

THE BEAUTIFUL DEKANDA VALLEY

Facing page 129]

The railway journey from Colombo is reputed to be one of the finest in Ceylon; and the tourist who has not much time to spare, but yet has enough leisure to permit of a run up to the Hill Capital, and a look at its Peradeniya Gardens, will have seen enough of beautiful Ceylon to dwell upon for the rest of his days.

The scenery along the route is quite different in its initial stages from what one encounters at the end of the journey. Starting with the lowlands, we begin with a few paddy (unhusked rice) fields and scraps of jungle, ere the track gets hillier and denser. But oh! how sparsely peopled and almost deserted seems the countryside of rural Ceylon compared to that of Egypt, teeming as ours does, with industrious peasants, and hardy labourers, and livestock of every description; and one wonders why Ceylon, an agricultural country, and so bounteously endowed by Nature, should nevertheless be so deplorably neglected agriculturally by its own inhabitants.

After passing Henaratgoda, with its well-known Botanic Gardens and noted rubber trees, and Veyangoda, which holds the ancestral property and domains of Sir Solomon Dias Bandaranayake, the Maha Mudaliyar of Ceylon, and the highest Ceylonese dignitary of the land, we approach Mirigama, where one gets his first experience of the many railway tunnels in Ceylon. Even as the train emerges from utter darkness into broad daylight, one never feels more acutely as then, the striking contrast from utter darkness to the light of day; and with a full heart he gratefully offers thanks to the Almighty that he retains intact the supreme blessing of his eyesight, without which life would be unendurable—or, at any rate, unenjoyable.

Beyond Mirigama, after passing Polgahawela, the junction for the Northern Railway to Jaffna, and that *via* Talaimannar on to India, and in the vicinity of which one can see the famous Talipot Palm (*vide* Cave's description later), the landscape is now transformed into hilly districts, and the very slopes, unlike the moss-covered, and sometimes scarped, acclivities on the Nuwara Eliya line, are now one wealth of luxuriant foliage and verdant vegetation.

The panorama soon after almost verges on the sublime; and when at Rambukkana, about 300 feet above the level of the sea, we begin the ascent of the Kadugannawa incline, climbing higher and higher up, we have practically attained the quintessence of the grandeur of the Tropics, culminating, on the one side in the far-famed and most beautiful Dekanda Valley, lying far, far below, a thousand feet down; and on the other side in scowling Alagalla, majestic and eërie as ever amidst its solitude, towering another 2,500 feet above us, from the altitude of a thousand feet we have already attained in our upward climb.

And as if romance must spin its halo round this famous peak, the legend goes that in the nebulous ages of the past, when kings were more of a power in the land, criminals met with short shrift at the hands of their sovereign who, divesting himself of all the paraphernalia of courts of law, judicial investigations, pleadings, and the like, meted out summary justice by simply having the offenders hurled from the dizzy summit of frowning Alagalla to be dashed to pieces in the depths far below.

In these regions one misses the grand waterfalls and rapids one meets with on the Nuwara Eliya line, though on this track, here and there the trickling crystalline water from up some slope, a miniature cascade, is not without its picturesqueness.

At last past Kadugannawa, set amidst such beautifully wooded country and enchanting scenery, followed immediately after by Peradeniya with its world-famed Botanic Gardens, the train dashes into Kandy; and once more anew come crowding all the sensations I experienced on first landing in Colombo. Kandy, most beautiful of all cities, lies before me, and as familiar as ever are its Police Headquarters, its Post Office, the Market, the pleasant Bogambara Recreation Ground which I pass as I drive on to the Queen's Hotel. Yes, while there is life there is hope, and patience hath yielded its reward in this fulfilment of a lifelong dream.

. . . . .

I have made but a few remarks on this railway journey, a bird's eye view of it, as it were; but I think it would be fairer to do full justice to the claims of this incomparable route, if only to advertise the charm of this beautiful land; and it is only a Cave who can successfully do so, as he has done in his admirable work: *The Book of Ceylon*. His account, accordingly, I give in *extenso*, and his pen-picture of the ascent into the Kandyan country I would in particular call my readers' attention to, a masterpiece of description as it is.

. . . . .

Cave's Account of the Railway to Kandy

"Leaving Colombo, the main line passes through marshy lands and backwaters until at the second mile the River Kelani is crossed and a fine view afforded on either side. At the fourth mile the first station (Kelaniya) appears. The agricultural products are coconuts, paddy and vegetables. The women of the villages are chiefly occupied in carrying the vegetables upon their heads to the markets of Colombo, and large numbers of them will be noticed in this useful work.

"But the chief object of interest to the visitor is the Kelani Wiharé (Buddhist Temple), which is held in great veneration by all the Buddhists of the lowlands, and to which many thousands come on full-moon days, bearing gifts of fruit, money and flowers for the shrine. This building stands near the river bank, and contributes its full share of picturesqueness to a scene that offers irresistible attractions to many an amateur photographer. . .

The image of Buddha, thirty-six feet in length, and the brilliant frescoes depicting scenes in his various lives, are fittingly found in the place which he is supposed to have visited in person during his life. A tradition appears in very early records that at Kelaniya in the fifth century B.C. there reigned a Naga king who was converted by the preaching of Buddha. A few years later he revisited his royal convert, who entertained him and his attendant disciples at Kelani, providing them with a celestial banquet. It was upon this occasion that Buddha rose aloft in the air and left the impression of his foot upon the mountain of Sumana, which is known to us as Adam's Peak.

"HUNUPITIYA is best known to Colombo people for its rifle range, where practice is carried on by the military and police from Colombo.

"At RAGAMA cultivation increases in variety, and we notice both tea and cinnamon in addition to the coconut and paddy. The reason for the existence of the observation camp here is found in the fact that Ceylon is dependent upon India for the supply of labour for the tea estates involving a constant immigration of Tamil coolies to the extent of about 150,000 *per annum*. In order that these newcomers should not import diseases into the various districts of Ceylon, they are, immediately upon disembarkation at Colombo, placed in quarters specially provided at the root of the Breakwater. Here they are subjected to a thorough inspection, bathed and fed. Next day they are entrained on the spot and conveyed to Ragama, where they are kept under observation until it is considered safe for them to proceed to their various destinations. During the Boer War a large number of recalcitrant prisoners-of-war were removed from the delightful camp of Diyatalawa and placed here in order that they might not infect the rest with their discontent.

"HENARATGODA is a busy little town . . . situated amidst well-watered fields and gardens whose products are of considerable variety and importance. Gardens devoted to the culture of the betel vine[1] are the most in evidence. . . . The district also produces areca-nuts, pepper, cinnamon, rubber, tea, paddy and coconuts. Its chief interest to us, however, centres in the Botanic Gardens where we may see some of the finest Para rubber trees in the colony. Many passengers from various countries who call at the port of Colombo make a trip to Henaratgoda for the special purpose of seeing these trees. The railway and other facilities afforded render the journey easy and comfortable. There is a good rest-house[2] near

[1] "The habit of chewing betel (made up of betel leaves, chunam-lime and areca-nuts) is almost universal (in Ceylon), and to say that they take the place of tobacco amongst Europeans falls much short of the truth; for while smoking is fairly common among the civilised races of Europe, it is not generally common among both men and women as is betel chewing in Ceylon. The method is as follows. The areca-nut is first sliced and then cut into tiny pieces by means of nippers. A few of these pieces, together with a small quantity of lime made from calcined shells or coral, are wrapped with a piece of betel leaf and placed in the mouth. The chewing of this mixture is said to be pleasant and to produce a soothing effect, and also serves the useful purpose of a prophylactic for those whose diet consists almost entirely of rice or other vegetable foods. The origin of the habit is a very ancient one, being mentioned by historians in times preceding the present era. It is very likely that in the first instance utility gave rise to the custom, which, like many others, has in time grown to be abused by excessive indulgence.

"A disagreeable effect of betel-chewing is the discolouration of the teeth; the betel leaf and areca-nut together colour the saliva a deep red, with the result that the lips and teeth acquire a blood-stained appearance. This does not strike the natives themselves as being in the least degree objectionable; although to the Europeans it seems a great disfigurement, especially as the Sinhalese have excellent teeth which are naturally pearly white, as may be seen in the few who provide the necessary exceptions to the general rule. Every man and woman of the humbler classes, young or old, carries somewhere in the folds of the waistcloth or concealed in the turban a little box or basket containing the three necessaries, and from morning till night on every favourable opportunity the munching goes on. Those among the wealthy who have adopted European customs have to a considerable extent given up the habit, generally in favour of tobacco, nor do these stand in need of the corrective to an exclusively vegetarian diet; but they are the exceptions. The native gentleman as a rule has his ornamental betel box of silver, and it is the duty of his chief servant to keep it replenished. He does not take wine, but he extracts as many of the pleasures of conviviality from the well-prepared betel, which is offered at ceremonial visits, as does the European from his wine . . . Leaves of betel are also used to enwrap the offerings of money presented in temples.

"The fruit of the areca palm is about the size of a small hen's egg, and grows in clusters beneath the crown of feathery foliage at the top of the stem. The so-called nut is the seed, which is found within the fibrous husk or rind. It is a pretty mottled grey and brown colour. It needs very little preparation; generally it is only sliced and dried in the sun, but sometimes it is previously boiled." (*Vide The Book of Ceylon*, by H. W. Cave, pp. 86–88).

[2] One of the welcome features of the highways and byways of rural Ceylon is the resthouse at every fifteen miles, which caters to the needs of the benighted wayfarer or the traveller of the daytime, and what a welcome retreat it proves at all times, and the Ceylon Government is certainly to be thanked for its thoughtfulness in this direction. These resthouses owe their origin to the Dutch, who instituted them during their rule in Ceylon.

And in this connection the Egyptian Government might do well to emulate the example of Ceylon, and seek to erect a greater number along its country roads,

the station, and refreshments are procurable without previous notice. Buggies or hackeries[3] can be hired near the station for driving to the gardens about a mile distant. The drive is pretty. . . . The garden is one of a number of such institutions that are under the Government Department of Botany and Agriculture, with headquarters at Peradeniya, where its director and extensive scientific staff of experts reside. The Henaratgoda gardens were opened in 1876 for the purpose of making experiments in ascertaining suitable subjects for cultivation in the heated lowlands. It was about this time that the Para rubber seed was planted, and many of the trees that we see there to-day(1907) are therefore upwards of thirty years old. . . . Although the Royal Botanic Garden at Henaratgoda has recently been so much regarded as the show place of rubber trees to the neglect of all else, the visitor will find many fine specimens of other useful trees and plants, including ebony and satinwood. The cultivated area is about thirty acres.

"VEYANGODA is the first stop of the fast trains to Kandy. The village itself is about three miles from the railway station. . . . Near it, at the twenty-fourth mile from Colombo is situated the historic residence of Sir Solomon Dias Bandaranaike, the Maha Mudaliyar of Ceylon (a title signifying the head of the Mudaliyars or low-country chieftains). The present Maha Mudaliyar is also native aide-de-camp to his Excellency the Governor of the Colony, and amongst the duties of his office is that of presenting on State occasions the various native dignitaries to the Governor. . . . Sir Solomon Dias Bandaranaike has added to the attractions of the ancestral property at Veyangoda by the addition of a horse-breeding

especially that now the advent of the motor car renders the need for such all the more necessary. But whereas the few that now exist are invariably reserved for Government officials only, and the "big wigs" in particular, the resthouse should, as a matter of fact, be of universal use, and thue have its doors thrown open to all, and not reserved for a privileged few only.

[3] The hackery is a small carriage, something like a crude dogcart, drawn by a hardy little bull; and its pace is sometimes quite fast. It is the conveyance which the villagers in Ceylon generally use, and it is to them the means of locomotion such as the donkey is to the Egyptian peasant, or the Arab steed to a well-to-do personage in a village.

establishment, a deer run, and modern arrangements for the breeding of high-class stock.

"To the traveller proceeding to Kandy for the first time the lowland scenery from station to station is an ever fascinating panorama. He cannot fail to feel enchanted by the alternating scenes of primitive husbandry, glimpses of villages embosomed in palms, magnificent groups of tropical trees, and particularly with the effect of the masses of thick forest, broken up at frequent intervals by deep recesses devoted to the cultivation of paddy. From November to January, when the corn is rising from its watery bed, snipe and other aquatic birds appear in large numbers between Veyangoda and Rambukkana and afford excellent sport. . . .

"The country round MIRIGAMA[1] is very favourable to the cultivation of the coconut, as is evidenced by the remarkable yield of fruit on many of the trees. It is not often, however, that the traveller can spare the time to inspect the various features of interest in this important branch of tropical agriculture, but he may, as he passes through it, welcome some account in these pages. . . . Its ubiquity is often the only thing noticed by the visitor about the coconut palm, and from this arises the erroneous supposition that it is an indigenous plant, whereas the native saying that it will not flourish away from the sound of the human voice is nearer the truth. The coconut is the chief source of Sinhalese wealth; but unlike the cinnamon, it depends upon man for its existence, and if left to nature pines and dies. It is true, therefore, that wherever you see the coconut palm there is population. Although European colonists have considerably extended its cultivation, it is pre-eminently the national tree, the friend of the natives, all of whom share in its benefits, from the wealthy owner of tens of thousands of trees to the humble possessor of a tithe of one. There are few gifts of the earth about which so much may be said; its uses are infinite, and to the Sinhalese villager all sufficient.

[1] At Mirigama is a fine coconut estate belonging to Mr. W. H. Wright, who has succeeded, more than others, in the cultivation of the mangosteen as well.

With the trunk of the tree he builds his hut and his bullock-stall, which he thatches with its leaves. His bolts and bars are slips of the bark, by which he also suspends the small shelf which holds his stock of home-made utensils and vessels. He fences his little plot of chillies, tobacco and fine grain, with the leaf stalks. The infant is swung to sleep in a rude net of coir-string made from the husk of the fruit; its meal of rice and scraped coconut is boiled over a fire of coconut shells and husks, and is eaten off a dish formed of the plaited green leaves of the tree with a spoon cut out of the nut-shell. When he goes fishing by torch-light his net is of coconut fibre, the torch or chule is a bundle of dried coconut leaves and flower-stalks; the little canoe is the trunk of the cocoa-palm tree, hollowed by his own hands. He carries home his net and string of fish on a yoke, or pingo, formed of a coconut stalk. When he is thirsty, he drinks of the fresh juice of the young nut; when he is hungry, he eats its soft kernel. If he has a mind to be merry, he sips a glass of arrack, distilled from the fermented juice, and he flavours his curry with vinegar from this toddy. Should he be sick, his body will be rubbed with coconut oil; he sweetens his coffee with jaggery or coconut sugar, and softens it with coconut milk; it is sipped by the light of a lamp constructed from a coconut shell and fed by coconut oil. His doors, his windows, his shelves, his chairs, the water gutter under the eaves, are all made from the wood of the tree. His spoons, his forks, his basins, his mugs, his salt-cellars, his jars, his child's money-box, are all constructed from the shell of the nut. Over his couch when born, and over his grave when buried, a branch of coconut blossoms is hung to charm away evil spirits.[1]

"The marvellous bounty of the coconut palm has been gracefully summarised by the poet as

> "clothing, meat, trencher, drink, and can,
> Boat, cable, sail, mast, needle, all in one."

[1] This charming description of the Sinhalese villager's necessities supplied by this bountiful palm is (Cave says) from the pen of the late Mr. John Capper.

[Photo by the *Author*

A NATURAL ARCHWAY—THE WELL-KNOWN LANDMARK ON THE COLOMBO-KANDY ROAD

Facing page 136]

GIANT BAMBOOS IN THE PERADENIYA GARDENS, OVERLOOKING THE MAHAWILA GANGA

From " A Handbook of Tropical Gardening and Planting " (Colombo: Cave & Co.). *By courtesy of the Author, Mr. H. F. Macmillan,*

Facing page 137]

"ALAWWA is one of the least important of the main line stations. The scenery, however, becomes more varied in character as we pass through this district. The railway runs parallel to the Maha-oya, which affords opportunities to the snap-shotter; for there are many exquisite vistas between the clumps of bamboo that decorate the banks; and with the present day rapid lenses and focal-plane-shutters photography from a moving train is not impossible, as many of the illustrations in this volume prove.[1]

"POLGAHAWELA is the junction for the northern line. Passengers are afforded every facility for comfort. There is also a rest-house quite near the station with bedrooms and provided with light refreshments. The agriculture of the district is the same as described in connection with Mirigama, with the considerable addition of plantains which are grown here extensively for markets which are brought into reach by the railway, about one hundred and fifty tons being despatched in the course of each month.

"A large number of Talipot Palms[2] are to be seen between Polgahawela and Kandy; and fortunate will the traveller be who happens to pass through this district when a large number of them are in flower. The botanical world offers no more beautiful sight than this. The period when it may be enjoyed is, however, quite uncertain, as the flower bursts forth once only in the lifetime of the tree when it is approaching its hundredth year. It occasionally happens that scores of trees are in flower at one time, while at another not one may be seen. . . . It will be observed that in its (the Talipot's) youth it devotes itself to producing only huge fan-shaped leaves; later a trunk begins to form, which grows straight as a mast to a height of about one hundred feet. The grand white stem is encircled with closely set ring-marks,

[1] One of the features of Cave's excellent book is the large assortment (756 in number) of lovely illustrations adorning his admirable work.

[2] If a person wishes to have a closer view of the Talipot Palm and enjoy its sight more amply, there in the Peradeniya Gardens he will find the famous Talipot Avenue near the river.

showing where it has borne and shed its leaves from year to year. The semi-circular fans often have a radius of fifteen feet, giving a surface of about three hundred and fifty square feet. The uses to which these leaves are put are computed by the natives at eight hundred and one, the chief being raincloak and sunshade. Three or four of these leaves form an admirable tent, and are often employed as such. The literary purpose to which they have for thousands of years been applied is perhaps the most interesting. For this they are cut into strips, and afterwards boiled and dried when they become what the natives term *ola* or paper.[1] On these strips of *ola* the history of the people and their religious systems have been handed down to us. I have seen manuscripts of this material more than a thousand years old, and yet in perfect condition, with the characters so clear and distinct that it is difficult to realise their vast age.

"When the Talipot attains full maturity, it grows somewhat smaller leaves, and develops a gigantic bud some four feet in height. In due course this bursts with a report, and unfolds a lovely white blossom which expands into a majestic pyramid of cream-coloured flowers, which rise to a height of twenty feet above the leafy crown. The fruit which succeeds this magnificent bloom consists of innumerable nuts or seeds. Their appearance indicate that the noble tree is nearing its end. It now begins to droop, its leaves wither, and within a year it falls dead. . . . It may, however, be observed here that its leaves are much used in the construction of camps for the officers of the Survey Department, and the supplies for this purpose are mainly drawn from the neighbourhood Polgahawela.

"At Rambukkana the ascent into the Kandyan mountains begins, and the beauty of the landscape approaches the sublime. If Ceylon presented no other spectacle of interest to the traveller it would still be worth his while to visit Kandy, if only to see the panorama that unfolds

[1] These remind me of the *papyri* of my own country, and the similar uses to which they have been put; but in as good a state of preservation as ours also are, they are still of even greater antiquity, dating back several thousands of years.

itself as the train moves upward in its winding and intricate course on the scarped sides of the mountains overlooking the lovely Dekanda valley. Two powerful engines are now attached to our train, one at either end, and so sharp are the curves that it is frequently possible for the passenger in the train to see both; or from his seat to take a photograph, including in the landscape a large portion of the train in which he is travelling. At one moment, on the edge of a sheer precipice, we are gazing downwards some thousand feet below; at another we are looking upwards at a mighty crag a thousand feet above; from the zigzags by which we climb the mountain sides fresh views appear at every turn; far-reaching valleys edged by the soft blue ranges of distant mountains and filled with luxuriant masses of dense forest, relieved here and there by the vivid green terraces of the rice fields; cascades of lovely flowering creepers hanging in festoons from tree to tree and crag to crag; above and below deep ravines and foaming waterfalls dashing their spray into mist as it falls into the verdurous abyss; fresh mountain peaks appearing in ever-changing grouping as we gently wind along the steep gradients; daring crossings from rock to rock, so startling as to unnerve the timid as we pass over gorges cleft in the mountain side and look upon the green depths below, so near the edge of the vertical precipice that a fall from the carriage would land us sheer sixteen hundred feet below; the lofty Talipot is flourishing on either side; the scattered huts and gardens, and the quaint people about them, so primitive in their habits which vary little from those of two thousand years ago—these are some of the features of interest as we journey into the Kandyan district.

"The precipitous mountain of Alagalla . . . is the most conspicuous feature of the landscape. Our train creeps along upon its steep side of granite. The track is visible like a belt passing round the rock. The peak towers aloft 2,500 feet above us, while the beautiful valley lies a thousand feet below. On the far side of that peak lies Hataraliyadda, a warm but radiant valley, where primeval manners and customs are yet uninfluenced by the march of western civilisation. . . .

"ALAGALLA is always majestic, but most beautiful immediately after excessive rainfall, when it is literally besprinkled with cataracts, some of which burst forth many hundreds of feet above the railway, and dash into the valleys some thousand feet below, increasing in volume and gathering enormous impetus as they pass under the line in deep fissures. The height of Alagalla is 3,394 feet. Tea grows upon its acclivities, and those who are occupied in its cultivation on these giddy heights are enviable spectators of the most varied and beautiful atmospheric scenes that are to be found in Ceylon. Unsettled weather is extremely frequent and is productive of an endless variety of cloud and storm effects over the wonderful valley which undulates below, until, in the far distance, it is backed by the rugged mountains opposed to Alagalla and which reach a greater height. At one time a vast sea of mists is rolling in fleecy clouds over the lowland acres, and the summits of the hills are standing out from it like wooded islands; at another every shape of the beautiful landscape is faultlessly defined and every colour is vivid beneath the tropical sun; then an hour or two will pass and rolling masses of dense black vapours will approach the mountain while the sunbeams play on the distant hills; now the sun becomes obscured, a streak of fire flashes through the black mass and immediately the whole mountain seems shaken by the terrific peal of thunder—thunder of a quality that would turn any unaccustomed heart pale. Then follows a downpour at the rate of a full inch an hour; the cascades turn to roaring cataracts, the dry paths to rushing torrents, and the rivulets to raging floods. The rice-fields suddenly become transformed into lakes, and the appearance of the valleys suggests considerable devastation by water; but it is not so; the torrent passes away almost as suddenly as it comes, and the somewhat bruised and battered vegetation freshens and bursts into new life as the heavy pall of cloud disperses and the gleams of the golden sun return to cheer its efforts. That tea or anything else should grow on these rocky slopes is one of the marvels of this wonderful land.

"Our attention will perhaps be mostly attracted to the Dekanda Valley. The terraced rice-fields, the beautiful trees, plants and creepers upon the slopes beneath us, the distant mountains rising in tiers on all sides and o'erhung with vapours whose forms and contrasts of tone from the deepest black to the purest white are almost always present, the curious shapes displayed by the heights, the Camel Rock, the Bible Rock, and Utuwankanda—all these contribute to make our slow progress seem all the more rapid. Utuwankanda, the curious crag observable . . . was in the early sixties the stronghold of a famous Sinhalese bandit, who for years terrorised the district, and whose exploits in robbery and murder have already reached the legendary stage. Sardiel was of small stature, and one could have expected an ordinary boy of fourteen to prove his match. Originally a barrack boy in Colombo detected in theft, he fled and adopted robbery as a profession. He appears to have gathered around him some kindred spirits, and to have fixed on Utuwankanda as his home. He was dreaded by Europeans and natives alike, showing marvellous resource in stealing arms and ammunition and using them with deadly effect in his nefarious expeditions. After he had so terrorised the district that no contractor would undertake the transit of goods from Colombo to Kandy without an escort, a reward of £100 was offered for his apprehension. The police were powerless against him. He shot six of them on a single occasion. At length he was taken by Mr. F. R. Saunders (now Sir Frederick Saunders), then district judge of Kégalle, who, accompanied by some men of the Ceylon Rifles, fearlessly entered his stronghold. His career ended in his execution by hanging at Kandy.

"We are now in the freshness of mountain air and have left behind us the steamy low-country, where the simmering heat, although the efficient cause of the beautiful features of the landscape, is nevertheless very trying to our energies. For thirteen miles we have been slowly crawling round the mountain sides, ever moving upwards, till at length, through a narrow pass, we emerge upon one of those ledges of the mountain system which were referred to in the introductory part of this work. There also we saw how the brave Kandyans held their capital for centuries against all the attempts of Europeans to take it. There was an ancient prophecy current amongst them that whoever should pierce the rock and make a road into Kandy from the plains would receive the kingdom as his reward. The prophecy was at length fulfilled by the British, who made the road, pierced the rock and secured the safe and permanent possession of the prize. The scene of the exploit is now before us. From the train we may see the road and the pierced rock. The eminence rising from the rock is known as Scouts' Hill from the circumstance that the Kandyans jealously guarded this gate to their kindgom with their forces always in readiness, should an enemy appear from the low-country. Each inhabitant was subject to sentinel duty and thousands were kept at posts overlooking the plains around, many even having to keep their watch on the tops of trees commanding extensive views of the whole country round, so that no person could get either in or out of the kingdom unobserved and without permission. Indeed, so jealous were the apprehensions of the Kandyan monarch when the British appeared in Ceylon that a strict system of passports from one district to another was adopted.

"The lofty column observable . . . comes into view as a signal that we have arrived at the top of the pass. Both road and rail here converge and make their entrance into the Kandyan country together, the road being most picturesque at its entrance to Kadugannawa. The monument is not, as is often supposed, in commemoration of the railway, but a memorial to Captain Dawson of the Royal Engineers, who planned and superintended the construction of the road. It was erected by public subscription in 1832.

"At KADUGANNAWA we are at once in most interesting Kandyan country, its chief attractions to us being the singular beauty of the road scenery and the historical temples in the district. . . .

"Kadugannawa is said to have been a health resort in earlier times, and with its salubrious air, its good supply of pure spring water, the grandeur of its scenery and its proximity to interesting places it is still deserving the attention of the Kandyans as a charming suburb.

"At PERADENIYA JUNCTION the fast trains of the main line are divided, the Kandy and Matalé portion proceeding northwards, and the Bandarawela part to the south with the passengers for Nuwara Eliya and the Uva country. Proceeding in the Kandy train we next come to PERADENIYA NEW where we cross the Mahaweliganga (the great sandy river). . . . It will be observed that a modern stone bridge has now replaced the historical satinwood bridge which for threescore years and ten was a conspicuous and beautiful ornament in the landscape. This bridge was a remarkable structure; it crossed the river with a single span, in which there was neither nail nor bolt, the whole of the massive woodwork being dovetailed together. It was constructed entirely of yellow satinwood, which fifty years ago was so plentiful in the forests of Ceylon that it was commonly used for building purposes. The present structure is of pleasing design, and is perhaps the most ornamental bridge in Ceylon, but it lacks the æsthetic qualities of its predecessor. Under normal conditions the river flows seventy feet below the bridge, but at the burst of the monsoon such a mighty torrent rolls between the banks that the bridge then clears the water by about ten feet only.

"PERADENIYA NEW is the station for the Royal Botanic Gardens of Peradeniya, world-famed for their usefulness and their beauty. Here, in a situation perfectly ideal from whatever point of view it is regarded, is a marvellous collection of living specimens of the flora of the whole tropical world, as well as a great herbarium and museum of Ceylon plants The term Royal Botanic Gardens, however, stands for something vastly more important than the great show-place of floral wonders which has gained their wide repute. From their inception a century ago they have been organised to foster and assist agricultural enterprise; but in recent years the scope of their usefulness in this direction has been so widened and developed that the title now indicates a government department of botany and agriculture presided over by a director and staff of scientific specialists in botany, chemistry, mycology and entomology, under whose direction all agricultural possibilities are put to the test, and experimental culture carried on in various parts of the country. Thus not only are all useful and ornamental trees and plants of other countries introduced into the colony, but technical and scientific advice and instruction are given as to every condition that makes for success in culture, in the treatment and prevention of diseases of plant life and the destruction and prevention of insect pests. In no country is more assistance for agriculturists provided by the Government, whose attitude to the native is truly paternal; for it supplies him with seeds, advice and instruction free of cost; it cares for his prosperity; finds what it is desirable for him to grow and experiments upon the product for him; advises him upon every point, and periodically inquires how he is getting on.

"The Gardens, with an area of one hundred and fifty acres, and at an elevation of about 1,600 feet, are rather under four miles from Kandy, and the visitor has choice of road or rail. If he chooses the former, the drive to and from Peradeniya will not be the least interesting part of the excursion; for the road is not only exceedingly picturesque . . . but presents many quaint scenes. The variety and aspect of the native dwellings, some squalid, others with considerable pretensions to luxury; but all nestling amidst glorious shrubs, trees and creepers, and having their own little gardens prolific of papaws, curry seeds, garlic, pepper, pumpkins, cocoa and sweet potatoes—all in wild profusion. Some are embowered

[Photo by the Author

THE PINGO CARRIER

Facing page 144]

[Photo by the Author

The Famous Dalada Maligawa, the Temple of the Holy Tooth—at the Time of the Perahera

Facing page 145]

in bread-fruit trees, the foliage of which is in marked contrast to the waving plumes of the coconut and other palms amongst which it grows. The fruit, which is very abundant, grows in large green pods, about the size of melons, which nestle beneath each separate crown of leaves. It is used as food by the natives in various preparations; but, as a rule, disliked by Europeans. Swarms of little brown urchins frolic on the roadside, and add not a little to the picturesqueness of the scene. Pingo bearers walk to and fro with their burdens of fruit and vegetables, representing many varieties quite strange to us. The pingo is a long and flat piece of wood from the kittul palm, very tough and pliable. The coolie, having suspended his load to the two ends in baskets or nets, places the stave upon his shoulder at the middle, and is thus enabled by the elastic spring and easy balance of the pingo to carry great weights for a considerable distance. Some pingoes are made from the leaf-stalk of the coconut palm, which is even more pliable than the kittul. This is a favourite means of carrying liquids, placed in earthenware chatties attached to the pingo by means of coir. Another familiar roadside character is the gram vendor (" hommos "). She sits patiently during the greater part of the day selling gram by the half-cent's worth (less than a farthing) to passers-by. As might be conjectured from the size of the little bamboo measure, the gram is sold in very small quantities as a delicacy. It resembles dried peas in appearance, and tastes rather like them. The village silversmith will also attract our attention as we pass along the road; for he works serenely in his open shed with tools of his own construction, and for his furnace a couple of simple native-made earthenware bowls. He does a roaring trade in anklets, nose-rings, bangles and earrings, converting the silver savings of the modest villager[1] into these articles and securing them upon limbs or features, where they continue to represent savings and to gratify vanity until an evil day comes when they are

[1] It may interest the reader to know that also in the Egyptian villages and towns a similar practice exists amongst the lower middle and lower classes, but their ornaments are, as a rule, of gold, not silver.

removed by the same hands to be sold and transferred to another thrifty and vain person. This modest worker is more skilful than his primitive methods would lead you to suppose, and can convert your gold or silver coins into useful articles of jewellery while you wait, and wait you should lest by accident the quality of your metal should deteriorate.

"Another thing which the stranger will notice upon this road is the temporary Buddhist shrine, erected to receive offerings from the devout wayfarer. It is frequently a very modest erection, consisting of a chair surmounted by a frame of bamboo sticks, covered with a few strips of calico, forming a canopy within which is placed a small image of Buddha and a bowl of offerings; at the close of the day the offerings are conveyed to the Temple of the Tooth at Kandy.

"For obvious reasons we cannot describe here all the thousand and one things which seize the attention of the traveller upon this interesting road. A day should be given to Peradeniya by every visitor who stays sufficiently long in Kandy to afford it. The best time is to set out in the early morning. There is an excellent rest-house near the entrance to the garden where breakfast and lunch may be obtained.

"In Kandy and its neighbourhood the gem of the earth sends forth her most exquisite rays. . . . Kandy is incomparably beautiful; but let it be at once understood that in thus describing it we are not limiting the epithet to the town and its immediate surroundings. It is rather the Kandyan country as a whole that is thus distinguished, and this must be seen from the hill-tops which command the far-reaching valleys where the Mahaweliganga rolls over rocky channels and through scenes of almost majestic beauty; from the Hunasgeria peak; from the Mattanapatana; from Lady Horton's walk and other steep acclivities that encircle the town itself. Travellers too frequently, either from want of time or lack of energy, obtain but a faint idea of the varied beauty of the Kandyan district. . . .

"As we ascend the steep acclivities the beauty of the landscape approahces the sublime; we gaze across far-reaching valleys where the Mahaweliganga rolls over channels strewn with massive rocks; we see the Hunasgeria peak towering above vast stretches of vivid greenery where cacao groves are interspersed with masses of lofty palms, with here and there patches of the most lovely colour of all vegetation—the emerald hue of half-ripe paddy; the grandeur of the Matalé hills and the whole surrounding country which, when viewed from the heights that embrace the town, is a panorama of surpassing loveliness."

. . . . .

Even at the risk of repetition, I might conclude this chapter by reiterating what Cave has so truthfully said: "If Ceylon presented no other spectacle of interest to the traveller, it would still be worth his while to visit Kandy, which (in itself) is so incomparably beautiful, if only to see the panorama that unfolds itself as the train moves upwards in its winding and intricate course on the scarped sides of the mountains overlooking the lovely Dekanda Valley."

CHAPTER XV

THE GEM OF THE EARTH

KANDY, of all places, is the one city in Ceylon that no tourist should ever miss. When we speak of the beauty of Ceylon, it is not the beauty of Colombo or Mount Lavinia that one generally thinks of—for many Colombos and Mount Lavinias, with as many attractions, can we find in many parts of the world—but it is the picturesqueness, the incomparable beauty, the infinite charm of the Kandyan country that springs to the mind, a magnet, as it were, to draw all to this earthly paradise.

Most beautiful in this beautiful land is Kandy, the brightest gem amidst all jewels. Her Dalada Maligawa she may revel in—sacred shrine of millions of the Buddhist Faith—as also in her world-famed Peradeniya Gardens; but it is in its majestic natural beauty, the incomparable loveliness of its everlasting amphitheatre of hills rising in terraces, interspersed with enchanting walks and drives, that this gem of the earth excels.

Here has bounteous Nature clothed it with all the wealth, all the luxuriance, and all the grandeur of the Tropics; and a kindly equable climate has not failed to add its share. Who is there indeed who does not stand spell-bound, bewildered, as he gazes from up Lady Horton's, or the Catholic Seminary on the heights behind the Tennis Club round the Lake, on to the wonderful, entrancing view of the famous Dumbara Valley far, far below? And the Reservoir, or the view from Wace Park, or that from "Arthur Seat" farther up—my home of one time—what other wonders they unfurl!

But no! gentle reader, ask not of me to portray to you such magic scenes. Go thither yourself, and let Ceylon but once come your way, and ever will you be thankful. It is not only Europe with her untold treasures and manifold attractions that can to you be a lodestone, but here in "The Pearl of the Eastern Seas", the Serendib of Sindbad, the supposed Tarshish and Ophir of Solomon, the Taprobane of the Romans, "The Brightest Gem in Britain's Diadem", will you find a land most wondrous to behold, most exquisite in its charm.

England may have her Lake District, and Germany her Rhineland; France her Bois de Boulogne, and Switzerland her Alps; Italy her lakes, and Norway her fjords; America her Yellowstone Park, and Hawaii her Honolulu; Java her Buitenzorg, and Japan her Fuji Yama; Tahiti her Papeete, and Australia her Sydney Harbour; India her Darjeeling, and Turkey her Golden Horn; Syria her Lebanon, and Egypt her Delta Barrage; but far above all, grand, majestic, unsurpassable, is Kandy of the Kandyans.

Some of Ceylon's lovely drives and walks have been named after the Fair Sex—the soul and embodiment of all that is beautiful the Great Creator has moulded for us. And fitfully have the roads reflected the charm of the ladies whose names they bear, perpetuating as these roads do the memory of the respected wives of the various Governors of the Island, who in their own way and sphere loyally and admirably supported their husbands in their onerous duties of the administration of the Island. Lady Blake's Road, starting at Katugastota, where one can see the Maligawa elephants bathing, alongside which flows the Mahawila Ganga, now a muddy stream, at other times a raging torrent dashing over a hundred boulders, as if it were another Asswan Cataract; Lady Horton's Road; Lady MacCarthy's Road, and a host of others, a veritable paradise to the photographer all of them, who has not tasted of their delights?

Here bounteous Nature unites with the hand of man to blend all the beauty of the forest with the comforts of a prosaic age, and thankful surely must be those who betake themselves to such haunts of bewitching charm to revel in the sublimity of an Eastern enchantment. Even the screech of the jungle fowl, or the grimaces of some wanderoo, or the rustling of the undergrowth as some denizen of the forest makes good its escape, shed their additional charm; and as if not to be left out in the cold, the voracious little leech must sometimes make its unwelcome presence felt.

Even the darkest of nights brings its recompense. There up the verdant, overhanging slopes of Gregory Road, Upper Lake Road, and the adjacent ridges of " Arthur Seat " twinkle the lights of many a home; and when a million fireflies join in the picture, uniting with the canopy of heaven, lo! what a ravishing sight, what a scene most wondrous to behold, most exquisite in the extreme, lies spread before our spell-bound gaze!

But the moonlight brings another picture, some remembrance from memory's holy shrine; and even as the fireflies twinkle, as if competing with the bright orb's silvery rays, and Kandy's lovely lake shimmers in the restful gleam, to Cairo's Royal Opera House and far-flung Nippon my thoughts wander. Once more there lives to me, incarnate as it were, that scene at the close of the First Act of Puccini's tuneful and charming opera, *Madame Butterfly*, and even as the fireflies twinkle now, and the moon sheds its silvery beams, I visualise the faithless Pinkerton, almost beneath the porch of his new home, locked in the arms of his credulous and innocent wife, as they sing that famous duet plighting their troths, and in the ecstasy of love pour out their hearts to Venus, firefly and silvery moon sole witnesses of this idyll.

CHAPTER XVI

MY VISIT TO KINGSWOOD

Soon after arriving in Colombo I had to hurry to Nuwara Eliya. But could I go past Kandy without having a peep at the dear old town, the beloved old School, and the kind old Head Master? To the Hill Capital accordingly I first directed my footsteps, if even for a few days, for Kandy, above all places, deserved to be visited first in my rambles throughout the Island, so close and attached were my associations with it.

At Kingswood I immediately called within a few minutes of my arrival, and here at last was the fulfilment of a dream I had so often seen in my sleep on Egypt's hoary soil. Quietly I slunk in, unknown, unnoticed, true to the letter of my hope and desire. A short query of the pupil in the playground, a gentle knock at some room, a whispered announcement, without mentioning names, of someone wishing to see the Principal, and the door opens, and out comes the tall, thin, familiar figure of Kingswood's famous Head Master, the youngsters he happened to be taking at the time, gathering in a group towards the entrance, and gazing in some wonderment at this stranger in the bright scarlet fez—quite different from the dark and short ones in vogue in Ceylon—who seemed so unceremoniously to have interrupted their lesson.

There at last within the walls of old Kingswood, and beneath the shadow of the Kandyan Hills we warmly greet each other once more, as I reiterate to him my most profound gratitude for meeting me on board the *Mantua*. To the Queen's Hotel I then drive back, as suddenly as I came, the carriage that bore me away carrying a heart that went out in deepest thankfulness to the Almighty that I had lived to see this happy day.

But even as I drove away I could not help moralising on the fact that, whereas I had expected to find Mr. Blazé taking the topmost form, I found him with one of the juvenile classes. But then, Mr. Blazé is not only an erudite scholar, but he is a maker of men as well, for he knew what it is to have a sound solid foundation on which to build the fabric of a successful career, for, "Well begun, is half done," as goes the familiar saying. Well, therefore, might those who in their early years were blessed with the Blazé touch thank their stars that they had such good fortune to pass through the hands of such a fine moulder of men.

. . . . .

It was the time of the Perahera, however, that I planned for a prolonged stay in Kandy, and amply did it justify my fondest hopes and expectations. On this occasion also I came into closer and more intimate touch with Kingswood, for, now that I had broken the ice, I could get over my shyness and nervousness without difficulty.

Several times I visited Mr. Blazé, but only when there were few pupils about and he was not engaged, and many a pleasant and enjoyable chat we had together after so many years. But no! I must see the boys he always said, and he insisted on presenting them to me formally, and when a Head Master insists, though we have left school his request is still authoritative, and we cannot but comply with his desire. Thus, once or twice, though I had summoned enough courage at the outset, I could not help shirking at the last moment, especially when I was told that the pupils were expecting me to propose a

[Photo by the Author

THE RAPIDS IN THE MAHAWILA GANGA, NEAR PERADENIYA

Facing page 152]

[*Photo by the Author*

THE LOVELY KANDY LAKE—FROM WACE PARK

Facing page 153]

half-holiday for them. But who was I to presume to make such a claim? No wonder, therefore, that I could not be brought to face the music, eager as I was to meet each Kingswoodian personally and talk together as one big family, tied as we were by the common and sacred bond of the same school.

Finally I did go, but it was on the last day of the Midsummer Term ere they broke up for their holidays, and instead of having one paltry half-holiday, they now could have a goodly forty days! How nervously I entered the school, and shyly and timidly entered the Hall where the whole school was assembled, and how warmly they greeted me in the true Kingswood fashion, my readers need not bother about—nor could I in all decency deal with it. But how my heart throbbed, and my courage failed me when, instead of quietly taking up my place in some unobtrusive corner, not even the most earnest pleadings availing, I found that I was being actually led to the platform where Mr. Blazé stood—tall, imposing, notwithstanding the pallor of a broken constitution, and the creeping pitiless years of Father Time, which seemed to wrestle with the fiery, indomitable spirit within.

The holidays were at hand, and Mr. Blazé was, accordingly, summing up the term's work. Here a hint, there a remark; now a piece of kindly advice, and occasionally some criticism; and so on paternal-like he dispensed valuable "Blazéisms" to all and sundry. "Make your vacation a real holiday," he would say, "and try to enjoy it to the utmost and in the best manner possible," he proceeds; "but be careful always to behave like true Kingswood gentlemen: honourably and manfully," he adds. "You will be going to camp in a few days, and you have won the *Hermann Loos Cup* on the last two occasions, and three times out the four since it was given; I hope you will be able to win it again this year; at any rate, do your best."

He next turns to a little youngster, addressing him by name, for he seemed to know every boy personally, thereby proving his solicitude and keen interest in the welfare of each of them personally. " What is the most important thing after you come back from the holidays?" he asks, expecting of course the reply of " Kingswood Week ", which covered the Prize Distribution, the School Sports, and " Kingswood Sunday ", or any one of them. But what was our surprise when " Caning, sir," comes the feeble reply in a nervous, tremulous voice, and out burst the whole school laughing; and whether this lad was another wag, like my friend Mr. Abdel Halim El-Shamsy, and was thus bent on producing a comic effect, or Mr. Blazé was another Eton Dr. Keate of caning fame, I cannot definitely say.

" By my side," he then proceeded to conclude, or in some such words as far as I can remember, " is a gentleman who is no stranger to this school, for he was with us many years ago. He now comes from Egypt to visit us, and we heartily greet him, and bid him welcome. I present to you, gentlemen, Ali Foad Toulba, one of our oldest " Old Boys ", and I remember the time when his father, the late Toulba Pasha, who was an exile here, first sent him to me. . . .", and so in this vein he waxed reminiscent about the late Arabi Pasha's sons—themselves Old Kingswoodians—and myself, with flashes of humour here and there in his narrative.

But horror of horrors! There, as I sat complacent, and complimenting myself that the proceedings were soon drawing to a close, and that after all my position did not seem so embarrassing as I had feared, Mr. Blazé all of a sudden launches the thunderbolt he had up his sleeve. " And now, gentlemen, Ali Foad Toulba will say a few words to you."

And now indeed it seemed as if I had to face the music in grim earnest. I, however, summoned up courage and resolved to face the situation as best as I could, inspired by the feeling that all eyes were watching me, and a Kingswoodian must try to prove equal to all emergencies.

Photo by] [*the Author.*

Lady Blake's Road, overlooking the Mahawila Ganga and the Rapids near Peradeniya.

p. 154

A few appropriate words I open with, expressing my joy at being present amongst them after so many years, but greater joy that I had lived to see Mr. Blazé still as Principal of Kingswood. The *Hermann Loos Cup* also gave me my cue. "Gentlemen," I said, "I have just heard that you have won it twice running. Will you let it slip out of your hands when it is almost within your grasp?" And the Cup happening to lie near me, I at once seize it, and holding it aloft, continue: "Here it is with us, and here in the school let it remain for ever,"—for I was under the impression that by winning it three times consecutively the school was entitled to permanent possession of it, as is the case generally in such instances, though unfortunately such happened not to be the case in regard to this Cup. "For the sake of good old Kingswood bring it back, and you will surely gladden the hearts of us all by doing so," I proceeded. "If I may say it, can I hope that you bring it back that I may return to my distant home with the satisfaction that I had happily witnessed one of the triumphs of Kingswood during my stay here?"

By my side was Mr. Edwin Boulton, my good old friend and former classmate, now the Vice-Principal of Kingswood, to which the Wesleyan Missionary Society had appointed him to help Mr. Blazé. Here was another inspiration. Round the Hall hung Rolls of Honour of Kingswood's *alumni* who had achieved distinction in various directions, and amongst them prominently figured my old friend. Who better, therefore, than this distinguished son of Kingswood, trained and educated in the atmosphere of Kingswood and under such a great Head Master as Mr. Blazé, could better appreciate the spirit of Kingswood? The pupils, indeed, were lucky to have such an able coadjutor to their great Principal, and, a good sportsman, he was as helpful a colleague. I had heard that he was somewhat strict. But then, Head Masters cannot be too lenient, and, horror of horrors, before I could realise what I was doing, I had actually let the cat out of the bag! Mr. Boulton who was now so strict, was he the same Boulton who wrote to me twenty-four years ago in a letter dated March 14, 1898, I still possessed:

"Mr. Wendt[1] is very strick (*sic*) to us and making us come to school on Saturdays (*sic*) and giving us to learn a lot of lessons."

That was enough; the Hall was roaring loudly, and Mr. Boulton the loudest of all.

. . . . .

A few days after the Cadets leave for Diyatalawa on the annual Camp. At the Station we meet—Trinity College, St. Anthony's College, and Kingswood College. Each group is accompanied by its own partisans who come to see their favourite school off, and we, a knot of Kingswood, are also there. All seemed to be in high spirits, but Trinity with its larger contingent is more in the picture.

I notice some pupil carrying the case of the *Hermann Loos Cup*.

"Is this the Cup?" I ask.

"Yes, sir," he replies.

"But surely you are not going to part with it?"

"No, sir," replies J. O. Mendis, "we'll do our best to bring it back."

"Yes, please do bring it back; it will delight us all, as it will gladden the heart of Mr. Blazé in particular." And then walking up to T. B. Herath, the sergeant of the company, I address him:

"You have won the Dornhorst Prize[2] already; let me hope you win the *Hermann Loos Cup* as well; so that when I go back home I shall always be able to think of you and your comrades as the winners of the Cup during my stay here."

[1] The reference here is to Mr. Victor A. Wendt, our Form Master during our time, who has since, however, given up the teaching profession, and is now attached to the Survey Department.

[2] The annual "blue riband" of Kingswood scholarship, thanks to the generosity of Mr. F. Dornhorst, the well-known Colombo Advocate.

Cheers here; cheers there; cheers everywhere; but none for Kingswood, so far. Is it that the over-modesty of the Principal has infected his pupils as well? I wait, but no one takes the lead. Surely this will not do. In a flash I have made up mind, but bide my time. The bell rings; the shrill whistle sounds; and slowly as the train begins to move, "Three cheers for Kingswood," I call for, and three lusty cheers all Kingswood and lovers of Kingswood respond to. And as their reverberating echoes die in the distance, I cannot help feeling gratified at this *coup* for the sake of the old school. Surely, there is, after all, some truth in the common saying, applied rather loosely in the present instance in a somewhat analogous sense, that he laughs longest who laughs last.

. . . . .

Never does one realise, until he has left school, how much he owes to it. But maturer years and a more balanced judgment soon bring their recompense, and he then never fails to recognise the undying debt under which he lies towards his *Alma Mater*. Big school or small school, famous school or unknown school, it is always *the School* one affectionately thinks of. Can we wonder, therefore, when even in the remote parts of the world there is still always a warm corner in one's affections for his former beloved school? His foster mother it has been, as it has nurtured him with its spirit and its lore when he was young and the world for him so rosy. If now to grown-up manhood he has attained, and to affluence, and power even perhaps, can he forget its beneficent influence and its paternal solicitude?

In some such light therefore stood beloved Kingswood to me, and as its loyal son, in duty bound, did I come over the seas to visit her once more, and to renew those fond associations so dear and sacred to my memory.

Khedivieh and Nasrieh I love, as I do the Royal School of Law and Kingswood, for each in turn has done its share by me. But if I have singled out Kingswood on the present occasion for especial mention, it is because in it I first tasted of the glories of school life, passing from the apron-strings and drudgery of private tutorship. Where else indeed, where better than in the maelstrom of life in some splendid school can a boy find a training so useful and more wholesome for the struggle of life to come?

More prosperous than when I entered it, and more flourishing than when I left it, did I find dear old Kingswood; but to find her so dignified as she was, honoured and esteemed by her sister-schools, thanks to her Grand Old Man, Mr. L. E. Blazé, was a thing every Kingswoodian looked upon with feelings of the deepest thankfulness and joy. Indeed, one has but to quote the handsome tribute of a brother Head Master, equally distinguished, in the person of the Rev. A. G. Fraser of Trinity College, at the Prize Distribution of the Wesleyan Missionary Society's Girls' High School in August last (1921) to realise still further what a fine character Kingswood was fortunate enough to be blessed with:

"He could also congratulate the Wesleyan Missionary Society on the personalities it had in Kandy running its educational work. He thought, though the person concerned would object to his saying so, that the most powerful and inspiring personality was the Principal of Kingswood College, Mr. Blazé. There was no school in the Island where the loyalty of the old boys was greater or more steadfast than at Kingswood. Yet is was almost phenomenal because of the remarkable fact that there was no other school in the Island that was worse backed or worse equipped than Kingswood.[1] It was a triumph

[1] No more, however, thank God, will Kingswood have to labour under such drawbacks, for, thanks to the generosity of the Wesleyan Missionary Society, and the munificence of Sir John Randles, these defects have been made good, and a newer and grander Kingswood, standing in more extensive grounds, and revelling in more palatial premises, and enjoying a view beyond compeer, graces Randle's

of personality. It was the biggest thing in education to have that sort of personality."[2]

Hill, midway between Kandy and Peradeniya. The inaugural ceremony was presided over by Sir John Randles himself on February 4th, 1925, and a great success the function proved. And may the new Kingswood continue to prosper and flourish, as of yore, and march from success to success.

[2] *The Ceylon Observer* (Wkly. Ed.), No. 34, August 24, 1921, p. 20.

CHAPTER XVII

TRINITY COLLEGE

Speaking of the Rev. A. G. Fraser, I necessarily find it incumbent upon myself to acknowledge with gratitude my most enjoyable visit to the great school at the head of which he rules. It was one August morning that I was accorded the privilege of a visit to this great school, and an institution worthy of the finest traditions of a great Public School did I find it.

A most conspicuous position occupies Trinity College, standing as it does on a hill overlooking Trincomalee Street, Kandy, and not the least striking feature of it is its pretty Chapel on a mound almost abutting on the street a little below. For all we know it might safely be Trinity-on-the-Hill, as if it were a counterpart of great Eton's famous rival Harrow, or Harrow-on-the-Hill, as we might call her here for the sake of the simile; and as worthy as her great counterpart just outside London is Kandy's splendid school.

Yes, like Harrow, it also has its own swimming bath; and like the famous "Ducker," and all that it stands for so fondly in the life and memory of every Harrovian, that of Trinity might even in its turn prove as dear in its associations to its own sons. Indeed, when, on seeing Trinity's swimming bath, which at the time was unused pending some alterations to have it renovated and fitted into a better one, I likened it to Harrow's famous "Ducker", the Rev. Fraser evidently seemed not a little pleased and gratified at the comparison, and, if I am not mistaken, I think my reference to it reminded him of a son of his at Harrow.

[Photo by Platé, Ltd., Colombo

KANDY—A PICTURESQUE CORNER OF THE LAKE

Facing page 160]

Mr. L. E. Blaze—The Founder of Kingswood College, Kandy

Facing page 161]

To us Kingswoodians, in particular, Trinity was more closely knit than several other schools in more senses than one; and, accordingly, did both come to regard each other affectionately. For, was it not within its walls that our great Head Master Mr. Blazé in his time drank of her lore, and beneath its watchful gaze and benign care, developed that character he brought into play with such conspicuous success in later years in his own turn in the school which now stands as a living monument to his great name? Happy, therefore, must Trinity be that she has produced such a fine character as Mr. Blazé, as Kingswood is grateful to Trinity for the part she indirectly played in her own development and fame.

Long may Trinity and Kingswood march hand in hand, worthy pioneers of the sacred cause of learning. If, in the field of play, or in the examination hall perchance, they are ranged on opposite sides, still in the cleanest and friendliest spirit of rivalry may each attain its goal, and both for ever, loyally standing by their respective ideals, prove that though opponents for the moment, they are none the less gentlemen above all.

Indeed, what a lovely picture would it have made had I been able, unknown to them, to snapshot both the Rev. Frazer and Mr. Blazé, as from my hotel window one morning I saw these two familiar figures walking side by side, quietly engaged in conversation. Here indeed was a picture to grace the walls of any school—two great headmasters of two great schools, in quite unconventional mood, and evidently shorn of every care and worry in the fresh morning breeze, now exchanging the thoughts of two great minds.

. . . . .

If to the reputation of a leading school we can add the glamour of a great name, how fortunate indeed must such a school be. And of such Trinity is now the happy possessor, for in their distinguished Principal, the Rev. A. G. Fraser, they have a name as honoured and esteemed in the Island, as it is noted far and wide, known even with distinction and prominence in the Great Peninsula as it is in Merrie England. And to his great learning and wide experience he has brought the full weight of his distinguished social position and great name to bear to the credit and benefit of Trinity.

Other schools have sent their sons to the Great War, in even greater numbers than Trinity in some cases, yet it alone of all the rest was singled out by H.M. King George for a war trophy, as witness the captured German machine gun that now graces her precincts. To whom does she owe it? To her great Principal. Wide and extensive premises she already possessed, and fine playing fields as well; and yet another big slice has she acquired, including the site of the Industrial School, and a quite big plot opposite, next to the Asgiriya Buddhist Temple, which the Rev. Fraser ultimately secured, in spite of great opposition at first. Is it not owing to his great influence, therefore, that she has thus succeeded, where others might have failed? Happy, therefore, is a school that can count on a headmaster with the glamour of a great name, the priceless asset of a fine education, and the welcome influence of a great personality; but what is more, one who knows how to utilise all these advantages wisely and judiciously.

. . . . .

Three points of the Rev. Fraser's character seem to have struck me most forcibly. First, he was none of that stiff, priggish, pedantic, scowling type of headmaster; and the easy, natural, jaunty, energetic air of his, coupled with the suave, courteous, and charming manner in which he most kindly showed me round and explained the various objects, only served to make me admire all the more his well-known and commanding personality. Indeed, he seemed to take his years very well, and the sprightly, elastic gait and step of his, and the hale and hearty appearance, spoke more likely of the right side of forty.

Again, games seemed to be his forte, as conducive to a healthy constitution and a good physique. Certainly,

" All work and no play makes Jack a dull boy," and he, therefore, naturally tried to live up to it. But in doing so was he inspired by a blind regard for games to the exclusion of work? No. His theory seemed to be that he valued games highly owing to the big role they played in the moulding of character, inasmuch as they gave boys a greater relish for work, for, as he told me, to get a few hours of real sound work, from good healthy boys, was sure to pay in the long run, than from the poorly built, fagged, weedy, myopic, bookwormish sort of youth.

Lastly, he impressed me most strikingly by a total absence of the self-consciousness and self-assertiveness, or what we commonly speak of as " side ", one sometimes stumbles across in conceited individuals suffering from " swollen head ", consequent upon any distinction they may happen to be revelling in at the time. If anything, in word as in deed, in the letter and in the spirit, he was out to preach the gospel of good fellowship and of common brotherhood. To him there was no colour question, no shibboleths of race or creed. The one dominating factor with him was the " Brotherhood of Man," and goodwill towards all fellowmen. And if there were no other outstanding feature about his fine character but this, it is still enough that in this lofty ideal he represented the teachings of the Almighty in their truest, highest, and noblest form.

To such a worthy gentleman I therefore most respectfully raise my cap, and long may Trinity be blessed with so distinguished a Headmaster.[1]

[1] Providence, however, seemed to have decreed otherwise, for notwithstanding his great attachment to the school he served so long and so well, he was called away in 1924 to the Gold Coast to assume control of Achimota College—8 miles from Accra—the nucleus of the future university there, which Sir Frederick Guggisberg, the Governor of the Gold Coast, in his very laudable desire to further the cause of learning, sought to found, and the aims and ideals of which he so lucidly outlined in his admirable little book *The Keystone*. This book I had the pleasure of reading on board the *Maloja* during my voyage to Ceylon in June 1924, thanks to the courtesy of a fellow-passenger, Mr. Robert Elliot, of Melbourne, whose acquaintance I was so delighted to have made on the occasion in question. And, no doubt it was the Rev. Fraser's wide experience and great knowledge of education in the East, that caused him to be singled out, of all others, for this highly significant, yet none the less heavy task. With what a sore heart, therefore, must Trinity have parted with her great Principal.

CHAPTER XVIII

QUEEN'S HOTEL

In Kandy I stayed at the Queen's Hotel, and an excellent sister it formed of a worthy trio in company with the Grand Oriental Hotel and the Galle Face Hotel of Colombo—in fact, they might most fitly be triplets for all we know. Her situation also, overlooking the beautiful lake, and abutting on the pretty Bund, is quite unique, and serves to enhance all the more its well-merited popularity, and the loveliness of its picturesque environment.

The comfortable feeling I experienced at the Grand Oriental Hotel I found here amply reflected, and her popular and genial manager, Mr. W. J. Byrne, as pains-taking as ever in his untiring efforts to uphold the reputation of this splendid hostelry, as he was courteous and obliging in the extreme to whosoever had the pleasure of enjoying a stay at this Hotel. The cuisine was beyond all reproach; but how much more enjoyable it would be if this hotel, first-rate in every other respect, were graced by a dining-hall worthy of its leading position. The staff also were polite and dutiful, due no doubt to efficient management. Splendidly Mr. Byrne had set the tune, and loyally his mermidons responded.

Thus, I sometimes even recall with gratefulness how I used to find my room redolent of the fragrance of flowers neatly placed in a dainty vase—thanks to the voluntary attentions of the considerate head servant of that section; and a mere hint was enough for any services required. Thus when I once unwittingly expressed the difficulty of reading or writing at night owing to the light being in the middle of the room, and thus at some distance from the writing desk, the evening saw a most welcome portable electric reading lamp on the table in question. And to pay a handsome tip for such small services one is certainly only too willing.

A scrutiny of my room revealed something beyond my expectations. Here was a stool, but a stool as a rule is a very commonplace thing. What then was it that attracted my attention? Here indeed was an Arabesque stool, worked out in the well-known "mushrabieh", beloved of the tourist; and here certainly was the home touch. I almost hugged it with joy, for did it not carry me back to my loved Egypt far away? But how did it creep in here? Did a considerate management put it there as a compliment, or was it there by sheer coincidence, or did it actually walk in to greet me when it knew that a compatriot had arrived, and thus share with me the ties of a common nationality?

Its silk covering had perhaps seen a better day, even as Egypt had once in a dim and distant past. But never mind; even with that it was welcome. But wonder of wonders! What is the inscription on it? "*Nasr min Allah, wa fath qareeb.*"[1] Was this again a coincidence, or was it the Divine promise of the fulfilment of a nation's aspirations in the near future? Still, there it was, and as it cheered me beyond all description, gladly likewise did I accept the welcome omen.

. . . . .

And to cap all, the room I had with a bay window was an ideal one, overlooking the lake in front; another side facing the clock tower of the Victoria Commemoration Building of the Ceylon Planters' Association, which sometimes chimed me to sleep whenever I happened to sit up late unconscious of the hours creeping on; and the

[1] This is a text from the Holy Koran, which Sale has translated into: "And" (ye shall obtain) "other things which ye desire: assistance from God, and a speedy victory."

other corner looking down Ward Street in the direction of the Buddhist Temple. Sunken in one of the huge upholstered wicker chairs, I would sometimes find food for reflection as I sat by the window and surveyed the prospect around.

It was in some such contemplative mood that I occasionally sat and peered yonder where the placid waters of Sri Wikrama Raja Sinha's lovely lake shimmered in the silvery moonlight. Could it be that such a tyrant as he should have been endowed with such æsthetic taste?

But why wonder? The last King of Kandy is not the only case of this kind, for history abounds with instances as singular. Lorenzo the Magnificent, tyrant as he was, yet lives as a great patron of art and literature; and the famous Italian city flourished in his time to such a degree that his rule came to be styled the "Golden Age of Florence." And here, in the history of my own country, we have but to go back to the time of the cruel Mamelukes to recall how the people suffered beneath their heavy yoke. Yet to these very Princes Cairo owes some of the finest specimens of Saracenic Art extant to-day!

Surely there must be something uncanny, something enigmatic about such men that there should seem to be some bright invisible spot, some redeeming feature, some saving grace in them that acts as a set-off to shortcomings on their part! Or is it that they take after Shakespeare's well-known lines:

> "Which like the toad, ugly and venomous,
> Wears yet a precious jewel in his head."[1]

Perhaps psychology is advanced far enough nowadays to be able to throw some light on this subject.

. . . . .

Sometimes also the very stillness of the night called for meditation of another kind, and to my mind would come

[1] Shakespeare's *As You Like It*, Act. II. Sc. I.

the words of the lovely poem of T. Moore: *The Light of Other Days*, so poignant, yet so true:

"Oft in the stilly night
  Ere slumber's chain has bound me,
Fond Memory brings the light
  Of other days around me:
    The smiles, the tears
    Of boyhood's years,
  The words of love then spoken;
    The eyes that shone,
    Now dimm'd and gone,
  The cheerful hearts now broken!
Thus in the stilly night
  Ere slumber's chain has bound me,
Sad Memory brings the light
  Of other days around me.

"When I remember all
  The friends so linked together
I've seen around me fall
  Like leaves in wintry weather,
    I feel like one
    Who treads alone
  Some banquet-hall deserted,
    Whose lights are fled,
    Whose garlands dead,
  And all but he departed!
Thus in the stilly night
  Ere slumber's chain has bound me,
Sad Memory brings the light
  Of other days around me."

CHAPTER XIX

PERADENIYA GARDENS

"NATURE's great garden by the river bank
Thou hast no rival fit with thee to rank!
The stranger sauntering through the leafy glades,
Starts at the beauty of their lights and shades,
What colours flash upon his dazzled gaze!
Amherstia gleaming gold amidst the haze,
Brownea with rich dependent red bouquet
Helping to make her own dark foliage gay,
Bright Cassia floribund with sulphur flowers.
Above her dwarfish neighbours proudly towers,
The Royal Palms whose stems like pillars grow—
Gaunt silent sentries standing in a row.
Canarium—with radial buttress'd roots
And Saraca—with drooping tender shoots,
Lianas strong that climb without restraint,
Coourupita—with blossoms rare and quaint,
Tall pines whose sombre weeping boughs recall
The sadd'ning mem'ries of the funeral pall,
Proud Auracaria rising high and square
As if to reach a rare, purer air,
The feathery bamboo bending from her seat
To kiss the rippling water at her feet.

. . . . .

In this grand home of Nature as I lie,
I feel within my soul that God is nigh;
And when to leave the glorious scene I rise,
I go as though expelled from Paradise."[1]

[1] *Flotsam: Verses Grave and Gay*, by C. Drieberg.

[Photo by John & Co., Kandy

KINGSWOOD COLLEGE, KANDY

Facing page 168]

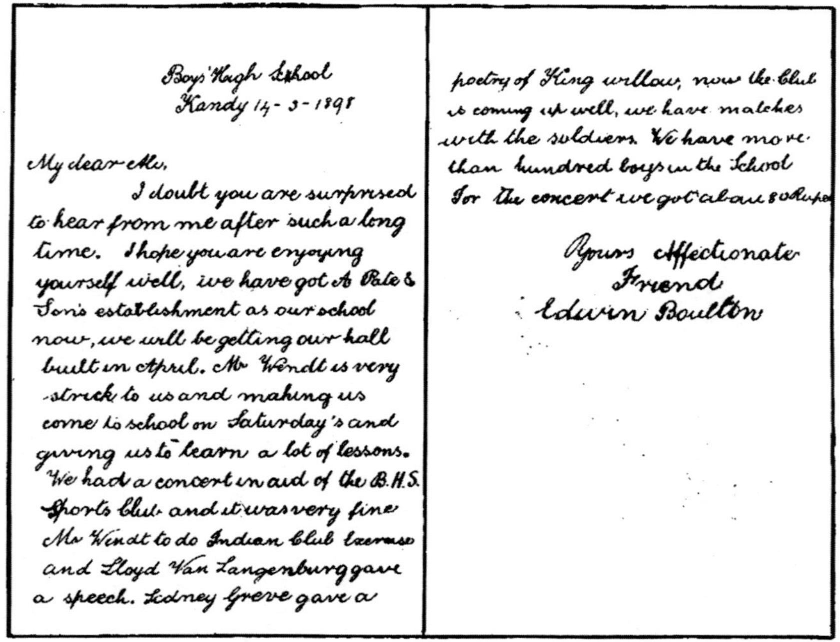
Boys' High School
Kandy 14-3-1898

My dear Mr.

I doubt you are surprised to hear from me after such a long time. I hope you are enjoying yourself well, we have got A Pate & Son's establishment as our school now, we will be getting our hall built in April. Mr Wendt is very strick to us and making us come to school on Saturday's and giving us to learn a lot of lessons. We had a concert in aid of the B.H.S. Sports Club and it was very fine Mr Wendt to do Indian Club exercise and Lloyd Van Langenburg gave a speech. Sidney Greve gave a poetry of King willow, now the Club is coming up well, we have matches with the soldiers. We have more than hundred boys in the School For the concert we got about 80 Rupees

Yours Affectionate
Friend
Edwin Boulton

FACSIMILE OF LETTER BY MR. E. BOULTON TO THE AUTHOR, IN MARCH, 1898, WHILST STILL A SCHOOLBOY

From letter in possession of the Author

As inevitable are the Peradeniya Gardens to Kandy, as Mount Lavinia is to Colombo, and as surely will the passenger visit Colombo's popular seaside resort, as the tourist will these famous Botanic Gardens. But whereas the reputation of the one is local, the other enjoys a prominence equalled by few.

Seeing is believing; and one has but to go to this Eastern paradise, this Elysium of the Tropics, to realise how its exquisite beauty transcends even the wildest fancies of one's imagination, and that only too truly do they bear out their world-wide fame. But not only is it a show place, and the rendezvous *par excellence* of picnic parties, but it also faithfully fulfils a utilitarian function of the most useful and approved kind. Deeply indebted therefore must Ceylon be to it botanically, horticulturally, and entomologically for its invaluable work in research and the experimenting and propagation of plants.

Fortunate have the Royal Botanic Gardens at Peradeniya been in the distinguished and capable line of curators that have controlled their destinies, and on a worthy superintendent has their mantle fallen, for in Mr. H. F. Macmillan, erudite as he is, courteous in the extreme, and popular locally as he is prominent abroad, Ceylon is blessed with a gentleman who conscientiously carries out his onerous duties true to the best traditions of this historic institution.

To this gentleman I had the pleasure of being introduced by Mr. C. Drieberg, himself a great authority on botany and horticulture; and I cannot adequately express my lasting obligation to him for the fine fruit plants he selected for me on my way to Egypt. Unfortunately, the majority of these fell victims to the baleful influence of an extra dose of over-zeal and "red tape" at Port Said —and this after I had brought them all the way from Ceylon, and they were landed in a flourishing condition!

. . . . .

Curiously, what I touched upon in regard to Mount Lavinia in connection with the question of communications I might allude to here again. Why not link up Kandy with Peradeniya with a fine tramway system—with two-decked cars thrown into the bargain? The favourite resort of picnic parties these Gardens are, there is hardly any cheap conveyance or means of intercourse schoolboys would relish so much as a tram-ride to get to their destination; and the welcome car will not only cater for their needs, but also prove a boon to the people of Katukelle and Peradeniya, and even the outlying districts hard by. And an extension in the opposite direction up to Lewella Ferry would not be a bad step.

The City Fathers, who seem to have done little for Kandy since I was in it a quarter of a century ago, now that the Great War is over, and they have no plausible excuse to fall back upon, might accordingly embark on a more active and progressive policy, and inaugurate the new era auspiciously. The centenary of these Gardens might even prove a fitting and appropriate occasion to present it with something of a birthday present, so to speak, in the nature of a trim, up-to-date tramway fitted with all modern comforts.

Indeed, Kandy will have to look to her laurels if she does not want to yield her outstanding position, as the leading mountain resort of the Island, to Nuwara Eliya. For, as a matter of fact, the latter has forged ahead within recent years in leaps and bounds, whilst Kandy has deplorably lagged behind. Even now Nuwara Eliya continues to go strong, gaining in popularity year by year; and if Kandy is not careful, and fails to awake from her torpor and take time by the forelock, why, at any moment she may find herself ousted from premier place, and actually playing second fiddle to her vaunting rival, Nuwara Eliya.

CHAPTER XX

THE PERAHERA

HAPPY is he who is fortunate to visit Kandy at the time of the Perahera. Suddenly from a rather sleepy existence does the Hill capital awake to welcome from far and near the myriads who flock to it, and rarely is a sacred shrine visited with greater religious fervour, or hallowed with such devout veneration as is the Dalada Maligawa on this momentous occasion by the Buddhists. But to the visitor of other creeds the Perahera lives as a spectacle of barbaric pomp and splendour, a pageant of "The Gorgeous East." No wonder that the Queen's Hotel is packed to overflowing, with bookings long in advance and accommodation elsewhere almost impossible to obtain.

For two weeks in the month of August does the Perahera thread its way at night through the streets of Kandy in a grand procession of elephants, to the sound of music and dancing, starting from the Temple, as the Dalada Maligawa is known in English, and every day it enlarges its circuitous route, increasing proportionately in grandeur until at last during the closing nights the climax is attained, and one can see it at its best.

On the last day, however, the Perahera is held in the daytime, and is known as the Day Perahera; but though on this occasion also the ceremony is gone through with all the customary pomp and splendour, still, I think, that from the spectacular point of view, the processions held at night look more picturesque and impress one more favourably.

In the evenings before the Perahera starts one may hear the ding-dong of the bells which announce the approach of the elephants from the outlying villages, on their way to the Maligawa. When all the elephants have arrived at the Temple, they are decorated with rich embroideries and costly trappings.

Each rider then gets on the back of his elephant with a tray of flowers in his hands, while another stands by the elephant's trunk holding a spear. The elephants then line up, usually three abreast, now that they are so many, and not in single file, as in my boyhood, when they hardly exceeded twenty-five. Then led in the van by torch-bearers, musicians, dancers, and whip-crackers, the Perahera starts, the first three class of people, barring the fourth, also figuring throughout the various ranks of elephants, the sound of the cracking of whips being in evidence only in the vanguard, as if to clear a way for the holy procession and to announce to those afar its approach.

But the cynosure of all eyes is the magnificent "Maligawa Elephant", resplendent as ever in the glare of a thousand torches, and glittering with all the rich and costly trappings of gold and silver—a giant of his species and the king of his troop. Followed immediately by the Diyawadana Nilame—the Warden of the Temple—and the Kandyan Chiefs in picturesque national garb, and dancers contorting and jingling to the weird shrill sounds of pipes, and flanked by a pair of consorts almost as gorgeous, this richly caparisoned, silver-tusked monster slowly and majestically keeps his way over the white cloth spread along his route, so that the soiled earth may not pollute the feet rendered sacred for the moment by the holy burden borne aloft; and there, in a gilded dome or howdah, beneath a canopy of gold, tinsel, and brocade, which gives to this pageant of August its title of the "Esala Perahera", is the sacred Tooth of Buddha, the Holy Relic of the Buddhists.

To those in other climes who see only an odd elephant now and then at some local zoo how wonderful must be this sight of sixty-three elephants in line doing honour to this sacred festival of Gautama Buddha, and even Hannibal might have wept for joy had he such a mighty phalanx to pit against the Romans.

But more numerous though the elephants on this occasion were, than the twenty-five that usually figured in my time, yet the Perahera of my day presented a better show and superior organisation—at any rate its trappings and embroideries and accoutrements did not show such palpable signs of wear and tear, which a rich Sinhalese Community might well attend to.

The town itself—as distinct from the ever beautiful surrounding country—usually drowsy and lethargic, now seems to awake from its torpor, and take on the aspect of a huge fair; and from all parts of the Island, and even from distant lands, come people in their thousands and tens of thousands, some to ply their trade, many on pilgrimage bent, and not a few to seek some welcome relaxation from the toils and worries of their daily work. Near the market side-shows spring up with unfailing persistence, and mirth and merriment find a ready outlet in the swings, the roundabouts, the mat slide, and the houplas that provide amusement in this time of joy-making to old and young alike. And the climax is reached with the grand Fancy Dress Ball at the Queen's Hotel on the last night, when the gravest and busiest man must relax and join in the general fun.

But lucky is he who can find any accommodation available if he has not had the forethought to reserve a room in advance. Indeed, I could not help feeling a little amused when I saw one tenacious gentleman, who would not hear of missing the ball, but doggedly stuck to his guns and changed near the lavatories, thoughtfully bringing the necessary kit in a suit case he handed the servant on duty there pending the termination of his high jinks.

CHAPTER XXI

THE CREMATION OF A HIGH PRIEST

FORTUNE favoured me on my first day in Kandy, as it had so heartlessly deserted me only so recently on the Racecourse. The High Priest of Malwatte had died, and that afternoon he was to be cremated with all the pomp and circumstance of his creed. Here indeed was the chance of a lifetime.

The very word cremation suggested a gruesome spectacle, but then, the world is an immense show place, and life itself not all honey, nor its scenes one unbroken chain of pleasant sights.

> "All the world's a stage,
> And all the men and women merely players:
> They have their exits and their entrances;
> And one man in his time plays many parts,
> His acts being seven ages,"[1]

truthfully says Shakespeare; and to-day, to all intents and purposes, we were to ring down the curtain on one who had played his last part. If the world is a stage, and all the men and women merely players, so is its background the scenery, and every curtain a scene in the drama of human progress or degeneration. As the players act, and then flit past us on the stage, so does each of us play his part and melt away, one scene giving place to another, even as the setting of our transient lives flickers for a moment and then vanishes swallowed in oblivion.

. . . . .

[1] W. Shakespeare's *As You Like It*, Act II, Sc. VII.

The High Priest is a very important personage in the Buddhist Community, and correspondingly great was the significance attached to his demise. Even the Perahera, if I am not mistaken, was not held on the day of his funeral, as a mark of respect and mourning for such a high dignitary.

Directly after lunch I drive to Katugastota, where the cremation is to be held. The funeral cortège, a very imposing and elaborate affair, is already making its way to its destination by circuitous routes round the town. Meanwhile, Fortune smiles on me again. By the roadway, as I wait for the procession to pass, so that I may follow it, a venerable Sinhalese gentleman quite unexpectedly accosts me:

" You are waiting for the funeral procession, I think? "

" Yes."

" And you want to see the cremation no doubt? "

" Yes; I should be only too delighted."

" Do you know the way to the spot? "

" No; but I am waiting for the funeral to pick my way up there."

" Then, would you like me to take you there, as you seem to be a stranger? " But how he spotted me for such, I cannot say, though he might have inferred this by overhearing me ask one of the bystanders, in English, for the way.

" It is very kind of you indeed, and I shall be very thankful; but I am afraid I shall be troubling you."

" No, no."

" Then, kindly step in, please," and with that we drove further on, and then got out at the foot of a hill, my kind companion turning out to be the great-grandson or some descendant—which, I cannot exactly remember now—of the Prime Minister of the last King of Kandy, as he told me.

. . . . .

Through winding paths, past rubber trees and cocoa groves, interspersed here and there with some tall coconut palm or the graceful slender areca-nut, we at last reach the holy site. Roped in on four sides is an enclosure rising in a conical pinnacle, something like a *pandal*, and wrapped with red and white bunting alternately, like the posts and decorations of a wedding in Cairo; and to me it was a singular sight, this contrast in the two situations. In the middle is the funeral pyre. First twigs, and then logs are being piled on it; gradually it rises higher and higher, as fuel for the fire increases. In the middle of it is a cavity wherein the coffin is to be placed—gaping ominously like the pitiless maws of some terrible monster. Another few logs and some resinous wood, and the pyre is ready for its distinguished victim. Kerosene oil is being copiously poured haphazardly through the chinks to make the pyre as inflammable as possible. On the adjoining footpaths is a large concourse of people, growing larger and larger gradually. Thanks to my companion, we take up our post at a fine vantage-point, just next to the temporary shed erected for the Government Agent of the Central Province (the Mudir or Governor), to which the populace, save for a few privileged individuals, can have no access.

. . . . .

The sound of music, or rather that of some doleful dirge, announces the approach of the cortège, and a sudden rush of people actually heralds its arrival. Almost immediately after it comes into view, a few shots meanwhile ringing out in the air at random as a salute, but not in the regular methodical fashion at military burials. Solemnly the coffin is borne to its last resting-place, and gently it is thrust into the cavity after having been carried round the funeral pyre a few times.

Now start the priests in Sinhalese, some chanting a panegyric or dirge, others making some address, but all recapitulating and eulogising the merits and fine qualities of their great chief, and exhorting us to follow in his footsteps. Ah! if only someone could have given one

[Photo by the Author

TRINITY COLLEGE

Facing page 176]

[Photo by Platé, Ltd., Colombo

THE QUEEN'S HOTEL, KANDY

Facing page 177]

of the priests such a splendid "tip" as Longfellow's famous lines:

> "Lives of great men all remind us
> We can make our lives sublime,
> And departing, leave behind us
> Footprints on the sands of Time,"

what a golden chance he would have stood for promotion, in the keen competition consequent upon the election of a new High Priest to the vacant post, and the series of promotions following thereupon. If anything, they seemed to be too long-winded in their various addresses, undertaken no doubt with the best of intentions to pay a tribute to the distinguished deceased, but, too, transparent enough to show the way they were trying to outvie each other in their rhetoric and eloquence, oblivious of the fact that dusk was fast drawing near, and that they had already actually used up a good part of the afternoon with their panegyrics.

. . . . .

At last with a huge flaming torch the pyre is set afire, and up spurt the flames, voracious, glowing, relentless. Gradually the fire eats through, and now and then one hears, at one time a sputtering, at other times the crackling of the logs as they are consumed in the merciless furnace. Mohammed, who stands just in front of the coffin, even sees the fire attacking its contents. But it will take hours ere the pyre is reduced to ashes, and by then all present will have practically turned homewards. *Sic transit gloria mundi !*

And so, from dust we are created, and to dust we go.

. . . .

The High Priest of Asgiriya, the candidate-elect to the vacant post, I am kindly introduced to by my good companion, and I fully appreciate the honour. He seems to be highly pleased that I should have come all the way to re-visit my natal land, and doubly so when I tell him that I had especially come at that time to have a chance of seeing the far-famed Perahera—so pleased indeed that he invites me to Asgiriya Temple, and even condescendingly offers to show me the sacred Tooth of Buddha if I should call on the last night of the Perahera at about 2 a.m. But fool that I am, in spite of my expressing my hope of doing so if possible, I do not avail myself of so generous an invitation, and thus miss a rare opportunity very few ever enjoy the chance of having.

. . . . .

Vanitas vanitatum! If the heartless woman who seeks with her wiles to enmesh within her deadly coils some thoughtless profligate or worthless wastrel, or the faithless wife or husband who respects not the sacred bond of wedlock, or the most hardened criminal, to whom robbery and murder are but an everyday pastime, or a degraded *jeunesse dorée* weltering in a pool of sin, and so on, all the debased types of humanity that go to swell the ranks of a demoralised and tottering world—if all these could but realise that even such transient ravings of a depraved mind and nature must also pass away even as there is an end to all things. If they could but recall Shakespeare's well-known lines:

> "And, like the baseless fabric of this vision,
> The cloud-capped towers, the gorgeous palaces,
> The solemn temples, the great globe itself,
> Yea, all which it inherit, shall dissolve,
> And, like this insubstantial pageant faded,
> Leave not a rack behind: We are such stuff
> As dreams are made of, and our little life
> Is rounded with a sleep . . ."[1]

Ah! if such a sight as I had just witnessed, or the yawning mouth of some open grave cannot provide food for reflection, and drive home to them in all its bare

[1] Shakespeare's *The Tempest*, Act IV.

nakedness how vain and transient are all earthly things, then shame to them! But withal this might be but the aberration of some diseased mentality; then forgive O God Almighty, those who have sinned, and deliver them, O God, from the jaws of evil, and lead them into the path of righteousness.

Not for nothing it might seem at first sight did Wolfe, as he contemplated the Heights of Abraham anticipating the coming struggle, give utterance to the famous lines of Gray:

> " The boast of heraldry, the pomp of power,
> And all that beauty, all that wealth e'er gave,
> Awaits alike the inevitable hour:—
> The paths of glory lead but to the grave."[1]

But the grave is not the end-all of our existence. In another world, in the Hereafter we have to answer for our actions in this; so, if the shadow of death stalks abroad, still to our death we can bravely go with a clear conscience if in this life we can do good, and live a Godfearing, upright, and honest life.

How true indeed then dawn upon us the words of our Prophet Seyyedna Mohammed; and in their reality and deep eloquence they even transcend the beauty of the lines of Gray:

" Do good in this world, as if thou wouldst live for ever; but for the Hereafter as if thou wouldst die tomorrow."

[1] Gray's *Elegy in a Churchyard.*

CHAPTER XXII

BAIRAM

BRIGHT and sunny o'er Kandy's Lake dawns the first day of Kourban Bairam, and this Feast will all Moslems celebrate, as Christians their Christmas. Facing towards Mecca, holiest of all holy places, will all devout Moslems turn, and right across the universe, wherever Moslems be, there will they meet on this auspicious morn in solemn prayer, even as on holy Arafat their pilgrims met in their thousands on the previous day from every rank and clime. And Islam, O God Almighty, in this its hour of dire peril, protect, and grant, Almighty God, that under Thy holy care it for ever flourish.

In the distance looms Hantenne, the mist and sun in battle royal grappled. Troubled are my thoughts—though happy they should be—but it is not of this land I now think, but of some other clime. Far beyond Hantenne they roam, far even beyond the verdant hills; and there past Socotra's stormy seas and Afric's burning sands looms another Hantenne, but barren and desolate. At its foot lies the desert, as silent as the grave; but in this very desert, undefiled by hand of man, lie those who have run their race, and now sleep their last long sleep. Perchance, in the stony silence of the grave some may find the repose they missed in their lifetime, for, to how many is life one long trial of suffering, if to all it should be a struggle for eternal good.

There at the foot of Gebel El-Giushi, in the Cemetery of El-Imam El-Shafei lie my dear parents, in two graves side by side, in death inseparable, as in life; through all the stress and storm and tumults of their time they remained faithful to one another unto the last. Miles and miles distant though I was, could I forget a mother's behest, and ignore the sanctity of their graves? No, a thousand times no! There, however, in my distant home were those who would faithfully act in my place, and carry out my instructions. Relieved, therefore, was my conscience.

In peace, therefore, rest O parents dear, my life to you consecrated; and hallowed ever be your graves, and green your memory.

But thy pardon, I crave, gentle reader; forgive me my melancholy. For, if in life we owe our duty to our parents, in death it is as sacred.

. . . . .

A treat I got on Bairam I shall ever be thankful for, Mr. A. R. Cassie Lebbé, a well-known notable and jeweller of Kandy, and brother-in-law to the late Mr. Mohammed Kassim Sidde Lebbé, and son-in-law of the late Mr. Mahmoud, together with M. C. Abdul Hamid very loyally renewed and maintained those traditions of hospitality and friendship which had once existed between the families of the two deceased gentlemen and ours; and it was thus with a real pleasure that I accepted their invitation. With them therefore I lunched on the first day of Bairam, though I had already dined at their house during my first and short visit to Kandy early in July soon after my arrival in Ceylon.

I appreciated this invitation all the more owing to the fact that I was able to spend this sacred Feast amongst people of my own religion, whose customs resembled ours in several ways. It gave me a certain homely sensation, and made me feel like being amongst relatives; and most attentive and cordial in all respects proved these gentlemen, as well as Mr. Cassie Lebbé's brother-in-law Mr. Mohammed Maarouf, a pupil at

Trinity College, and I shall always be grateful to them all.

. . . . .

One little surprise I did meet with here on this occasion. Noticing, during my last visit in July, that I was desirous of tasting some good Ceylon sweetmeats, which I inadvertently named, what was my delight when I found spread before me such Ceylon delicacies as *Kalu dodol*, *kawen*, but above all, my prime favourite, *sow dodol*. These, together with *bebekan* and *roti*, I had tasted at the Grand Oriental Hotel, thanks to Fernando, the second steward, who used to get me a plate of one or the other now and then, when he came to know that I cared for them very much. But his were sometimes rather rancid; and though one might have been able to order any at some of the local *boutiques*, still, very rarely can they rise to the standard of those on which unusual care has been lavished in one's home. Thus, how much did I enjoy those made at Mr. Cassie Lebbé's, perfect as they were.

Indeed, I have such a liking for Ceylon's familiar dishes that I sometimes sighed that I had not a possibility of enjoying them more often, though now and then I partook of a plate of *pittu*, or *happu*, or *idiappu* (something like vermicelli, or Egypt's *kunafa*, but unsweetened) or Indian patés, during my breakfast, and the hotel waiters would seem not a little amused that a stranger should stoop to such common fare! But then, this is to the Ceylonese what the *ful mudammes* or *taamieh* is to the Egyptian; and even the richest pasha will sometimes hanker after these dishes.

And the curries also—not the miserable, insipid, tasteless thing we get here, going by such a misleading name, as if reflecting the glamour of the East, but the real, hot, savoury stuff we get out in Ceylon. And, moreover, the way they eat it out there in the East, the curry and rice spiced, as it were, with such snacks as chutney, grated coconut, chopped onions in coconut milk, grated coconut mixed and pickled with chillies, and so on, called *sambol* out there; and one does feel that he gets a real, typical dish of what one hears termed rice and curry.

CHAPTER XXIII

THE CEYLON MOORS

Bairam did not pass off without its rather singular incident. Mohammed, always a pious and devout fellow, must certainly go and say his prayers in the correct orthodox way; so to a neighbouring Mosque he betakes himself in the early morning, little dreaming that Ceylon is not Egypt, and that even religious customs will sometimes vary in different places. But what was his surprise on going there to be told that the Mosque was one for the Hanafy Rite, and not the Maliki, to which he belonged; and besides, that prayers would be said at nine o'clock, and not in the early dawn, as is usual in Egypt on this occasion.

This was the first time that I had heard of such a thing, and, as a consequence, I was not a little astounded, and even amused. Yes, that the Moors of Ceylon should quibble with such trifles, and try to create that schism which divided the Christian Faith into Protestant, Catholic, and Orthodox, and the concomitant churches for each, when in our religion no such thing as separate mosques for each rite existed.

If, instead of wasting their energies on such trivialities, they devoted more of their time to the cultivation of the Arabic tongue how much more profitable and laudable it would be. Indeed, descendants as they are, of the great Arabs of the past who sailed the Eastern seas, and carried their trade, their name, and their religion even to the confines of China and the Philippines, when not even the British or French or Portuguese or Dutch flags were

[Photo by the Author

THE QUEEN'S HOTEL—FROM WACE PARK

Facing page 184]

[Photo by Platé, Ltd., Colombo

THE VICTORIA ESPLANADE, KANDY

Facing page 185]

seen in these waters, do they not feel ashamed that they have no tongue of their own to speak in, but have to use that of another community—Tamil—with the exception of a few words of Arabic essential for prayers? Why, have they not even bitterly felt the taunt of Sir Ponnabalam Ramanathan, when he wanted to show that they in reality were originally Tamils, though now of a different religion, but which, I was told, they eventually disproved successfully?

I remember, once, in a conversation with the Honble. Mr. W. M. Abdul Rahiman, the former Member for the Mohammedan Community in the Ceylon Legislative Council, asking him how, since they did not know Arabic, they proposed presenting the address of their own Community to H.R.H. the Prince of Wales when he visited Ceylon, and whether they did not find it humiliating to have to do so in Tamil—which they all spoke as if it were their national language—side by side with the English tongue, when a national language, as we all know, is an outward, real, tangible, living symbol of nationhood.

Arabic is to Islam what English is to a great part of the world; and from the borders of Morocco right across North Africa, and even in the Sudan right to the heart of Equatorial Africa, past the great Arabian Peninsula, on to the heart of Asia is the Arabic language spoken amongst the peoples of these lands, with but slight variations of dialect here and there. So, it is only meet that the Ceylon Moors should be more alive to the interests of their community in this direction, a wealthy and respectable section of the population of the Island as they are, and with such glorious traditions of their ancestors behind them.

In Egypt we have some very good Training Colleges, and several of the cleverest graduates go to England to prosecute their studies further at the Universities there at the expense of the Egyptian Ministry of Education. So, if the leading Mohammedans of Ceylon, with the full concurrence of the Ceylon Government, beg it to use its good offices to approach the Egyptian Government and seek its aid in engaging one or two capable Arabic Masters who know English fairly well, offering them at the same time fairly handsome emoluments, as the Universities of Oxford and Cambridge do in regard to the selection of Arabic Lecturers for themselves, they will in no time make a very creditable start, and finally earn the gratitude of posterity.

They have already come on immensely since we left them, and even now it is a pleasure to see practically the whole of the Moslem Community wearing the fez—which has grown to be the national headgear of Islam in more senses than one—where formerly there was barely any before the advent of the Egyptian Pashas to Ceylon; and what they have done in this direction, they can very successfully do in a more worthy cause.

And now that they have entered on a very ambitious education scheme, for which they proposed to collect Rs. 1,000,000, and which they announced to the world with such a flourish of trumpets, but which, most unfortunately, is not progressing favourably for the time being,[1] and seems to be in abeyance owing to factious recriminations and petty jealousies, when a united front and a common purpose would serve their community and such a noble cause more usefully, they should accordingly make it a point of introducing the Arabic language into their schools, side by side with English. They might also found a big college towering head and shoulders above

[1] At the time of my 1921 visit to Ceylon, the education movement amongst the Moors of Ceylon was in anything but a flourishing state. Since then, however, happily a turn for the better has taken place, and a complete transformation, which augurs well for the future, seems to have come over the Mohammedan Community.

It now gives me great pleasure therefore to record that one of the last acts of the retiring Governor of Ceylon, Sir William Manning, was to lay the foundation stone of the main building of the already existing Zahira College, in March 1925, the Principal, the Honble. Mr. T. B. Jaya, in thanking the Governor on that auspicious occasion for the Government's generous grant of Rs. 25,000 for the School, also alluding *inter alia* to the munificence of the Mohammedan gentlemen, who had thus enabled the School to bid good-bye to the lean years of the past, and enter on a new phase of life with all the best wishes for her prosperity and success.

Let us all hope that she may continue to flourish, as her very name so aptly betokens in Arabic; and that the Governor, in laying the foundation of the new building, incidentally also hermetically sealed beneath it the hatchet of discord that had unfortunately for so long been its bane, and that it is a newer and happier era that at last dawns on the Moslem Education Movement of Ceylon

the rest, not forgetting, of course, to give a proper share of their attentions to both Sinhalese and Tamil, which no doubt are quite necessary for purposes of trade and business, and in their personal dealings with the sister communities of the Island.

I have given vent to these few remarks, inspired by the best of intentions, and hope the Ceylon Mohammedan Community will not take them amiss, but generously accept them in the friendly and sincere spirit in which they are given. In any case, they are the best judges of their own interests, and as to the best methods of upholding their dignity and *amour-propre*, and are therefore in a more favourable position to investigate and tackle their various problems. If, however, as I sincerely hope, these remarks do not fall on deaf ears, but do actually bear fruit ultimately, then, if there were no other gratification in the publication of this book, it were still enough that it proved instrumental in the spread of the Arabic tongue amongst the Ceylon Mohammedans.

CHAPTER XXIV

SEYYID TALIB PASHA

In Seyyid Talib Pasha I had the pleasure of coming across an interesting personality during my stay at Kandy; and a worthy son of the great Arab race he looked. Indeed, with his tall, imposing figure, and stately mien, he seemed as if reflecting in his person the majesty and glory of the mighty Saracen Empire that once ruled the world.

Seyyid Talib Pasha is a man who has left his mark on the history of his country. A member of the illustrious Nakib family, as representative of his country he passes into the portals of the short-lived Turkish Parliament of pre-War days. But it is as a Minister in the stormy events of his country's most recent history that his name lives most prominently. Even on Egypt's hoary soil he set foot as an honoured guest.

But Mesopotamia claims its distinguished son, and to his distant home he " plods his weary way ". And even as he once more returns to the hearth of his fathers, and would from its ashes of to-day see rise phœnix-like the glory of the Saracen Empire of yesterday, behold, as if on Aladdin's magic carpet he is borne to Sindbad's wondrous Isle, Seredib! For politics is a dangerous game, and the dearest friends will sometimes fall out over some question, and brothers at times will not see eye to eye. Until the world grows purer, and big countries realise that even small nations must have their place in the sun—for is not sunshine conducive to good health, as the doctors say?—so long will the world be torn by conflicting passions and rent by opposing forces.

. . . . .

Behind the dark, spectacled eyes one could see the fiery, indomitable spirit of the Saracen that burned within. But tempered with this hard, implacable nature, one could easily find the polished touch of the chivalrous courtier. An honour as it was to make the acquaintance of so distinguished a personage, it was as great a pleasure to realise the condescension and courtesy with which he extended to me the hand of friendship.

And even as I bade him farewell, I could see through the thin mask of a wistful look how manfully he was wrestling to get the upper hand of a homesick feeling, which my impending departure so poignantly suggested to him. And even now, as I write these lines by the banks of the Nile, I heartily pray God that he may yet live to see his home once more even as other exiles have returned to their native shores.[1]

. . . . .

The deportation of Talib Pasha was carried out in such a remarkable way that perhaps the account given by *The Times*[2] might prove of some interest to my readers.

" The (Cairo) Conference decided that British interests made a Sherifian ruler for Mesopotamia a necessity, and that the Emir Feisal was the man.

" . . . At a dinner given in his house in April (1921) . . . he (Talib Pasha) declared that Mesopotamia would never accept Feisal, and that certain British officers who were working on Feisal's behalf were not acting loyally towards the Arab Administration which employed them. The speech was reported next day by one of his English guests to the British authorities. Sir Percy Cox

[1] If only every prayer were as speedily granted! For, it gives me great pleasure to record that, since these lines were written, Seyyid Talib Pasha has been allowed, on the plea of failing health, to go, first to Italy, and then to Egypt, returning finally to his native land in April 1925.

[2] *The Times*, December 28, 1921.

appears to have decided that if the policy of the Cairo Conference was to be made a reality in the teeth of local opinion, a demonstration of force was necessary and that Seyyid Talib must be removed. No time was lost. The High Commissioner and the Commander-in-Chief lunched together on the following day. As it happened, Seyyid Talib, in pursuance of an old invitation, was to take tea with Lady Cox at Government House in the afternoon. This gave the military authorities the chance for a neat arrest, for there is only one practicable route for vehicles to Government House. The unsuspecting Seyyid Talib duly took tea with his friend, Lady Cox, who, of course, was also entirely unsuspecting. The High Commissioner was opportunely absent at the Races, for Baghdad was having its " week ", in celebration of the fourth anniversary of Sir Stanley Maude's entry. When Seyyid Talib left Government House in his motor-car he found a motor-lorry drawn across the road, about fifty yards from the entrance, and was compelled to stop. He was immediately arrested by an officer from G.H.Q.; and two hours later was in a train bearing him southwards to a boat at Basra. Before he could recover from his astonishment he was on the high seas speeding to Ceylon."

Comment is useless; but who will not say that, after all, there really are times when " truth is stranger than fiction "?

CHAPTER XXV

UP THE MOUNTAINS TO NUWARA ELIYA

NUWARA ELIYA has always had a glamour of its own, and Englishmen who know very little of other parts of Ceylon seem to have heard a good deal of this place. It appears from what I have read in books that some believe it to resemble the Highlands of Scotland, and if to this we add its çold, crisp, bracing air, which acts as a tonic to the jaded townsman, and which even Sir Samuel Baker, so far back as the 'seventies of the last century, when Nuwara Eliya was practically unknown, said worked wonders on his health, which had broken down at the time, one does not feel surprised that it should appeal so forcibly to Britishers in particular. Indeed, so popular has it become, and so assiduously has its amenities been brought into the limelight, that it has even become a sanatorium of the East, people flocking to it, not only from India, but even from far-off places like Australia, Hong Kong, Malaya, and Mesopotamia in ever-increasing numbers to recover their health amidst its beautiful surroundings and bracing air, or to seek pleasure or relaxation from the stress of present-day life.

Indeed, even Mahmoud Samy Pasha, Yacoub Samy Pasha, and my father, an inseparable trio of boon companions and the staunchest of friends, could not resist its call and yielded to its temptation, availing themselves, in 1896, of the absence of their families in Egypt, to go up to Nuwara Eliya and see for themselves this wonder-land of Ceylon. Somehow or other, however, they seem to have found it boomed and " boosted " to an extravagant degree, or, perhaps, could not adequately appreciate its much-advertised glories owing unfortunately to their probably finding it in one of its unusual spells of extremely biting cold and gloomy weather; and so, instead of staying at " Alfred Cottage ", which they had hired for three months they hurried back after barely a month to their more congenial Kandy.

I, of course, wanted to see as much of Ceylon as possible, especially the much-talked of Nuwara Eliya, which I had never visited before. Undeterred, therefore, by the bad impression of it formed by my father and his fellow-exiles, I determined to put it to a personal test, and see for myself how it bore comparison with the rosy reports about it. Moreover, it was said to have come on immensely within recent years owing to the unremitting attention lavished on it by one of Ceylon's most popular Governors, Sir West Ridgeway.

Besides, the Diacono family were domiciled there, and I certainly could not come to Ceylon and miss seeing my best friends. Even the passing of years did not seem to have affected our lifelong warm friendship, for they would not hear of my going anywhere else in Nuwara Eliya except to their own place, Maryhill Hotel, as if I were a member of their family, in spite of its being closed to the public at the time owing to the end of the season then. And to them accordingly I went, and was as warmly and cordially received as of yore; and to see a place amidst friends, and in their genial company, is a boon not every tourist is blessed with.

. . . . .

The first stage of my journey from Kandy to Nuwara Eliya brings me to Gampola. In ordinary circumstances this town would not have appealed to me, except in so far as it was an ordinary wayside railway station; and not even the fact that it had once seen better days as the capital of Ceylon, and was even now the centre of rubber, tea, and cocoa plantations, and the best home of that

[Photo by the Author

KANDY LAKE—THE BUND, AND A SECTION OF ITS PRETTY PARAPET

Facing page 192]

[*Photo by Platé, Ltd., Colombo*

THE WONDERFUL VARIETY OF PLANTS IN THE PERADENIYA GARDENS

Facing page 193]

delectable Ceylon confectionery called " jaggery ", would have weighed very much with me. But though on my first trip to Nuwara Eliya and back it was not much to me, still, later on it acquired a sentimental interest, for, were not two of my friends living there?

Soon after my arrival in Ceylon, one day as I was lunching at the Grand Oriental Hotel, the waiter handed me a card, and whose name should it bear but that of my old friend and former classmate, Mr. W. T. Samaraweera. By his card he seemed to have blossomed forth into a planter, with such a fine estate as " Ranawella " belonging to him. And Mr. Samaraweera insisted on my going up to his place and staying with him some time, he having, as we say in Arabic " entered a new world ", and become the happy pater of several little Samaraweeras.

Again, the following day, quite unexpectedly at Cave's Tea Rooms whom should I meet but Mr. E. G. Jonklaas, the well-known Proctor of Gampola who, in my time, when I was still a little kid, was one of the " lions " of Kingswood, or what in Public School parlance one usually terms a Prefect of the School. And in his turn he pressed an invitation on me that I must come and see him at his residence at Gampola. He also had become a paterfamilias, and his son, a strapping young lad, whom he introduced to me, was soon leaving for Oxford to try and prove himself a worthy " chip of the old block ".

By Jove, the Fates indeed were kind! Here were invitations dropping like ripe plums fast into my lap, so to say, and I could not help feeling intensely gratified to observe how loyally our friendship had stood the test of time, and that my former friends were so generously extending their hospitality to me in so liberal a manner. I was indeed so delighted that I could not refrain from writing and telling Mr. Blazé about them, as I knew it would gladden his heart, so concerned was he as to whether I was enjoying my stay. To him therefore I wrote to reassure him on the point:

"I knew Kingswoodians to be loyal to their school," I said, "but I hardly expected them to be so generous and hospitable as well."

And there was no mistaking the pleasure he felt, by the tone of the reply he sent me:

"Don't be surprised at being welcomed by old friends. *K.F.E.* has plenty of magic in it!"

Could I, therefore, not have a warm corner in my affections for Gampola?

I, however, excused myself for a long stay for the ostensible reason that I had not much time to spare, but really owing to my not wanting to put them to any undue inconvenience, busy as they were certain to be. But paying them an afternoon visit was a different thing. And as if the Fates would still continue to smile on me, the Honble. Mr. W. M. Abdul Rahiman kindly gives me a "lift" in his fine *Opel* car right up to Gampola and back during one of the afternoons of the Perahera, and right glad was I to have been able to call on both Mr. Jonklaas and Mr. Samaraweera under such pleasant conditions and in such welcome company.

Mr. Samaraweera's house was a pretty one, right in the heart of his estate up the mountains, and perched on a hillock; the road leading to it overlooking a beautiful landscape; and as I passed the tea bushes I could not but wish them to thrive and prosper in a manner worthy of the generous nature which made him give me such a handsome present as the large quantity he sent me before I left for home. And to drink the tea that comes straight from the estate of an old friend is a pleasure one can fully appreciate.

And "Ernleigh", the bungalow of Mr. Jonklaas, oh! what a lovely one it was, and how fairylike, as it lay snugly ensconced amidst the surrounding foliage! Indeed rarely did I ever see a better and more picturesque site. It was simply ideal. Just above the town it was, situated on a grassy knoll; and right below, winding, meandering in serpentine coils through glens of leafy bamboo and matchless scenery, which was a real feast to the eye, flowed the Mahawila Ganga—the longest river in Ceylon. And as if land and water must combine to produce a perfect picture, there right ahead on the horizon, at times visible, at others shrouded in mist, towered the far-famed Peak of Adam. Indeed, if Mr. Jonklaas ever needed inspiration in the preparation of a *cause celèbre*, here surely was this idyllic spot which could serve such a purpose quite amply.

. . . . .

And now to return to my journey again, for this has been a pretty long digression from the main topic already. After passing Nawalapitiya, where another engine is added to the rear of the train, the next important stage is Hatton, to which a certain significance attaches in that it is one of the starting points for those wishing to climb Adam's Peak, the other route being *via* Ratnapura. The presence, however, of the fine Adam's Peak Hotel at Hatton makes this route the more favourite one for excursionists, inasmuch as it is the more accessible by rail.

From Kandy to Gampola rubber seems to rule supreme, though now and then a cocoa grove peeping here and there, and a fair proportion of tea estates seem determined to keep it company. But little by little the rubber plantations grow fewer, cocoa vanishing almost entirely, and the tea estates correspondingly increase, until, past Nawalapitiya and Hatton, only the bush of the "cup that cheers" lives in the picture, its familiar plant dotting the landscape and covering every hillside.

As we approach the heart of the tea country at Talawakelé and past it, some of the grandest views of Ceylon unroll themselves before our eager gaze. If on the way to Kandy we meet with one Sensation Rock, here we find a dozen; and as if the excitement of being on the edge of a giddy precipice were not enough, we must here experience the sensation of being suspended, as it were, in space, as the train passes over the slender girders bridging some wonderful mountain gorge. And how we hold our breath as we traverse such a cutting, only letting ourselves go as we pass on to *terra firma!* Indeed, in such rapid succession do these sensations follow one another that we hardly have time to catch them all.

Again, at one moment you hear a gushing stream, at another a raging torrent. And as you watch the crystalline water trickling down some hillside like a miniature cascade, a grander waterfall is on you ere you are aware. But before you have gazed on it in wonderment, lo! you are ushered into utter darkness! Even as you sit almost petrified, asking yourself whether it is a tunnel you are passing through, or you have had the misfortune to be stricken blind, a streak of light answers you, and dispels any qualms of creepiness that may have seized you; but ere you have the time to thank the Almighty that your eyesight remains untouched, the train is actually passing over another ravine with a raging torrent below, a veritable cataract, a Niagara in miniature!

But no! gentle reader, you have not reached the limit; something more wonderful and magnificent is in store for you. A little farther, and the distant sound of rushing, falling waters arrests your attention, and as you peer out of the window to detect the spot where the distant waters murmur, there, just before you reach Talawakelé, and about one or two hundred yards away are the St. Clair Falls, the apotheosis of all that is beautiful and sublime which human eye can picture, a mighty, sparkling brilliant, as it were, set in a bed of emeralds! But the St. Clair Falls must have their consort, for it would be a pity to revel in their grandeur all alone; and a little farther the Devon Falls come into view—equally sublime, glittering, and grand.

Even the scarped, moss-covered mountain slopes, now stripped for the most part of the jungle and the thick undergrowth of the Kandyan country, do not appear so bleak and cheerless as they might seem, for the very greenery envisages them with a more pleasing and restful aspect than the barren, sandy wastes of a dreary desert.

Even the skies must lend their share of the mystical, for a wonderful experience I had after passing Ambagamuwa—said to be Ceylon's rainiest district, averaging 200 inches annually as it does. It was raining cats and dogs, and the skies were dark and sullen as we were passing; but there, a couple of miles or so away on the other side shone the sun in all its brilliancy, flooding the mountain tops with all its warmth and radiant sunshine, the blue tones of the crests, as they merged into the fleeting mist, enhancing the beauty of the scene. It was, indeed, a remarkable contrast, and one must have the good fortune to see such a sight adequately to appreciate the sensation of such a striking phenomenon.

After Talawakelé the atmosphere begins to get colder, and one feels it to a certain extent; but it is not the biting cold that penetrates to your very bones, and keeps you indoors, but the crisp, bracing air that beckons to you to go forth and breathe its fresh, invigorating power. A pretty bungalow perched on some grassy knoll ("Blackwater" I think it was) tells you of the residence of some hardy planter who, in shorts, as if he were going to play football, goes about to inspect his estate. The path leading to his house is neatly flanked with trim hedges, and dotted here and there with pretty flower beds, as if it were some beautiful home of Merrie England transplanted to this distant corner of the Orient.

The creaking sound of something on a pulley next attracts my attention, and for the first time I notice the aërial tramways in vogue on the factories for communicating with the coolies at work on the slopes or in the depths far below. As I gaze on them in bewilderment I cannot help admiring the inventive genius of man, ever seeking resolutely and patiently to conquer nature and tame it to his needs.

The coolies themselves, Tamils all, as they industriously went about their work, were not without their insignificance and moral, and as I watched them I could not help wondering here why, when there was such a large population of Sinhalese, they should still allow others to come and fill the jobs which rightly belong to them. It is true that they are taken up with the arts and crafts, and the Sinhalese carpenter and craftsman is a real credit to the Island. But there is plenty of room for them as well in agricultural pursuits, and many of those who seem to be doing nothing in Colombo might as well turn their hands to more profitable work in this direction. But then, how can the sleek, comely Sinhalese of the Metropolis stoop to till the soil, and thus spoil the effects of a neat, trim appearance, even if he earned thereby only half of what he could gain in agriculture.

. . . . .

At last Nanu Oya comes into view. A few moments more, and we are actually in the station, having climbed by rail to an altitude of 5,300 feet in a journey of 128 miles from Colombo. Here as far as passengers for Nuwara Eliya are concerned, the journey is at an end on the broad gauge line, they having to change here, and travel on to their destination in what is a veritable toy oj a railway, even its shrill whistle in keeping with its diminutive nature and size. The original train then goes farther up on the main line, passing *en route* Pattipola, at an altitude of 6,244 feet—the highest point in the Island by rail on the broad gauge line—before dropping 2,000 feet in its gradual descent towards its terminus Bandarawela, thirty-two miles away from Nanu Oya, constituting thus one of the highest and most picturesque railways in the world.

To attain Nuwara Eliya, however, we have to ascend another 1,000 feet from Nanu Oya, and though the distance is only six miles, we take an hour to cover them by devious and circuitous routes cut away from the mountain sides,—so many snakelike coils of some huge python or anaconda as they looked like on the lower ridges from above, as we were climbing higher up. On our way we pass the hydro-electric power station, where electricity for the town is generated by the Nanu Oya waterfall; and as one contemplates this pretty corner, one realises how abreast of the times this pretty town has kept. No wonder therefore that Nuwara Eliya is coming on so fast.

And this journey from Nanu Oya to Nuwara Eliya, Mohammed very aptly described, when he likened it to the upward climb on the Scenic Railway at our Luna Park at Heliopolis, near Cairo.

The very fact that one can reach Nuwara Eliya from Colombo by rail, even with a bijou railway on the last stage, reminiscent of the *funiculaire* of the Swiss mountains, is a feather indeed in the cap of the Ceylon Government, for which all of us must be grateful.

But the approach to Nuwara Eliya is said to be far more magnificent by the Ramboddé Pass, than *via* Nanuoya, and the pity is that I should have missed trying this route as well, especially when the advent of the motor-car and Ceylon's splendid, smooth, and dustless roads make travelling on them a veritable delight, and more in the nature of a pleasure drive than the mere use of a means of communication. Indeed, pleasant as the railway journey is, still it would be worth the trouble and the outlay to travel by car whenever possible, provided one can afford the expense, as sometimes the country traversed by car is even more beautiful than that bordering the railway track. Moreover, certain highways and byways of rural Ceylon have not as yet heard the shrill whistle of " the iron horse ", though the horn of the car is no longer any stranger to them, and the very attractiveness of such localities calls for a drive through them.

. . . . .

To sum up, the journey from Kandy to Nuwara Eliya is, as a matter of fact, one kaleidoscopic panorama of arcadian beauty, a picture show, as it were, set off by the contrasts that mark its opening and its concluding stages; and if a traveller goes with his eyes open, and a heart full of enthusiasm for delights to come, but untasted of as yet, he will be thrilled by the sights and experiences that spring upon him at every corner, and be amply rewarded and feel only too glad that he ever made the trip.

As on our journey from Colombo to Kandy we began with the Low Country, and finished in all the grandeur of scowling Alagalla and the enchanting Dekanda Valley, so do we here on our way from Kandy to Nuwara Eliya start with all the wealth of the Tropics, and end in the scenery characteristic of a Temperate countryside. The luxuriant foliage and vegetation of the warmer districts has now given place to a wealth of greenery just as welcome and pleasing to the eye, but the trees and bushes that confront us dotting the landscape, are of a species more at home in these colder regions, the rhododendron and the wattle in this zone being as conspicuous here, as we miss the familiar coconut, areca-nut, mango, jak, cashew-nut, and a host of others of a lower altitude. Even the papaw and the plantain are but anæmic, almost wilted specimens of those sturdy counterparts of theirs elsewhere. And as one begins to despair of fruit in these parts, lo! rows of pear, plum, peach, apricot, apple, and strawberry, as if conscious and forewarned of our disappointment, point admonishingly with a rebuking finger to themselves as if saying: "Aren't we as good and delicious as those you come across in Colombo and Kandy, we who grace the orchards of Merrie England?"

The very mountain slopes seem at times to be clad with an undergrowth so dense, unlike what one expected, owing to the nature and look of the country before reaching Nuwara Eliya, that in certain parts even the thickest jungles in the Kandyan Hills seem to pale into insignificance by their side. One sometimes asks whether they have been left standing there as remains of a virgin

[Photo by the Author

AVENUE OF CABBAGE PALMS, PERADENIYA GARDENS

Facing page 200]

[Photo by the Author

THE LOTOS POND—A PICTURESQUE CORNER OF THE PERADENIYA GARDENS

Facing page 201]

forest, or must they also one day yield to the hand of progress, and succumb to the inroads of tea's triumphant march, the elk and the leopard, that so long sought cover within their impenetrable depths, for ever banned to farther wilds?

CHAPTER XXVI

NUWARA ELIYA

If the town of Kandy—as distinct from the surrounding country—is supposed to be dull compared to Colombo, how much duller might Nuwara Eliya be. But it depends upon what perspective you approach it from. True, here we have not the animated scenes of the quarters of the Pettah or Borella buzzing and throbbing with the bustle of local life; but then, Nuwara Eliya is not a business town, nor a flourishing port, but a mountain resort of the first order. What it lacks in one direction it compensates for in other ways, and the bored or fastidious can hardly complain of a lack of amenities to suit every taste and condition.

If angling has not got its thrills and cannot claim a fair number of votaries—and angling, too, for real trout from the Scottish Lochs—then there is tennis or golf or football or hockey or cricket to satisfy the fancy of the devotee of each game; and if one is a good shot, or can make any pretension to being one, in his hankering after adventure, why, the adjoining jungle and thickets just beyond the Moon Plains will receive him with open arms. Not even racing, " the sport of kings ", can be denied its share in dissipating any boredom that may have settled on the town; and when its annual Agri-Horticultural Show takes place during Easter, the town simply hums with life, as if some electric current had been passed through the placid waters of its normal, tranquil existence, and galvanised it into scenes of unusual bustle and animation.

It is a relief also not to be pestered with leeches here, and it was only after I had been reassured on the point that I moved about without worrying about them to keep looking at my boots now and then. But in one respect my information was not correct. The belief that intense cold banished them to more hospitable regions, and did not give them a chance to survive here, proved wrong in the light of subsequent events. After I returned to Cairo, one day as I was reading *The Times* of September 23rd, 1921, what was my astonishment when I found in Colonel Howard Bury's account of the Mount Everest Expedition that leeches actually thrived and attacked the members of the Expedition in a most voracious and troublesome manner at an altitude of 12,000 feet, that is to say, twice that of Nuwara Eliya! Here indeed was a revelation and a record, and an addition to my general knowledge. So, next time when I go to Nuwara Eliya I shall not take things for granted, but be wary about these beastly little pests, even though I did not come across them at Nuwara Eliya this time.

Even in pleasant walks and drives is Nuwara Eliya amply provided for, and as if its splendid park, and its fine maze, and pretty ponds where the fish spring and jump tantalisingly, knowing that they are immune from the depredations of any keen angler were nsufficient, Nuwara Eliya must needs have its Hakgalla—for has not Kandy her Peradeniya, and Colombo her Henaratgoda? So why should a rising town like Nuwara Eliya not have its own Botanical Garden in turn? And the very drive to Hakgalla in a car is a trip pleasant enough in itself. These Gardens are well kept, and prove a welcome attraction and adornment to the surrounding country; but in their grandeur the Peradeniya Gardens tower above the others.

From Hakgalla one can also enjoy a rare sight not to be obtained elsewhere. From it, as one gazes on the undulating Downs of Uva culminating in Diyatalawa—where the Boer prisoners were once interned, and where now the Aldershot and Bisley of Ceylon are combined—

and Bandarawela, a rising mountain resort which aspires to be a rival to Nuwara Eliya, one realises what a wondrously lovely view one has gazed on, and what a marvellous country Ceylon is! Another curious phenomenon associated with these districts is, as I have been told, that when it happens to be raining in Nuwara Eliya, just across at Bandarawela there would be beautiful weather and lovely sunshine, and *vice versa*, according as to how each town is affected by the monsoons. My readers will recollect my allusion to some such sight in the preceding chapter after the train passed Ambagamuwa.

. . . . .

But it is the British who generally benefit by all these delights, for as a British stronghold Nuwara Eliya seems to have developed into a sort of " Gezireh Enclave ", as Lord Milner so aptly and ironically dubbed Cairo's aristocratic Island suburb where our British reside in blissful exclusiveness in a world all their own! And even the Ceylonese who own bungalows in Nuwara Eliya seem to lease them for the most part, whether because they are handsomely paid for them, or owing to the exclusive and inexplicable aloofness of the British, Heaven and the proprietors only know.

But why the Britisher should always fall under the bane of such adverse criticism I cannot understand. One believed that the Great War was waged for the good and weal of the human race as a whole, and as such it was therefore a fight against the influences of evil, a fight against aggrandisement—at any rate, these were the lofty ideals we were given to understand for which the Allies warred. If for these, therefore, men passed through the furnace of the greatest war of modern times, the struggle in which millions offered their lives in the service of mankind, if these ideals were but a mockery and not a reality, then might the human race well perish.

Indeed, one believed that the Great War was to herald the dawn of a new era, doing away meanwhile with many of the old-time shibboleths, and paving the way for a better, a more generous, and a more broad-minded spirit and age. But alas! in the heat of the moment how many golden promises one often makes, and how many solemn pledges and rosy prospects he holds out, but how often and how quick does the morrow bring disillusionment! A fine race the British are in many respects, but it is a pity that in their dealings with Orientals in particular they still labour under so lamentable a drawback as their extreme aloofness; and it seems that if they are slow to learn, they are even slower to change.

. . . . .

The weather at Nuwara Eliya is cold, it is true, but it is the crisp and invigorating quality of the cold which makes it so welcome to many. But it is not everybody who would relish it; and in this respect again does Kandy act as the golden mean, for, whereas at Colombo the nights are rarely ever pleasant, and at Nuwara Eliya the nights usually call for a thick blanket, and even a cosy fireplace, at Kandy sleep is a real delight, and one welcomes his bed only too eagerly.

. . . . .

And the lake, or whatever goes by that name—what a poor specimen, what a mockery of what a real lake should be, and of all places in a well-known mountain resort! If anything, it is more like some large woebegone pond; and Nuwara Eliya might first send someone to Kandy to study what a pretty lake, which is an adornment to a town, should be like, and then reproduce it here. If a town can provide pretty ponds and pools for fishing, it can just as well attend to its æsthetic appearance.

. . . . .

When I was at Nuwara Eliya I expressed the desire to visit a tea estate. I actually had the "Scrubs" in my mind, presuming on my acquaintance with Mr. J. C. Van Langenberg, of the estate in question, who had been a friend of my father's. Unfortunately, he was ill at the time; and though he subsequently put me into touch with the superintendent, Mr. R. A. Paterson, who, in his turn, very kindly offered to show me all round his estate when next I came up to Nuwara Eliya, still, the rush on my time during my last days in Ceylon precluded any such possibility. Anyhow, on the present occasion I visited " Naseby ", thanks to Mrs. C. W. H. Duckworth, who knew its superintendent, Mr. E. Wilson Smith.[1]

This gentleman, although he had just returned from a Rugby match in a neighbouring district, very generously showed us all round the establishment and factory, and carefully explained the various stages the tea passes through, from the time it is plucked to the time when it becomes the cup that cheers. He took us also to his bungalow a little farther up, and showed us some of the trophies he had brought back from the Great War—for he was an officer in the Gordon Highlanders—such as German helmets, anti-poisonous gas masks, splinters and fragments of shells, and so on. Then came the cup that cheers, and seldom during my stay in the Island did I taste such delicious tea; for if a person cannot really enjoy it on the estate where it is produced, where then can he rightly expect to?

He then took us up by winding paths through tea bushes right up to the summit of his estate, until we were at an elevation of about 7,000 feet above the level of the sea, and only Pedrotalagala ahead on the opposite ridge, the highest mountain in Ceylon, towered another 1,300 feet or so above us. Oh, the sensation, the exhilaration, the crisp invigorating air, the sublimity and grandeur of

[1] Curiously, by a pleasant coincidence, when I failed, during my 1924 visit, to get my usual supply of tea from the " Scrubs " estate, which I always enjoyed so much, owing to the estate in question being under contract to supply a London firm, I fell back upon Mr. W. J. Byrne, the Manager of the Queen's Hotel, asking him to try and get me some of the best which he could kindly recommend, or even some of what was being supplied to the Hotel, the tea this time being superior to any I had tasted elsewhere in this trip. What was my surprise and delight when in the Superintendent of " Mooneragalla Estate," Pusselawa, from which Mr. Byrne ordered my consignment of tea, I recognised an old acquaintance in the person of Mr. E. Wilson Smith, who had taken up his billet there. And excellent tea I found his, and just as good as that of " Scrubs," he very kindly having taken particular care to supply me with the best.

the scene around! One felt as if one were on the roof of the earth! These sensations are better felt than described; and even the most graphic and vivid pen can hardly do adequate justice to such a superb spectacle.

But the ascent to Pedrotalagala is said to be even more wonderful, and the view obtained from it even more sublime. If a person has the enterprise and energy to go thither in the early dawn, what a sight awaits his eyes! If there were nothing else to encourage such an attempt, it were enough to realise that there, from Ceylon's highest point, at an elevation of 8,296 feet above the level of the sea, on a clear day, a person can see far, far away in the distance the waters of the Indian Ocean breaking upon Ceylon's spicy shores. The pity is that I should have missed such a grand opportunity. But then, how many things have I not missed! There is the consolation that this time I seem to have found my bearings; next time I shall be able to turn my trip to better account, and thus find it more enjoyable, for there is nothing like learning in the hard school of experience.

. . . . .

When I think of the tea I drank at "Naseby", and the poor, insipid stuff supplied elsewhere, I sometimes wonder whether I was really in Ceylon, drinking real "Pure Ceylon Tea", as it is vauntingly and tantalisingly thrust upon all and sundry! And of all places in Ceylon not to be able to enjoy a good cup of this beverage except rarely, as if it were a *rara avis* in its very home, or another myth, or some fabulous roc to exist only in our fertile imagination. Is it the old story of "Nobody is worse shod than the shoemaker's wife", or will the people of Ceylon heedlessly persist in undermining their own prosperity? How much ink has been spilt on this grievance, and how often shall we hear the bitter plaint of this shortcoming on the part of Ceylon! If anywhere in the world one should expect to enjoy a really good cup of tea, it should be here in its own home, and what an advertisement this would make!

I, for one, who have presented my friends in Cairo with tea as came from such fine estates as " Scrubs " and " Naseby ", what praises have I heard all round, and every one of them affirms that he hardly ever tasted any better quality, and that only on partaking of the right stuff did they realise what a delight good tea really was. Indeed, even every one of them wanted henceforth to get his tea straight from the estates in Ceylon, while the grocer or middleman could look after themselves.

True, there is tea and tea. But passengers and people abroad should be given a fair chance of acquiring their needs according to their own tastes and means, and not that every brand, just because it is produced in Ceylon, should be labelled and thrust on a credulous and long-suffering public as the "Best Ceylon Tea"! The act itself is a breach of honest trade, in which the best qualities suffer at the expense of inferior brands owing to such indiscriminate sorting; and it is high time that a stop was put to such tactics; for the passenger would like to find within easy reach a place where he can safely procure some really good tea to take home, without the fear that he has been " done ", or that the tea will turn out, as so often happens, when he returns to his country, only so much worthless stuff.

This subject has been so frequently threshed out already that it would be mere repetition to dwell upon it here again. But let the remarks of a real friend and well-wisher of Ceylon not fall on deaf ears. Above all, let the big hotels take the initiative and lead the way, for it is within their portals that a passenger or tourist usually gets the one chance to taste a really good cup of tea. Ceylon's reputation, as the country producing the best tea, is at stake, and I can even see " the writing on the wall ". She had better look to her laurels while it is still not too late, else a time will come when she will rue the day she did not take warning.

. . . . .

[Photo by the Author

THE MALIGAWA ELEPHANT INSIDE THE TEMPLE, BEING GOT READY FOR THE PERAHERA

Facing page 208]

[*Photo by the Author*

THE KANDYAN CHIEFS IN THE PERAHERA

Facing page 209]

The very mention of tea brings me to another grievance. I cannot comprehend why in an agricultural and pastoral country like Ceylon one should have to put up with tinned milk, to the exclusion of the fresh, natural article! It cannot be a dearth or shortage of cows—and this when they are so cheap! Nor is it conceivable that we can admit feeble plea of adulterated milk, for how can the responsible authorities answer to such a charge, or put up with such a stigma! Is it because the tinned milk—and even then a watery, anæmic dilution that parades under such a name—is more economical, or some fastidious palate cannot trust itself to the tender mercies of some fanciful, tubercular cow?

Or, does he fear that Ceylon's milk, like Egypt's water, is endowed with that wonderful, mystic power: *Qui aquam Nili bibit rursus bibit* (He who drinks of the water of the Nile, must return to the Nile), and so is afraid that by drinking Ceylon's milk he might likewise fall under its spell, and must needs thus emulate the example of his equally fatuous counterpart in Egypt, who will drink only soda water, and not hear of Father Nile?

CHAPTER XXVII

A MOTOR TRIP ACROSS CEYLON

PART I—LAKE KANTHALAI AND TRINCOMALEE

I SHALL never forget the kindness of the Honourable Mr. W. M. Abdul Rahiman, and words cannot adequately express what a lasting obligation I owe to him. We were introduced to each other one afternoon when we met accidentally at Mr. Macan Markar's well-known establishment, and exceedingly pleased I was to renew our former ties of friendship. Moreover, I was glad to meet again the gentleman in whose house in Union Place, Slave Island, Colombo, I was born. Accordingly, I cannot but avail myself of the present occasion to thank him once more for all his goodness towards me; and I wish Fortune would enable me to do something in return for him in my own country.

During the Perahera he very kindly arranged to take me down to Colombo in his motor car at its close, and I was delighted to get the chance of a trip along Ceylon's splendid roads and through its beautiful scenery. Later on, however, he hinted that he wanted to take me to Colombo, but by the northward route *via* Matalé, Dambulla, Trincomalee, Anuradhapura, Puttalam, and then down towards the metropolis. But this was offering too much; and I, accordingly, did my best to dissuade him from this plan, for the expense and trouble entailed in the new route, and the possibility of its also carrying him out of his work, would scarcely have been fair on my part were I to take advantage of his generosity.

Even on the day preceding our trip, when he kindly took me round to Gampola to call on both Mr. E. G. Jonklaas and Mr. W. T. Samaraweera, he left me under the impression that we were going to Colombo on the morrow, with the result that I sent on all my luggage ahead in advance by rail to the G. O. H. Anyhow, the morning of our trip dawns; the car drives up, and we get into it. He still divulges nothing, and it was only after passing Katugastota, to which he made a feint of going to lay in some petrol, instead of going by the usual route to Colombo *via* Peradeniya, did he make it plain to me that we were going northwards to Trincomalee; and a pleasant surprise indeed it proved; still I could not help fearing that I was taxing his kindness too much.

A veritable joyride was this trip, and there was only one drawback to mar it to some extent. Had I known for certain that we were really going by the route he had sedulously planned unknown to me, I would have looked up Cave's *The Book of Ceylon* beforehand, and thus would have ultimately been in a better position to appreciate all the better the various places and sights we were passing through. But then, it was no use regretting now, and one had to make the best of the situation.

. . . . .

Our first stage took us through the beautiful country of the Matalé District, and as we passed through it we could see estates of various descriptions—tea, rubber, and cocoa following each other in regular sequence, like the famous vicious circle, or cyclic order x, y, z. The trim, pretty town of Matalé itself lay nestling amid its well-kept play fields, its lovely arbours, and overhanging hills, and I regretted that I had not spared a few hours previously to pay it a more leisurely visit. Nowhere as in this quarter did I notice such a profusion of cocoa groves, and their very abundance seem to have supplied the *raison d'être* of Messrs. Barber's well-known chocolate factory at Ukuwella near by, since rivalled by the newer establishment at Peradeniya.

From Matalé we proceeded to Dambulla, where we arrived at noon. But though I seem to have heard something of the famous Dambulla Rock Temples, and the equally famed Rock Fortress of Sigiri, somewhere in the neighbourhood, still, lack of sufficient knowledge about them, and their exact whereabouts, did not make me venture to pay them a visit. Besides, we wanted to reach Trincomalee in good time before dusk. At the Resthouse we had a good lunch, ordered in advance; and after resting for a while, we resumed our journey in the early afternoon.

The route from Kandy to Dambulla passed through a most beautiful countryside, the road itself being in excellent condition. Thenceforward, however, the landscape changes. No longer is the way so thickly peopled, or the rural scenery so enchanting. We now miss the charming hills, and the pretty terraced paddy fields, as also the luxuriant vegetation of cultivated areas where man has united with nature to present a vista of surpassing loveliness and extreme usefulness. Even the baying of dogs is now less noticeable, and fewer wayside villagers rush out from their thatched cottages or huts to gaze in some wonderment at the car dashing along. It is a different region we now enter.

The road continues good, but it is not up to the standard of the previous section. The wayside is still thickly wooded, but it is the mass of scrub of virgin forest growing on less raised ground, not that covering the slopes and steep acclivities of the hilly districts; and lest the dense undergrowth might serve as cover or traps for lurking beasts of prey, the Ceylon Government has very thoughtfully made clearings of about four or five yards on either side of the roadway to preclude the possibility of any prowling animal attacking wayfarers suddenly. The very region of Habarane, I was told, was not far from the preserves beloved of the big game hunter; and if a person armed with a trusty gun yearned for sport or thirsted for adventure, why, he had but to penetrate a little deeper into the jungle through by-ways, and there he would find enough to glut the greediest appetite.

But these are not the only districts for big game, for down in the south-east of Ceylon, somewhere between the regions of Ratnapura and Hambantota, even better and more approved stretches await the ardent hunter of the wilds, and those hankering after a shot at an elephant, bear, leopard, wild boar, elk, or minor prey, can be assured of a handsome bag.

We are now fast approaching one of Ceylon's greatest ruins. All vestiges of human life have meanwhile practically vanished, and but for some hardy coolie or forlorn wayfarer, it is the denizens of the forest that are now our sole companions. The huge towering ebony tree I see for the first time in its natural guise amidst the wilds, as also Ceylon's fine satinwood. The crackling of some bough overhead shows one of "man's poor relations" springing from branch to branch, and as if vexed that his betters should encroach upon his sylvan haunts, he sometimes pelts us with berries, at other times whole troops of them—father, mother, and baby monkeys—will cross our path. The mongoose also—dread enemy of the serpent—we now and then see; as also the fleeing jackal; and, ere we are aware, some beautiful, bushy squirrel has scampered up a tree, or, all of a sudden, the heavy flap of some big bird, or its sudden screech proclaims the huge buzzard that flies to seek shelter in the depths of the forest. Butterflies there are, butterflies of every size, and of the gaudiest hues; and even the sight of parrots of the brightest plumage, or the trill of some bulbul are not unwelcome in this solitude. The charred remains of some logs, or sleepers neatly stacked, portend the approach of the Maho-Trincomalee railway, and even some clearings for hundreds of yards indicate a section of the route the proposed line is to traverse.

A little farther, and the famous Kanthalai Tank bursts upon our view—a sheen of placid waters, like the broad expanse of some boundless inland sea. And even as we skirt it on the parapet, I recall that vivid description I once read of these regions when I first received Cave's book:[1]

"No European resident or visitor in Ceylon can be said to have availed himself of all its attractions who has not passed through the wilds of the northern parts, explored its most interesting antiquities, shared in the sport which the almost uninhabited regions afford, and, last but not least, visited its most beautiful port, Trincomalee.

". . . Trincomalee may be reached *via* Vavuniya, Anuradhapura, or Matelé. The Matalé route, though the longest, affords the best road. A mail coach runs from Matalé to Trincomalee daily. . . . The journey is also quite practicable for motor cars and bicycles.

"After leaving Dambulla we arrive at 'Habarane', which is really in the centre of some excellent hunting grounds, and although it is the fashion to say that game in this locality is getting scarce, there is plenty of evidence to the contrary. Here is a vast wilderness of two or three thousand square miles, consisting of beautiful and valuable forest trees, interspersed with strips of open plain and vast artificial lakes, the remnants of bygone ages, which not even the destructive tooth of time has been able to obliterate.

"Let us now visit one of these secluded spots not too frequently disturbed by the white man, and we shall be surprised at the countless number of living creatures that haunt the vicinity of a stretch of water in these remote solitudes. Here a telescope may be of greater interest than a gun. Concealed beneath the shade of some beautiful tree, one may watch the habits of animals in their natural freedom. This occupation has a wonderful charm on a calm evening, with a tropical sunset glowing upon the dense jungles, whence all manner of creatures are seen to emerge and steal gently down the open glades

[1] *The Book of Ceylon*, by H. W. Cave, pp. 618–622.

to refresh themselves by draughts of water. A distant sound like the blast of a horn reaches our ears, and we scan the thickets of the opposite shores: a majestic elephant is trumpeting to his herd; they obey his summons to the evening bath, and some six or eight are seen to disport themselves in the shallow waters, which they hurl over their bodies in great showers. Noises betoken the approach of greater numbers as the sun gradually disappears below the horizon. The shrill bark of deer, the grunt of the boar, and the screams of a myriad birds mingle as the congregation increases. The reptiles and the birds are not the least interesting; crocodiles, kabaragoyas and iguanas are present in great numbers; but the endless variety of the large birds is the most astounding feature of these lonely shores. There are cranes nearly six feet high; pelicans like little heaps of snow gently propelling themselves over the smooth surface of the water; the pretty little water-pheasants and their glittering heads, standing over the lotus leaves; the adjutant stalking after reptiles; ducks innumerable and of finest plumage; teal of the most delicious species; while the gaudiest peacocks strut about the plain. Here is a paradise for the naturalist as well as the sportsman. We must, however, pursue our journey to Trincomalee.

"Every fifteen miles brings us to a resthouse, and from every resthouse we can make a sporting excursion into the jungle if that is our will. The traveller who is merely journeying to Trincomalee will need very little commissariat. If he is cycling (a method of locomotion pleasant enough on this road)[1] he will need to carry only a change of flannels, and will find most of the resthouses provisioned with such light refreshment as he may need; or he can travel through by coaches, of which there is a regular service carrying His Majesty's mails.

[1] This was written in 1907 before the motor car had become so extensively used as at present, else the writer would have recommended it very strongly. Even the Government mails are now conveyed on the roads alluded to by motor buses, as we had occasion to see.

"From Habarane to Alutoya forms the next stage. The road here is very beautiful, owing to the undulations and the character of the forest, which is rich in fine timber trees. Occasionally we come across a straight mile or two in length, and in the distance we see herds of wild hogs cross from one side to the other; here and there grey jackals put in an appearance, while monkeys and large squirrels are surprisingly numerous. Troops of wonderoos abound all the way, and at frequent intervals numbers of them leap from the branches of trees on one side of the road to those on the other.

"Another stage brings us to the lovely lake of Kanthalai. Many a sportsman has felt that he would not mind spending the balance of his life here. After several hours of travelling through the dense forest, it is with a shock of delight that the monotony is broken by the sudden appearance of a beautiful lake stretching away for miles to dreamy ranges of distant hills, whose beauties are reflected in its calm waters. Life and light combine to greet us as the gay birds are startled by our approach. We stand enchanted by the scene. All is still save the voices of the creatures that dwell on these beautiful inland shores. Spotted deer are browsing; peacocks, airing their gaudy plumage, strut o'er the plain; the majestic elephant is enjoying his evening bath in the shallows; herds of buffaloes leave the shade of the woods to slake their thirst; grim crocodiles are basking on the shores watching their prey; troops of chattering monkeys are skylarking in the trees; while the sturdy cranes and pinky flamingoes stalk the shallows. Such are the scenes that surround the tank or lake of Kanthalai.

"And now let us, for a moment, go back a couple of thousand years for the origin and purpose of this gigantic artificial stonework embankment on which we stand. The history of Ceylon contains authentic records of a system of irrigation which, for engineering ingenuity and the rapidity with which they were executed could not be

[Photo by the Author

TEMPLE ELEPHANTS BATHING AT KATUGASTOTA

Facing page 216]

[*Photo by Platé, Ltd., Colombo*

CREMATION OF A BUDDHIST PRIEST

Facing page 217]

surpassed by any conceivable means at the present day. We know that such works were constructed, because the evidence remains in the imperishable barriers of solid masonry that we find stretched across the valleys to secure the heavy rainfall of certain seasons; but so wonderful are they, and so intricate yet perfect the system of conveying the precious water to the field, that we cannot realise the conditions which placed such magnificent works within the sphere of the possible.

"The forest now spreads over a network of these ruined lakes and tanks, tens of which are of giant proportions, while the smaller ones number thousands. Embankments eight feet high and three hundred feet wide were carried for many miles at a stretch. The dam of one of these is eleven miles long, and is faced with steps built of twelve-feet lengths of solid granite. That on which we are standing are constructed by King Maha Sen about A.D. 275. The same monarch is said to have made no less than sixteen of the large tanks, including Minneria which, like Kanthalai, is about twenty miles in circumference. When it is borne in mind that in addition to the formation of the necessary embankments and sluices in this wholesale fashion, hundreds of canals for the distribution of the water formed part of the scheme, the stupendous nature of such an ancient undertaking is manifest. Wonderful as are the remains of ancient monuments, palaces, and temples in these now deserted provinces, nothing is more impressive than the great works of irrigation, or attracts one more to the study and consideration of early Sinhalese history."

And we Egyptians, who revel in the magnitude of our great irrigation works of to-day, such as the famous Assouan Dam, of the beautiful, yet none the less remarkable and useful Delta Barrage, little dream that once in ancient Lanka, when Ceylon flourished as a nation, there existed irrigation works equally stupendous and useful.

. . . . .

And now to return to my original account. After Kanthalai we steer for Trincomalee, and the roads are now not so lonely. Just as we approach Trincomalee what a wonderful sight did I behold of the golden orb of the sun trying to fight its way through a sheet of clouds, at one time King Sol, at other times, the clouds, gaining the upper hand. Never in my life did I witness a more gorgeous phenomenon of the heavens, no, not even counting the glorious and superb sunsets viewed from the top of the Mokattam Hills behind the Citadel of Cairo, which no tourist should ever miss.

Even before we enter the precincts of the town proper the landscape on its outskirts assumes a different aspect, the countryside being for the most part dotted with the Palmyra Palm; but of pleasing greenery and vegetation there is very little about—I almost said nothing. At one corner as we are making for the Resthouse, what a malodorous stench we smell from afar—which we soon find out to be that of fish being "cured"—and one feels inclined to believe that after all "Stinkomalee" was not an inappropriate name to have been applied to it in a sense. At last we reach our haven and drop anchor in the Resthouse for a few minutes, making arrangements for spending the night there.

Knowing that we were to leave early next morning, we try to see as much as possible of the place in the short space of daylight still left. We accordingly start almost immediately, but early in our drive we seem to have motored right into a *cul-de-sac*, for right in front of us there was no egress, and we come to a dead stop—as if we had struck another Land's End! It was all we could do to get ourselves out of the predicament we found ourselves in, and at last we succeeded in getting on to the right track.

Along the sea route we then drive past the town into the heart of the erstwhile naval quarters. There they lay the barracks, forlorn and abandoned, and the fortifications overhead dismantled and deserted. The very roads themselves seemed dejected and gloomy, as if weeping for neglect, and not even the adjacent bushes could hold up their drooping heads, so sorrow-stricken they looked. Even the beauty of the far-famed harbour, the exquisite loveliness of the grassy headlands that commanded the approaches to its entrance, or the pretty islets, like so many verdant knolls set in a silvery sea, or the equally famed Saami Rock—which we failed to visit owing to the lateness of the hour—were lost in that air of intense depression which the town seemed to wear. Trincomalee, forlorn and desolate, looked as if some blight, some dread hand had laid its fell touch upon it.

The town itself looked more like a village than a one-time flourishing naval station, and the Tamils and Moors, who make up the bulk of the inhabitants there, do not seem to have any great conception of the æsthetic or civic life—if anything, they seemed to be almost as moribund in spirit as the unfortunate town in which they lived. Of industries and trade there seemed to be little, apart from that of the stinking dried fish which so kindly offered its hearty welcome to the approaching visitor.

And as if the gloom and dreary aspect of the town must also be reflected in the buildings, the Resthouse seemed to partake of the dismal atmosphere pervading. As a matter of fact it was anything but a Resthouse in the real sense of the word—it might more correctly have been nearer the appellation of a torture house, and as long as I live I shall never forget that night I spent at Trincomalee which I shall add to the company of an equally awful night I once spent at a village near Beni Suef, that I did not even wait for sunrise, but fled in the early dawn to take the first train to Cairo.

Trincomalee, divested as it is of its former glories, can ill afford to suffer any more of Government neglect, and this lack of a decent building in a good site, and of proper and comfortable accommodation inside, might very truly be the proverbial last straw that broke the camel's back. If the benighted traveller, coming all the way to such a distant and out-of-the-way place, cannot be assured of a comfortable night, well, there are other places more worthy of a visit, and Trincomalee, for all he knows, can be dropped out of his itinerary without any qualms of regret.

One bright spot in the prospect was the playing fields, and it was a pleasing sight to notice the life infused into the place by the football match which had just been played by bluejackets from a British warship in the harbour against a local eleven.

But one isolated event will no more pull out a town from the rut it has sunk into than one swallow a summer make. Not that Trincomalee cannot admit of development. No, on the contrary, it enjoys a unique harbour, and a fine stretch of sea front; and these added to its pleasing surroundings, plenty of neighbouring land which can be opened up for cultivation, and a dozen other possibilities, can render its revival and rehabilitation a very likely thing. The hope of the projected railway to it, and the promise of a brighter outlook, engendered by the prospect of its blossoming forth anew into the one-time naval station, are enough to foretell happier days to come. If to these we can add such enterprising souls who have the foresight and courage to take time by the forelock, and bestir themselves, why, it will not be long ere Trincomalee is established on a pedestal far sounder and more conspicuous than she once enjoyed, and the prosperity of the new town cannot fail to strike its visitor then, as compared with the stagnation and dreariness that once pervaded its stricken shores.

Let us also hope that even the Resthouse will receive its share of the new broom, and that a more commodious and up-to-date structure, fitted with all modern conveniences and ideas of comfort, will grace the view of the visitor, and that its situation will not itself call for any more criticism. The Resthouse should be on a site where one can get the benefit of the cool, refreshing sea breeze, and feel that he is really by the seaside, not stuck up in some hole in a tumbledown, ramshackle, old building with rickety beds in low, stifling rooms, whose very ceilings, bare and uncovered, make him feel that at any moment he would receive the unwelcome, clammy attentions of some rat, snake, or lizard through the hundred-holed mosquito nets, or what once passed for such.

CHAPTER XXVIII

A MOTOR TRIP ACROSS CEYLON

Part II—Anuradhapura and Puttalam

We were up betimes the next morning to get along on our way, or rather the Hon. Mr. Abdul Rahiman and Mohammed, for I did not get a wink of sleep that night, but kept counting the minutes and waiting for the first streak of dawn to get up and dress without disturbing the other visitors. After a fair breakfast we resume our journey.

We pause for a short while at some hot-water wells near Trincomalee, which are reputed to be of wonderful curative powers for rheumatism, gout, and kindred diseases. If such were the case, as many assured me, it is a pity that here again was a fine opportunity thrown away, and great possibilities allowed to languish, instead of being supported.

It is not only the poor who suffer from such ailments, but it is the rich who, as a rule, are the more afflicted with these maladies owing to their easy life and inaction; but whereas the poor, impelled by necessity, do not mind bathing in the open, pouring a few buckets of the precious fluid over themselves, and are thus the gainers by the process, so hard and fast are the rules of convention that no person with pretensions to the ranks of gentility could decently expect to strip out in the open before the gaze of all and sundry. And the result is that with such an effective remedy so near at hand, and this so cheap, a suffering mankind has, nevertheless, to put up with its ills because the dictates of convention, and the lack of sufficient enterprise of an otherwise paternal Government will not seek to extract the fullest benefit from these wells.

Perhaps in the happier days to come, when Trincomalee is blessed with an enterprising corporation or municipality, then might she tackle this problem with full energy, and see to these springs being fitted with suitable bathing accommodation to suit every taste and purse, and who knows, another Helwan-les-Bains, with its thermal establishment, might perhaps blossom forth near the banks of the Mahawila Ganga, even as its counterpart here, near Cairo, has proved such a blessing to mankind.

. . . . .

After these wells the road again acquires, for the most part, the aspect of the last stages between Kanthalai and Trincomalee, but now it is over flat ground that we travel. Even as we approach Anuradhapura the very fields and meadows look like an Egyptian countryside, minus the villages, and for the first time I see maize and millet. Cattle are even more in evidence, and there is more life about, and one begins to appreciate Ceylon's boast of once being a rich grain-producing country of the East, even as Egypt was the granary of the Roman Empire.

But one asks why, if in bygone ages such wide tracts were given over to agriculture, and irrigation works of the first order existed—as witness the remains of the Great Tanks—why indeed could not the present age, with its all vaunted boast of a superior civilisation, step into the breach? If the tanks cannot be renovated or improved in a way to fulfil anew their former functions, other means certainly can be devised. But, above all, let us hear less of the rice problem and hungry stomachs, and unemployment, and more of agriculture; then might Ceylon find an outlet for her idle hands, and solve one of the crying needs of her people, nor could an ungenerous India impose its imperious will on a neighbouring land.

. . . . .

A few more miles and Anuradhapura comes in sight. The fact that we were on the sight of Ceylon's ancient capital is not without its significance, and even as one gazes in wonderment on these remains of a civilisation that once flourished, how forcibly does one realise the vanity and transitoriness of all earthly things, though one cannot at the same time help admiring the grandeur of Lanka's great past.

Was this really the city of the King's Pleasure Garden of Mahagama of twenty square miles in extent? And those pillars there, 1,600 monoliths in all, as if they were another Stonehenge, were they the sole remnants of the once wonderful Brazen Palace—worthy counterpart of Amenemhat's Labyrinth of my own land—towering nine stories aloft, each with a hundred apartments, and all resplendent with the gems, gold, silver, and ivory with which it sparkled, the very roof glittering with the brazen tiles which gave it its name? And Ruanweli, mighty Dagaba of the past, towering 270 feet upwards, or Mihintalé, the birth-place of Buddhism in Ceylon, imposing in its solitude, yet wondrous as ever with the 1,840 granite steps leading from its base to its summit, a thousand feet further up, what stranger could not be impressed by their majesty? And how many another monument here claims our admiration!

. . . . .

At Anuradhapura one does feel the warmth, but it is to some extent like the dry heat of Egypt—at any rate so it seemed to me at the time of our visit—and not so much affected by the humidity of the air, as in Colombo, else the weather, already sultry enough, and that in a comparatively rather arid region, would have been well-nigh

THE EGYPTIAN EXILES IN CEYLON

From " Ceylon Illustrated " (Colombo : The *Ceylon Observer* Office). *By courtesy of the Author, Mr. J. M. Ferguson, and the " Ceylon Observer "*

Facing-page 224]

[By courtesy of Mr. H. F. Macmillan

TAPPING RUBBER

Facing page 225]

intolerable. As a matter of fact the butter at the hotel was so much liquid *ghee* more than real appetising butter which could be spread on the bread; but then, the hotel was not to blame, but the weather, for the butter would actually be brought nicely set in its dish, but it would hardly be placed on the table for a few moments ere, before you were aware of its presence, it melted!

The hotel here we found quite handy and neat, especially its verandah where palms, ferns, and hanging plants were tastefully arranged in a manner that augmented its daintiness, and served as a cooling and soothing set-off to the enervating atmosphere around. Indeed, as if true to its traditions of old-world sanctity and the life of a forgotten age, Anuradhapura did not seem to have yet felt the need of electricity, for here we renewed our former associations with the familiar punkah of another day. Yes, it did raise some semblance of a breeze, but of course it was no match for the more efficient electric fan; and the slight breeze that wafted overhead fluctuated according as the dutiful little lad—who, for all we know, might have been another Fat Boy of the genus immortalised by Dickens—energetically pulled the punkah to and fro, or relaxed his tug, according as he was wide awake or was lulled to dozing by the spell of the warm air.

. . . . .

Nor did our visit to this historic city pass off without its comic side. One of the living institutions of Ceylon's former capital is a well-known Moor guide, whose services had been utilised by Royalty on several occasions, as he proved by certain newspaper cuttings in his possession he guarded most jealously. I cannot remember his name now, but he was practically certain to be snapped by the sightseer, so familiar was he in the locality—or was it he who as often as not "bagged" the hardy visitor?

Ah, if recitation at school could have been by proxy, here was the man for the job! No more would we have had to put up with the tongue-twisting, ear-splitting, nerve-racking *Lotos-Eaters* of Tennyson, such a stumbling block to so many, as it was at " Rep. " time such an excuse for malingering, that even Mr. E. G. Finch, our Master of English at Khedivieh, so patient and unsuspecting at first, ultimately saw through the subterfuge, and had as a consequence to treat defaulters to double doses of *Lotos-Eaters* in detention! But this by the way.

To return to our learned guide.

" The Brazen Palace, one of the wonders of the world, was originally of 1,600 pillars, and . . ."

But, stop! No, he won't! You may interrupt; you may raise your voice; you may shout; you well-nigh clap your hand over his mouth, but still he is mumbling, chattering! He cannot help it: habit is second nature. He has repeated this story hundreds, perhaps thousands of times; even in his sleep he might be muttering it, for all we know. He will not stop till he has got to the end of his reel, else he will lose the thread of his tale and have to begin all over again.

To another of the ruins he takes us.

"This Temple," he resumes, "was the place from which the priests used to fly to Colombo, and . . ."

But, stop! stop! I actually make him do so with a jerk, for he cannot have his way always. Here was a revelation; something wonderful, almost incredible! Flying in the ancient times! Who had heard of it! Come! come! Zaky Pasha,[1] you have bargained without your host, and for once we have caught you napping! Oh, shades of Ibn Firnas and El-Gowhari, Oh, Mouillard, how you must roll in your graves!

Was our friend the guide really pulling our legs, or was it that the West, and we into the bargain—for did not the celebrated Khedive Ismail most aptly say on the

[1] Ahmed Zaky Pasha, a well-known historian and scholar, on noting that a memorial was being raised to Mouillard—a French pioneer of aviation—at Heliopolis, near Cairo, proves that Ibn Firnas and El-Gowhari, two Arabs who flourished centuries ago, were the real precursors of flying, and thus has their names likewise inscribed on the memorial which stands as a monument to the genius of Mouillard.

occasion of the opening of the Suez Canal: " My country is no longer in Africa, we form part of Europe "?—in self-satisfied complacency thinks how backward and steeped in ignorance the East is, even the latter's boast of its superiority of a former age paling by the side of the Occident's present-day ascendancy, and thus limiting its perspective of the Orient as far as the Suez Canal, and ignoring the well-known platitude that there is nothing new under the sun, suddenly awakes to the shock of an inventive genius farther beyond, which gives the lie to its own vaunted superiority?

Anyhow, I, for one, falling under the spell of this pretension of the West felt inclined at first to ridicule such a claim.

" But how did they fly? "

Reply: silence. Probably the guide is unnerved and flabbergasted by such a poser.

" Was it by balloon or aeroplane? " I add somewhat amused, and with a view to making him resume his entertaining talk.

" I don't know," he meekly answers.

" But then, you said they used to fly? "

" I was told that."

" Oh, well, in any case I hope next time you will be able to give us fuller information."

Later on I was told that the man was only too truly recounting an historical fact, as the chronicles record that the priests did actually improvise some device to alight from the top of the temple on to the ground as if they were flying in a sense, but how this escaped the attention of the Western scientists I cannot understand. Perhaps the great distance of Ceylon from Europe and America accounts for its being so little known archæologically, and its buried treasures and ruins still waiting for another Champollion or Mariette or Flinders Petrie or Belzoni to unearth them and reveal their hidden secrets and wonders to the world.

. . . . .

To us Egyptians, with our unrivalled monuments dating back to over seven thousand years, those of Ceylon at Anuradhapura, Pollannaruwa, and elsewhere in the Island with 2,500 years to their credit may not, on the face of it, appeal so forcibly to our imagination from the point of antiquity. But even then they are not without their merits and noteworthy features, and in some respects they even surpass ours. Thus, where in the world can we come across the equal of those wonderful irrigation works of Ceylon's buried past? If only the same care and attention were lavished upon its remains as are usually devoted to ours and those of other climes, what untold wonders might not Ceylon reveal?

Again, in one other way can Ceylon boast of a quite unique distinction. In this once mighty city of palaces stands the oldest specimen of the tree world, for in her venerable, sacred Bo-Tree Anuradhapura glories in the shrivelled, decrepit, age-eaten stem of a once mighty overspreading giant that has stood the test of 2,200 years, and still defies Time. Yes, here also, as in my own country, can we aptly apply the familiar saying, "Man fears Time, but Time fears the Pyramids." Can we then wonder if the Sinhalese regard it with such awe and veneration, this tree which has sprung from the branch of that beneath which rested their lord Buddha, and have it carefully and jealously fenced in, the one solitary branch of the stem still extant, if I am not mistaken, being even adorned with a gold band round it as if it were a gold bangle round the shapely and pretty arm of some beautiful lady.

So sacred indeed is this tree that no one dare pluck a leaf off it, and happy is he who has the good fortune to bear away as mementos one or two of these precious leaves which will have fallen on the ground of their own accord inside the enclosure. The attendant there very courteously gave me two of these precious leaves which I carefully cherish now as a valuable and welcome souvenir.

In Egypt, it is true, at Matarieh, about seven miles to the north of Cairo, we have the sacred sycamore tree beneath which tradition says the Holy Family rested in their flight into Egypt. But then this tree is not so old as that of Ceylon; besides, unlike the Bo-Tree of Anuradhapura, which has existed these 2,200 years past in one unbroken line, that of Matarieh is not the original tree alluded to, but another which was planted later on in its place when the parent tree had died.

. . . . .

To give a detailed description of the wonderful ruins that now lie scattered and forlorn about Anuradhapura does not fall within the scope of this little volume. Not that this is no proper place for them, but the fact is that there are others who have done so quite adequately and in a most illuminating manner, as Cave in his *The Ruined Cities of Ceylon*, or Mr. John Still in his *Guide to the Ancient Capitals of Ceylon*. Besides, our visit to them was very brief, and practically in the nature of a cursory review of them in a manner which smattered of American hustling, rather than a leisurely scrutiny and examination of each in turn, so determined were we to get away in good time to reach Colombo by nightfall. We had been so fed up with our experiences of the previous night at the Trincomalee Resthouse that we did not now wish to risk a second.

But not even the shortest of visits to Ceylon's former capital can fail to leave a deep and lasting impression on one's mind of the vista that lies spread before us. Gone is Anuradhapura, city of palaces, gone its glories and its grandeur. Vanished is its kingly line that built these mighty and stupendous works, vanished the Court that echoed to the sound of music and revelry. Its pillars tottering to their fall—mere shadows of their pristine greatness—are now the sole vestiges of the Anuradhapura that once was, and the city that once throbbed and rejoiced with prosperity now lies buried beneath the overspreading jungle. Now will even the wild beast spare the sanctity of its quondam greatness, but must needs with brazen effrontery pollute the very pools that royalty once graced.

Anuradhapura, farewell! In ruins you may be, but on these very ruins in clear, indelible characters is thy glorious history writ, and thy grandeur carved. Rest majestic amidst thy solitude, awe-inspiring and imposing in thy desolation, and in thy splendour of another age may thy sons of this day seek inspiration for the future, and with the help of a benign Government achieve anew the glory that once was.

. . . . .

From Anuradhapura we went on to Puttalam, tearing away for all we were worth, and reaching it late in the afternoon. Even before arriving there we could feel the soft, cool touch of the zephyrs of the Western coast, and a welcome change it proved from the enervating heat we had just left behind. Under ordinary circumstances we should have spent the night at Puttalam, but, as I have already said, we had planned otherwise.

A hasty tea we had there at the Resthouse which, unlike its counterpart on the Eastern coast, was here suitably situated to receive the full force of the soothing sea breezes of the Indian Ocean. As a matter of fact the Resthouse did not actually overlook the ocean, but abutted on the famous lagoon, with many of which Ceylon abounds in these parts, even as the northern littoral of Egypt is studded with them. But to the inexperienced eye, or rather to the person who is not conversant with the geography of the locality, it looked like some expansive landlocked inlet of the sea.

To us the significance of this place lay in that after proceeding northwards from Kandy to Trincomalee for 111 miles, we had now motored right across the Island from east to west another 111 miles from Trincomalee on to Puttalam. True, this was not the broadest part of the Island, which is said to be about 140 miles at its widest, but still it was to us sentimentally a quite noteworthy feature of our trip.

At Puttalam as I gazed far out into the waters I bethought myself of those pearl fisheries, somewhere about these regions, for which Ceylon is noted, that even on the stage they have come to live in the haunting melodies of Bizet's charming opera *I Pescatori di Perle*, and the once popular musical play of our day, *The Cingalee*, one of the lines of which ran:

" Beyond the bar of far Mannar the diver seeks for—Pearls."

. . . . .

From Puttalam, late in the afternoon, we now started on the last stage of our homeward journey, another ninety miles to the south. The route now lay parallel to the coast line, and as we dashed along, we went past many of the coconut plantations in which the districts of Chilaw and Negombo are so rich. A noteworthy feature also of the road was the carts or vans laden with returning parties of pilgrims, homeward bound after visiting the distant fair or shrine of some saint.

As we pass through Chilaw I think of one of Kingswood's most loyal and distinguished sons, Major S. Guy Sansoni, who was one of the " lions " of the school in my time, and now a leading light of the local Bar, and but for the fact that it was night, I would certainly have paid him a surprise call.

And when all seemed to be going well and events pointed to our reaching Colombo rather early in the night, what was our mortification when there at Negombo, just at the gates of Colombo as it were, our *Opel* car, which had faithfully borne us over all these miles, and stood the strain of two days' incessant travelling without a hitch, should now give way, and most disappointingly suffer a breakdown in its gear. But the chauffeur cleverly comes to our rescue; and though at one time it looked as if we should have to spend the night there, ultimately, thanks to his efforts and skill, we resume our journey, after losing over an hour by this unforeseen breakdown.

At the time it was to the old Resthouse that we went, for the fine new building had not as yet been commissioned for the service of the public, and right glad was I that we did not have to spend the night there, for the building was a quite unprepossessing one, and for all we know it might have been a faithful replica of that of Trincomalee.

One noticeable feature of Negombo's Resthouse however was that it overlooked a canal, and under ordinary circumstances there would not have been anything strange about this but for the fact that its very rarity made it not a little interesting in these quarters, even as the gardeners in Peradeniya had once pointed out a pair of date palms to me during one of my visits (little knowing where I came from) as some great curiosity of the horticultural world.

At last, close upon midnight, we reach Colombo, after one of the most enjoyable excursions of my life; and what a sigh of relief I give that I could thus be able to spend a comfortable night in my sanctum at the good G.O.H., a second home as it had grown to become to me.

. . . . .

Over 300 miles we had covered, and as interesting a trip as one could wish for, we had the ineffable pleasure of having had. We opened with the lovely Kandyan Highlands of the Matalé district; passed through virgin forest and one of Ceylon's big game preserves; saw some of the greatest engineering works of bygone ages; called at one of the world's finest harbours; visited Ceylon's ancient capital and its great ruins; and finished along the western coast amidst the lowlands of Ceylon and the waving fronds of her invaluable coconut. And this by the best of all means of locomotion, the motor car, and through a diversity of rustic scenes, interesting districts, and quaint sights such as do not fall to every traveller;

[*By courtesy of Mr. E. G. Jonklaas*

THE BEAUTIFULLY WOODED MAHAWILA GANGA AT GAMPOLA

[Photo by the Author

ADAM'S PEAK—FROM ADAM'S PEAK HOTEL, HATTON

Facing page 233]

and above all, in the company of as kind, as good, and as generous a friend as one could have, as the Honble. Mr. Abdul Rahiman. Can I, therefore, conclude this chapter without thanking him again most cordially? Certainly not.

CHAPTER XXIX

MY LAST DAYS IN CEYLON

My last days in Ceylon were fast drawing to a close. There is an end to everything, and even a pleasant holiday must enter on its last phase. With what sadness, therefore, does one often have to ring down the curtain on the last act of some delightful event.

My last days were, for the greater part, taken up with concluding the purchases of things I was taking to Egypt, and in rounding up friends and paying them farewell calls. But one thing in particular they appropriately closed with, a veritable climax to an already most delightful trip. The "Kingswood Week," which was one of the main inducements that took me to Ceylon, now wound up my tour in fitting fashion, and immensely as I enjoyed it, as it supplied me with the pleasantest of recollections to dwell upon for the rest of my life, still it was with no little poignant regret that I could find it in me to tear myself away from such pleasing haunts and such joyful and sweet remembrances.

. . . . .

On the afternoon of the 27th of August, soon after my return to Colombo from my motor trip across the Island, as I was having tea at the G.O.H., a telegram is handed to me. I open it with some trepidation, for telegrams occasionally seem to have something uncanny about them;

but what a delightful surprise it sprang upon me when I read the joyful news:

> "Won Hermann Loos,
> Gentlemen of Kingswood."

And so they had done it gallantly! Individually several did not seem to have much hope of lifting the Cup; but by concerted action, and a stupendous effort, they had all pulled together, and pulled to victory. All the more credit to them; and happy indeed must their sergeant, T. B. Herath, have been, that he had so successfully capped his academic career in gaining the "blue ribbon" of Kingswood, the Dornhorst prize, the previous year, by now winning in the field of sport as well.

The tea, of course, I leave unfinished, and fly to the telegraph office, and reply with a message of congratulation worthy of Kingswood's achievement.

For the third year in succession they had won the Cup, and the fourth out of the five it was competed for since its inception. Unfortunately, contrary to all expectations, and the rules generally in vogue in such instances, which stipulate that when a challenge cup or trophy is won three times outright, it passes into the permanent possession of the winning school or club, this was not the case in regard to the Hermann Loos Cup. But it is still not too late to remedy such a lacuna, by providing for a replica of it in miniature, which the winning school every year, or, at any rate, that which has won it three years consecutively might retain permanently as a memento of past triumphs.

I might add that the Kingswood contingent had kindly invited me to accompany them to camp at Diyatalawa, but much as I should have liked to avail myself of this kind invitation, I declined owing to my being afraid that I might be in the way of their activities to some extent.

. . . . .

During my stay in Kandy, few as were the old friends I could still find there, it was no less pleasing to renew our former ties; and I was particularly glad to meet my good friends and old school-fellows Mr. V. J. Claude Jonklaas, who had since taken to the surveying and levelling line, and Captain Percy W. Van Langenberg, a well-known member of the Kandy Bar, who both kindly looked me up at the Queen's Hotel.

But not only in old friends was I blessed, but the making of the acquaintance of new friends proved no less welcome. Thus, thanks to Mr. J. S. Perera, of Colombo, who kindly invited me to his house, I was afforded an opportunity of meeting his family, including his venerable mother, and his esteemed brother-in-law, Mr. Donald Obeysekera, and a real treat the afternoon proved.

This gentleman, a member of one of the foremost families of Ceylon, had received an education in keeping with his leading position socially, for it was to Trinity College, Cambridge, that he went and eventually graduated from, returning to Ceylon to join the Bar. His home "Rajagiriya" on the Cotta Road, just beyond Borella, on the outskirts of Colombo, was also a remarkable residence. It was as if it were in town, and yet at the same time like some grand country seat. Standing in grounds nearly fifty acres in extent, all carefully walled and fenced in, or rather in a thickly wooded park, it was something like the old ancestral manor of some English peer standing in its own domains; and here in this proud home of his Mr. Donald Obeysekera dispensed hospitality in a manner worthy of the finest traditions of his race.

In one respect we seem to have met on common ground. From what I had previously gathered from the papers and hearsay, I had learnt that he was an authority on poultry, a subject in which I also was keenly interested, and the fine specimens he had, especially of Indian game and turkeys, amply bore out such reports. How I wish I could have also come across some fine varieties of Orpingtons, or Wyandottes, or Plymouth

Photo by] [*Platé, Ltd., Colombo.*

The Perahera—showing the Maligawa Elephant bearing aloft the Holy Relic.

p. 236

Rocks, or what I have a greater fancy to, namely Brahmas and Cochins.

To Mr. Obeysekera I was also indebted in visiting my old home up the hills in Kandy, " Arthur Seat ", which belonged to his mother, Mrs. J. P. Obeysekera, a charming lady who invited me to tea there, and thus enabled me to renew my associations with the beautiful home where I had spent so many happy moments of my golden boyhood.

There it lay, the old portico, from which my parents and myself used so often to gaze on the lovely lake below and the beautiful landscape around, and what a delight it gave me to stand there again and gaze once more on the sights of my childhood, as I had longed for these many years past. Little did I dream, as often, when passing by this road, I used to gaze wistfully upwards at this fine residence and its incomparable site, and yearn to stand beneath its portico once more, that Fortune would smile on me so soon. But Fortune when she gives, gives with both hands, and a kindly Providence that can reach the innermost recesses of one's heart and mind must have heard my yearning, and as generously granted it.

Here, at this portico also, when I came, I found Lady Manning seated with Mrs. Obeysekera, and to Her Excellency I had the honour of being presented by the genial hostess, and though it was for only a few minutes that I had the pleasure of being in the presence of H.E. the Governor's Consort, I was pleased to have had the good fortune.

On the eve of my departure from Ceylon, thanks to Mr. W. T. Samaraweera, I am invited with him to have tea at " Siriwinesa ", the fine residence of Mr. and Mrs. L. W. A. De Soysa, in the Cinnamon Gardens, and it caused me no little pleasure to make a closer acquaintance with this distinguished Ceylonese family, as I had got to know another member in the person of Mr. R. E. S. De Soysa on the Havelock Racecourse through Dr. C. W. van Geyzel. To this well-known family stands the distinction of having the only statue raised in Ceylon to one of its sons in the person of their head, the late Mr. C. H. De Soysa, the great financial magnate and philanthropist.

. . . . .

Now that my departure was impending, as I was so eager to meet the Diacono family at Nuwara Eliya on my arrival, I could not now afford to leave Ceylon without bidding farewell to them—the more so that they had more than justified my highest expectations, and proved just as warm-hearted on this visit as they always proved throughout the years of our lifelong friendship. To this beautiful mountain resort accordingly I pay a flying visit, and right joyous I was to be thus able to see it once more ere I left, and say good-bye to its well-merited loveliness.

There at Nuwara Eliya I meet Mrs. W. F. Diacono, her eldest daughter Mrs. C. W. H. Duckworth, and her son Mr. Ezio Diacono, a budding flying officer who had just missed winning his spurs owing to the abrupt termination of the Great War, the other members of the family being in Colombo and elsewhere in the Island. By a happy coincidence, Mrs. I. M. Del Tufo, who has a fine studio at Colpetty, Colombo, happens to be there at Maryhill Hotel on a friendly visit, and through her courtesy, on the spur of the moment we have a fine group photo of us all taken together, and I thus succeed in having one of the very few snapshots of my visit to Ceylon during this trip, as I incidentally have the pleasure of making the acquaintance of such an esteemed lady as Mrs. Del Tufo.

From Nuwara Eliya I come down to Kandy on the 15th of September for " Kingswood Week ", which was to start on the following day with the prize distribution, but I think it only appropriate in the nature of things to allot a section by itself to this most important event in the life of all Kingswoodians, and the next two chapters accordingly I devote to this theme. Though they may not perhaps appeal so strongly to the general run of my readers as they will to Kingswoodians, still I have included them on the strength that they may afford some insight to people of other lands of what a rising public school and its spirit in distant Ceylon looks like.

CHAPTER XXX

"KINGSWOOD WEEK"

Part I—Through the Eyes of an Old Kingswoodian

"Kingswood Week" was timed to open on the morning of Friday, the 16th of September, with the cricket match between the Old Boys and the Present Boys; and aware as I was that my time would be practically all taken up with the next two eventful days, I decided to make use of the intervening period to attend to the last few courtesies so necessary on such occasions in view of my near departure, and also to visit once again for the last time, ere I left, the loved haunts of my happy boyhood.

Bright and sunny dawns the morning of the 15th, and up the lovely Kandyan Hills I motor for the last time—of this trip only, let me hope, but not for ever. To me, who was leaving so shortly, they appeared more beautiful than ever; and ah! the sadness, the intense grief with which I parted from them. Yes, there is always a certain deep poignancy in the last of anything, for in the very term lies, as it were, the sense of finality from which perhaps there is no return or escape. But still, O God Almighty, grant, as Thou hast stood by me so often throughout the years, that once again in my prime I may yet live to see these haunts and scenes which have gladdened my heart as nothing has done for many a long day.

On Mr. C. Drieberg I call, "Edge Hill", Peradeniya, to say goodbye, and personally thank again for all his

[Photo by the Author

THE ST. CLAIR FALLS

Facing page 240]

[Photo by the Author

THE DEVON FALLS

Facing page 241]

kindness. I call immediately after on Mr. H. F. Macmillan at the ever-beautiful Peradeniya Gardens for the same purpose, and to make the final arrangements for the safe despatch to Colombo for shipment, of the grand assortment of fruit trees and palms he had so kindly seen to personally and procured for me. On each of my other friends I call in turn, finally going in the evening to tea at Mrs. J. P. Obeysekera's charming residence " Arthur Seat ".

. . . . .

With the morning of the 16th of September opens " Kingswood Week ", which has always figured as one of the important annual events of Kandy—an event enhanced in interest by the personality of its noted and popular Principal, Mr. Blazé, and by its annual prologue at the prize distribution. One has but to observe how eagerly everyone looks forward to this clever epitome in verse of the year's most notable events to realise how inseparable an institution of Kingswood prize-givings the prologue has grown to be.

The cricket match between the Old 'Uns and the School ushers in the " Week ", and to Bogambara Recreation Ground[1] accordingly I repair rather late, after having been detained for some time by the presence of Seyyid Talib Pasha, who had kindly called to repay my visit of the previous day when I went to see him to say goodbye ere I left. On reaching the playfield I was told that a place had been reserved for me in the Old Boys' Eleven. Yes, some of the youngsters seemed eager to see how this Egyptian shaped at the game of King Willow, and whether he was good for a " century ", like another " Ranji ", or, well—a " duck "!

[1] Curiously, the Bogambara Ground seems as if it felt that it could not find it in its heart to depart from the general somnolence of the town to which it has the honour of belonging! For, there, I found still extant that same old, ugly, wretched, ramshackle shed that grandiosely parades for a Grand Stand or Pavilion; and a greater eyesore, a veritable disgrace, to an otherwise most beautifully set playfield I have never come across! The wonder is that throughout all these twenty-four years no one should have had the enterprise or courage to press for a really decent and more worthy substitute, which could be a real ornament to this lovely playground!

As a matter of fact, I hadn't handled a cricket bat for the last twenty-four years, nor had I ever laid claim to any proficiency in this game, it being "soccer" that I usually played during my school days in Egypt, cricket being non-existent in the Government schools, except for a brief spell when it was played at Khedivieh during the season 1899–1900. So, there was no question of my being able to join in the show, and thus whet the appetite of my eager onlookers, as I told Mr. Claud Jonklaas, who skippered the Old 'Uns—unless, of course, this match was going to serve as another Dingley Dell of Pickwickian fame!

The guests proved too strong for the school. Mr. M. K. Brantha, a rising police inspector, and one of the finest all-round sportsmen of Ceylon, proved the batting mainstay of his side, mercilessly trouncing the bowling of his quondam comrades, and another Old 'Un in the person of Mr. T. C. De Sylva, in his turn played havoc with the homesters, and like another "Razor" Smith of Surrey fame, kept simply "shaving" off the school, when the youngsters, failing hopelessly with the ball against Jonklaas, Brantha and company, tried to retrieve their position by a futile stand with the bat.

. . . . .

In the afternoon the prize distribution is held at the Town Hall, with the Rev. F. H. de Winton, M.A., Archdeacon of Colombo, in the chair; and curiously it takes place in the very room I attended twenty-four years ago, on October 17th, 1897, but in a different capacity. Then it was as a pupil of the school that I repaired to the Town Hall, and mixed amongst the audience; to-day it was as an Old Kingswoodian that I had the honour of being on the platform. Mr. Blazé had requested me to make a speech, and as I said in my opening words: (. . . To an old Head Master we still always owe a certain degree of duty and obedience, even as loyalty is due to Country, King, and School). To his desire, therefore, I could not but agree. And, as at Kingswood I received my first education, it was at a Kingswood Prize-Giving that I now delivered my first address in a public hall before a large and distinguished audience. And so once again the long arm of coincidence had stepped in.

At the close of the day's proceedings I had the honour of being presented to both Sir Anton and Lady Bertram by Mr. Blazé; as also to the venerable chairman; the Rev. J. Eagle—the manager of the school—and several other ladies and gentlemen; and it was very gratifying to me to observe the evident pleasure they evinced at meeting me. Perhaps it was this kindly disposition on the part of the audience that helped me in my task of delivering my speech, and thus spared me the embarrassment of stage-fright.

But this prize-giving was not without its funny sequel, though the aftermath took place in Egypt, not in Ceylon. On my return home, the *Egyptian Gazette*, the leading English paper in Egypt, kindly published a small item anent my visit to Ceylon, alluding *inter alia* to the fact of my having given a small scholarship to my old school, Kingswood. What was my amazement some time later when my friend Mohammed Ahmed Gad El-Moula Bey showed me a newspaper cutting from one of the Arabic "dailies", wherein the *Egyptian Gazette's* item was translated, and I was described as "having created at Kingswood College a section for the instruction of navigation" (*sic*)—meaning the scholarship!

Here indeed was a "howler", and a quite original one too; and not from a schoolboy, but from a dignified paper, with a translator purporting to have a fairly good knowledge of both the Arabic and English languages! And so the Kingswood prize-giving unwittingly supplied its share of the light side, and added yet another "howler" to the many that have brought joy to so many hearts.

. . . . .

The sports at Bogambara on the afternoon of the 17th were indeed most enjoyable. What a delight it must have been for Old Boys from far and near, long separated perhaps from one another, to assemble here again where they had met so often in the past. And a jolly reunion is this, a gathering of the Old Boys—and as gay as the "gathering of the Clans", as the Ceylon planters so lightheartedly word their annual reunion—and how all must delight to revive anew those boyish pranks and naughty escapades of their giddy and mischievous youth. Even the gravest and most staid of individuals must relax on such an occasion as this, even as the trammels of convention and make-believe must as often as not go by the board.

Now is the moment of gaiety and pleasure, and all must eagerly enter into the spirit of fun; they cannot help it; they are borne right in the maelstrom of amusement that sweeps, carrying them along, and high jinks is the order of the hour. But if, with all this, there still be the inevitable cynic or ineffable bore, why, he had better have kept away, or rather betaken himself to some wilderness, for the humming, buzzing, gay world is no place for him! After all, we are hardly better than grown-up children in a sense. Maturer years may bring a more balanced judgment, and a more responsible outlook may impart a certain gravity of demeanour. But once open the floodgates of amusement and rollicking fun, once let loose the pent-up passions of a careworn, hard, and bitter life, and we are only too glad and ready to find an outlet for them as boisterously and playfully as any child, in our search for relief from the heavy strain and manifold conventions of a strenuous age.

To me in particular the sports appealed in an even more irresistible manner, handicapped as I was by my distant home, and thus not in a position to undertake the annual trek to the "Kingswood Week", as those who were more closely and favourably placed. How exceedingly glad did I feel indeed not only to meet once more several of my former associates and schoolfellows, but also to make the acquaintance of several other Old Kingswoodians who attended school after my time.

The staff of the school also I came to closer quarters with on these occasions, and got to be on more intimate terms with; and it gave me particular pleasure to meet once more my old friend and classmate, Mr. Edwin Boulton, and together talk over old times. But in lavishing praise on Mr. Blazé one must not forget to accord due credit to his faithful coadjutors, who so ably supported him in his onerous duties. Kingswood certainly owes a great deal to her Headmaster; but he alone could not have stood the strain of his heavy burden, and succeeded so splendidly were he not loyally and dutifully backed by the efficient staff which he, with rare perspicacity and discrimination, had succeeded in selecting in the best interests of the school. That they all together should have combined and co-operated to raise Kingswood to the proud pedestal she now stands upon, cannot but reflect the greatest credit on all concerned.

. . . . .

On the present occasion I reaped the benefit of a rather pleasant surprise. During the afternoon Mr. Blazé kindly introduced me to one of the leading members of society in Kandy, Mrs. Martin M. Smith, and on hearing that I came from Egypt, she naturally expressed a desire to know whether I happened to be acquainted with a cousin of hers in my country, called Mr. Furness, who was said to be the Headmaster of some big school in Cairo. Here indeed was a coincidence, for in him I at once gladly recognised Mr. J. M. Furness, the Principal of Khedivieh, my other old school in Cairo! She in turn was highly delighted to find so unexpectedly that I was an Old Boy of his school. On my return to Cairo, therefore, when I spoke of Mrs. Martin Smith to Mr. Furness, how pleased he was, and not a little amused that circumstances had so conspired to make me a connecting link between him and a relative of his in a distant land, with whom he had lost touch for some time past.

. . . . .

The eventful day's proceedings were wound up by an equally welcome finale in the night, and to the Kingswood concert, held in its own hall in the nature of a quite homely affair, I had the additional pleasure of going. Quite enjoyable a function did this entertainment prove as that of the afternoon, and the high talent displayed all round by those who generously volunteered a part in the show reflects the highest credit on all who participated in it—not the least on that facetious and enterprising Mr. Somebody who helped to get the encores with a quite serviceable horn, and who might have made a very good *claqueur* at some Paris theatre.

In particular I was highly gratified by the unforeseen compliment paid my country by the gentleman who so kindly introduced a pretty song wherein " Cairo " predominated—C-a-i-r-o in a long, sing-song drawl, and even as I write these lines the echoes of those pleasant strains and the generous nature of that courteous gentleman who paid me such a handsome compliment now ring in my ears, as also the generous rôle of the gentlemen who formed the Nigger Troupe, amongst whom I could unmistakably spot the versatile and ever-jolly Charlie De Sylva, who in turn also would not omit to extend to me their greeting. No wonder that Kingswoodians cannot help being loyal to their *alma mater* when she greets them so warmly and hospitably in later years, as she watched over them with such paternal solicitude in the green days of their youth, and follows their doings so scrupulously even after they have left the school.

Another pleasing feature of the concert was the renewal of a link with a gentleman once closely connected with Kingswood. In Miss Dorothy Martinus, the daughter of Mr. O. E. Martinus, who was second master of the school in my time, the past seemed to live once more in the present; and her charming rendering on the violin of Mascagni's ever-popular *Intermezzo* from his opera *Cavalleria Rusticana* came as a real treat, indeed, in a land already poorly catered for in the shape of music. Perhaps, who knows? In the years to come on a future visit it may be the equally exquisite *Meditation* of Massenet's *Thais* that may grace the school's concert, and it is by this talented young lady again that we should most certainly like to hear it played.

At last even the pleasant concert ends, and I say good-bye to all present, and to the school and its hall for the last time—I say last time with reason, for when I go next it is probably to a newer and grander edifice in another locality that I shall proceed.

It is sad to break with the past, and part with old associations, especially when they are surrounded with such fond old memories as a school usually creates. But the march of events shows no mercy even to the sanctity of such buildings, even as the exigencies of a growing school, especially when it had not been thoughtfully provided for beforehand against any such future contingencies, impel such change. Sad as it must be therefore for Kingswood to remove to another place and be accommodated in other, though more convenient, premises, still she cannot help yielding to the demands of her position, and the ever-increasing claims of modern education, if only to maintain her place as one of the leading scholastic institutions of the Island.

After all, it is the right spirit and healthy tone of a school that gives to any institution the halo and brilliance of success, and the dignity and glamour of a worthy school. And if Kingswoodians have hitherto succeeded in carrying on so splendidly, and in abiding so nobly by the proud traditions of their school, let us hope that in like manner the present and future generations of all Kingswoodians, and all those associated with the school, will faithfully and loyally live up to such lofty ideals, and continue to make their school, amidst its new surroundings, the success it has always been.

. . . . .

Much as I would have liked to have seen the " Kingswood Week " right through, still I could not help having to forgo Kingswood Sunday, and the meeting of the

Kingswood Union of Old Boys. It was with much reluctance, therefore, that I decided to leave for Colombo on the morning of Sunday, the 18th, by the first train, the P. & O. liner *Naldera*, by which I had booked my passage back, having been originally scheduled to sail on the 22nd of September, with the sailing, however, subsequently antedated to the 20th, and then again quite unexpectedly being advanced another day. I, therefore, had not much time to spare, inasmuch as the antedating of the sailing from the 22nd to the 19th had upset my plans to some extent and forced me to rush many things I had kept to the last moment.

What was my surprise on going to the station to see a large crowd of Kingswoodians, including Mr. Blazé, several masters, a good many pupils, a fair sprinkling of Old Boys, assembled to see me off. As a matter of fact, I had expected to meet one or two of my friends there; but to see them all in such force was something I had never bargained for. Need I, therefore, affirm how deeply touched I was by the display of this mark of courtesy and affection on the part of all who had assembled there at the station to say goodbye to me? And I cannot but avail myself of this opportunity to express again how profoundly and most gratefully I appreciated this manifest proof and spontaneous expression of these gentlemen's warm-hearted cordiality and generous nature towards me. May God bless them all for the right hearty manner they had welcomed me once more in their midst after all these years, as for the generous and courteous manner they had seen me off.

The train is putting up steam—sure sign that it is about to start. With everyone I shake hands, bidding farewell; but how my heart sinks with grief at the sadness of parting. In this very farewell there was the moral of our transient existence: to everything there is an end in this vain world; it is in the Hereafter that one might hope for eternal happiness.

Into the train I jump, and even as I do so the station bell goes, indicating that the train is about to start, and

[Photo by Platé, Ltd., Colombo

NANU OYA ROAD AND RAILWAY TO NUWARA ELIYA

Facing page 248]

[*Photo by Platé, Ltd., Colombo*

RAMBODDE FALLS

Facing page 249]

I am accorded that rousing send-off which will never fade from my memory. Even as the train moves I, in my turn, take up the refrain and call for three lusty cheers for good old Kingswood, with another three for her Grand Old Man ere the echoes of the former have died away.

At last the train slowly moves out towards Peradeniya, and amidst waving hands and handkerchiefs it finally steams out of the station; and even as Kandy slowly fades away behind, there in the far distance I catch one last glimpse of the tall, familiar figure of Kingswood's great Principal, as also of the fine strapping form of her true and distinguished son, Major Guy Sansoni, another Gaafar Waly,[1] as it were, so scholarly in the domain of learning, as he shone so brilliantly in the field of sport.

. . . . .

And thus closed a memorable " Kingswood Week ", and one of the happiest periods of my life. In the following chapter, my readers, especially Kingswoodians, can read for themselves a fine report of the doings of these eventful days from a leading newspaper, which I reproduce *verbatim*.

[1] Gaafar Waly, or to give him his correct title, H. E. Gaafar Waly Pasha, who in less than fifteen years has risen to Cabinet rank, even now holding a portfolio in the present Ministry, is the most distinguished of the Old Khedivians of the younger generation. One of the finest sportsmen and athletes of his day, captaining as he did one of Khedivieh's best football elevens, and figuring as a member of its winning tug-of-war teams, in scholarship also he distinguished himself, topping as he did the Secondary Certificate Examination, and graduating second from the Royal School of Law, but first of the English Section which had just been incorporated.

CHAPTER XXXI

"KINGSWOOD WEEK"

Part II—Through the Eyes of "The Ceylon Observer"

KINGSWOOD, KANDY

Last Week's Great Rally Round the Old School

"It was a glorious rally of past and present at the old and unpretentious school in Brownrigg Street last week-end. Of the former, Ali Foad Toulba Bey (of His Highness the Sultan of Egypt's Cabinet, and a son of one of the Pasha exiles to Ceylon in past years) made Kingswood Week his special mission to Kandy; another Mr. T. de Joedt arranged a visit to his native place from Tanganyika synchronise with the Kingswood rally of this year; and yet another, Mr. C. S. Vitilingam came specially from Travancore. Prominent among the other old boys present were Messrs. W. E. Barber (Crown Counsel), Major Guy Sansoni (Colombo), and St. John B. Jonklaas (Superintendent, Niriella, Nivitigalla). Then there were prominent citizens of Kandy, who are past students of Kingswood. All these conspired with the present element to make the Kingswood celebrations the huge success it was.

"The programme opened with the

CRICKET MATCH

played on Bogambara ground on the first half of Friday, the 16th, and which resulted in a win for the Old 'Uns, as follows:

OLD BOYS

1st Innings		2nd Innings	
A. D. S. Laxana, b. Cranleigh	10		
A. F. de Silva, c. de Saram, b. Baie	1		
Z. A. Ahamath, c. Christie, b. Cranleigh	6		
M. K. Brantha, c. de Saram, b. Mylvaganam	56		
T. C. de Sylva, c. Christie, b. Mylvaganam	4		
V. J. C. Jonklaas, c. K. W. D. de Soyza, b. Mylvaganam	1		
G. F. Smith, st. Perusinghe, b. Mylvaganam	21		
R. Murray, b. Baie	6		
E. Dias, not out	7		
A. S. Isaac, b. Baie	0		
T. P. S. Laxana, b. Baie ...	0		
Extras	1		
Total	113		

PRESENT BOYS

1st Innings		2nd Innings	
H. A. Perusinghe, c. and b. T. C. de Sylva	1	Z. A. Razak, c. Isaac, b. A. D. S. Laxana .	4
E. L. de Kretser, c. T. P. S. Laxana, b. Ahamath	0	E. L. Kretser, c. Jonklaas, b. T. C. de Sylva	14
G. R. Christie, st. Smith, b. Ahamath	18	H. A. Perusinghe, b. Dias	22
K. V. Mylvaganam, b. Ahamath	1	G. R. Christie, l.-b.-w., b. Dias	3

1st Innings (contd.)		2nd Innings (contd.)	
R. Cranleigh, b. T. C. de Sylva	0	K. V. Mylvaganam, c. Jonklass, b. Dias	4
K. W. D. de Soyza, b. T. C. de Sylva	1	R. Cranleigh, c. Murray b. Dias	4
S. Baie, c. T. C. de Sylva, b. Ahamath	0	K. W. D. de Soyza, l.b.w., b. T. C. de Sylva	5
F. de Saram, st. T. C. de Sylva	1	S. Baie, st. A. F. de Silva, b. T. C. de Sylva	34
T. H. Gibson, c. Ahamath, b. T. C. de Sylva	0	F. de Saram, b. T. C. de Sylva	2
Z. A. Razak, not out	4	T. H. Gibson, c. Isaac, b. Ahamath	1
A. J. Samath, c. T. C. de Sylva, b. Ahamath	0	A. J. Samath, not out	0
Extras	0	Extras	10
Total	26	Total	103

The Prize Giving

"This important function took place at the Town Hall on Friday evening the 16th. The attendance was large and representative, and the rally round their *alma mater* by the old boys was more than significant of their loyalty and attachment to the old institution and the respect they bear to its adored Principal. The Ven. F. H. de Winton, Archdeacon of Colombo, presided; and the others on the platform were:—Sir Anton and Lady Bertram, Mrs. C. S. Vaughan, Mrs. Martin M. Smith, the Rev. H. Cornish, Miss Mallett, the Rev. John Eagle, Rev. Father D. L. Hyde, Mr. J. Dunbar Jonklaas, Dr. C. de Vos, Dr. H. Ludovici, the Rev. J. Simon de Silva, the Rev. G. S. Amerasekera, the Rev. Ernest E. Taylor, Mr. C. Drieberg, Ali Foad Toulba Bey and Mr. L. E. Blazé (the Principal). The proceedings opened at 5 p.m. with an opening hymn and a prayer offered by the Rev. G. S. Amerasekera.

"The following report was next presented and read by the Principal:

"This report must begin with an expression of our gladness at the presence in the chair of the Venerable the Archdeacon of Colombo. 'I was very pleased to hear,' writes the Hon. Mr. Denham from Mauritius, 'that you had got the Archdeacon—a true and genuine Oxford man—to preside.' As an Oxford man, representing the scholarship, the culture and the sanity of outlook of which Oxford holds the secret, we specially welcome our chairman this evening; but not less do we remember the esteem and reverence in which he is held for his high position and personal worth by all classes in Ceylon, and not least in Kingswood, to which he is not altogether a stranger.

"The persistence of our manager, the Rev. John Eagle, has secured for us a definite hope—to be very soon realised—of new buildings and other urgent necessities. He has also helped us to make improved arrangements for the regular supervision of classwork, and we are grateful to him for his constant personal attention to our requirements. The establishment by the Mission of an Advisory Council of its Colleges, with a committee for Kingswood, makes a substantial advance by which we hope to profit largely. One of the first acts of our committee has been to sanction a Kindergarten class which we hope to begin next year.

"The four representatives of the Wesleyan Methodist Missionary Society who visited us last year were deeply impressed by the needs and possibilities of the school, and left with very definite views on the subject. The Rev. Mr. Goudie (whom we congratulate on his appointment as President-elect of the Weselyan Methodist Conference) has since assured us of the sympathy of the Home Committee; and I am satisfied that before the next prize-giving Kingswood will have begun to work under better conditions.

"So much for externals. In the school itself, in the things which matter most, I find no cause for undue anxiety or complaint. Our examination results, on the whole are not unsatisfactory. Our Cambridge Senior candidates failed to get through last year. In the Junior Examination three passed, one of them (Roy Keegel) with honours in Class III and a distinction in religious knowledge. Two candidates passed the Elementary School-Leaving Examination, and one (T. J. Saldin) the Government Clerical.

"Our Junior Cadets won no first places at the February sports in Colombo; at Diyatalawa, last month, for the third time in succession, and for the fourth time in five years, our Senior Cadets won the Hermann Loos Challenge Cup.

"The Dornhorst Prize is awarded this year for the twenty-fifth time; the Hill Memorial Medal (given by Mr. R. H. Ferguson) for the seventeenth time; and the Denham Essay Prize for the second time.

"The Special Scripture Prizes this year is the gift of an Old Boy, G. B. de Vos. Another Old Boy, not resident in Ceylon, gives the new prizes for General Knowledge, 'because in my estimation,' he says, 'a sound general knowledge is more useful.' Ali Toubla has given us a scholarship. These spontaneous gifts from Old Boys are not in place of, but in addition to, their ordinary contributions to the expenses of the Kingswood Week.

"Some of our boys are still on active War service, and I deeply regret to record the deaths of V. C. Cook, of the Royal Garrison Artillery, and of Walter de Moor, of the Queen's Royal West Surreys. Both these boys were on active service from the beginning of the War.

"K. A. Chunchie, who also went from Ceylon on War service, is in England, taking an active part in the new brotherhood movement, and he is much in demand as a platform speaker. W. E. Schokman in Poona has been promoted Sub-editor of the *Advocate of India*. Collin Cook has obtained employment in Calcutta, where A. E. Bogars has long established himself; V. C. Wanigasinghe and S. Rajaratnam are employed in the Colombo Census Office; and S. N. Lisk in the Post and Telegraph Department. T. C. de Sylva and M.

Boange have been appointed Agricultural Inspectors. G. Boulton has been promoted Inspector of Police. M. Ismail, Sub-inspector of Police, is in charge of the Police Training School, Colombo. A. Wanigasinghe and M. B. Abeykoon have passed the Intermediate Examination for Proctors. E. Boulton has been appointed Headmaster of Kingswood. Dudley J. Barthomeuse has been elected to represent the Old Boys on the Advisory Council's Committee for Kingswood. Captain Guy Sansoni of the C.L.I. has been promoted to the rank of Major.

"There are two more Old Boys whom I must mention. They have come to Ceylon from North and East Africa, so arranging their official leave that they might attend 'Kingswood Week'. C. T. de Joedt, of the Postal Department, comes from German East Africa (now the Tanganyika Territory), where he teaches the pupils in the Government Telegraph School. Ali Bey, the son of Toulba Pasha, who accompanied Arabi Pasha to Ceylon in 1882, holds an office in the English Department of the Sultan of Egypt's Cabinet. They are both here this evening, and all I need say is that we in Kingswood honour them for the fine example they have set of unswerving loyalty to the school and the ideals of the school.

"I have now the pleasing duty of offering our thanks to those who have so readily assisted us in various ways; to Mr. A. M. Spaar, who audited the school accounts; to Mrs. J. Eagle and Mrs. W. J. L. Rogerson, who marked the papers for the Denham Essays Prize; to Miss Eaton for her help in the church service; to all the generous donors of prizes; and once more to our honoured Chairman.

. . . . .

The Prologue

"The Principal's clever and charming annual Prologue, an institution of Kingswood, was then read by

T. B. Herath, the best all-round boy of the School. It ran as follows:—

Unrest, Transition, Change! Things must get worse
Ere they get better. This vast universe
Goes by fixed laws; and this is doubtless true,
Till some fixed laws, grown old, give place to new.
Just when you are settled, and your books are writ,
When doubt means want of sense or want of wit,
Just then some grave Copernicus will shew,
And cynic Galileo prove—things are not so.
Thus Einstein proves our science out of date,
That straight is crooked; crooked may be straight;
Aryan, Dravidian; and what statesmen mean
For butter but politic margarine.
Small wonder that with all mental shocks
Men flounder in a world of paradox.
We don't complain. 'Tis easier for us
In School, that certain things should happen thus,
Our faults, unpunished, are now backward traced
To some far ancestor who us abased.
Vex'd teachers let no angry passions rise,
But calmly sit to psycho-analyse!
Change, and Unrest; the New World all a-make,
Men seek new paths and older paths forsake.
Shaken and toss'd, our vex'd, bewilder'd Earth
Thrills with the hopes of Karma and Re-birth.
All shall be new; yet we, who stand between,
Talk o'er grave issues, wondering what they mean;
And, peering thro' the loopholes of retreat,
Watch the fierce play and players at our feet.
Now, self-assertion flings its arms about,
Uncheck'd by fear, untramell'd by a doubt.
Strikes, raids, rebellions, war's remorseless pains,
From Moplah land to blood-steep'd Soviet plains,
What dreams, what schemes, our restless thoughts engage
In this tempestuous, mad, high-flying age!
An age of great adventurers—when the mind
Soars high, roams wide, a resting-place to find;

[By courtesy of Mrs. W. F. Diacono

MARYHILL HOTEL

Facing page 256]

[*By courtesy of Mr. H. F. Macmillan*

GIANT FERNS, HAKGALLA GARDENS, NUWARA ELIYA

Facing page 257]

For hidden truths to search; known truths to test,
So that the new shall better all our best;
New Everests to climb, whose peaks shall shew
More than contented mortals cared to know.
Our pearls are cultured—those we daily wear
In Church, School, Councils: the true pearl is rare.
Ev'n learning's peerless pearls may cultured be
In a new "Shoddy University".
Our clothes don't suit us: yellow's the right hue,
Once it was nought but Boadicean blue.
But why object, if some in tropic noons
Prefer the bifurcated pantaloons.

Let manners change; let laws and customs change;
Let old things change for better things, though strange;
But keep unchanged, O Kingswood! love, and truth,
Honour, and that proud soul of loyal youth;
The generous instinct homing o'er wide seas,
True to the School, and its fond memories.
Thro' war and wreck, thro' cares that never cease,
Thro' subtler lures of wealth and greedy peace,
Keep the same heart you bore from land to land,
O'er ravaged Europe and o'er Mespot sand;
Which with passion none can now mistake
By Egypt's Nile, and Tanganyika's lake,
In Indian jungles, by Malayan seas,
And here at home, in Men as true as these."

. . . . .

The Chairman then delivered his speech.

The Archdeacon's Opening

"The Venerable F. H. de Winton in his presidential speech detailed the pleasure it gave him to accept the Principal's invitation to preside that evening. Allusion had been made in the Principal's Report to certain remarks from the Hon. Mr. E. B. Denham, from Mauritius as to the Principal's choice of the speaker as chairman at the Kingswood Prize-Giving. He (the speaker) represented Oxford University in a humble way, being still on the foundation of Jesus College, having won his degree from Balliol. He had a lifelong interest in education ever since his boyhood. Beyond these matters, he had always been impressed with the newspaper reports of the annual Prize-Giving at Kingswood, wherein he, as often as it came round, read of the loyalty and attachment of the old boys to their school and its Principal; also the Principal's summary of the year rendered in choice verse. Another reason for his wishfulness to accept the invitation of the Principal to preside was that the late Mr. John Blazé was at Merton, Oxford, when the speaker's brother was at Balliol between 1871 and 1875.

" The speaker went on to say that the aim of education in Ceylon should be to prepare and fit young people for the work that came in the paths of life by forming and developing character. In the recent war, it was a display of this education in character, not only in England, but also in Ceylon, that made it possible to Lord Kitchener to raise an army of 3,000,000. Kingswood was principally engaged in the moulding of character of her boys.

" The speaker quoted from *Our Boys; the Kingswood Magazine*, for the Christmas term of 1916, as follows:—

" ' The School was started on the 4th May, 1891, as a private school, not as an " adventure school ", but with the definite aim of establishing, if possible, an institution, where in following the usual course of studies, more attention should be given to the general advancement of the pupils, individually and collectively, than to exceptional brilliance in competitive examinations. There was no thought then, and there never has been since, of competing with other schools.' The speaker proceeded to say that Kingswood had always worked with fixed ideals. The work at Kingswood reminded the speaker of the aims and objects of the celebrated Edward Thring, of Uppingham, who aimed at producing, not class-men, not even gentlemen, but men, though he welcomed University distinction. Still not many distinguished men hailed from Uppingham, although in the War, and not more than four years ago, two thousand from Uppingham had gone to the War, of whom 300 got placed on the roll-of-honour. The greatness of ancient Rome was achieved by the ordinary deed of her ordinary men. A marked feature of Kingswood was the interest of the Old Boys in the School's concerns, and the great interest the school takes in its past scholars. This condition of affairs recalled to the speaker's mind the ways of Uppingham and St. Thomas's College, especially during Warden Miller's time.

"The speaker went on to remark that the Classics were too dominant in the old days, and that too much time and energy were devoted to Greek and Latin. Then came a time when the educational mind turned away from the necessity for the Classics in the schools, and especially then did Sir Henry McCallum scoff at Greek. Now a re-action has set in in favour of the Classics, as evidence the following quotation from the *Ceylon Churchman*, extracted from *St. Thomas's College Magazine* of recent issue:—

"'During the War a conference on the new subject was held at Princetown, and a volume was put forth under the title *Value of the Classics*, containing, besides reports of speeches and addresses, some hundreds of testimonials from leading men in all walks of life. The witness borne by principals of colleges and universities might be discounted to a certain extent on the ground that they were professionally interested in their maintenance in education. But, by far the most impressive testimony, to the value of a classical education came from the heads of great business concerns—bankers, directors of insurance companies, engineering works and so forth. In their view the most effective results in specialisation were attained where pupils were grounded in Latin and Greek; also they held that those studies furnished the best training in leadership and character. With us the defence of the Classics is carried on in a far more apologetic way. It has been reserved for the most go-ahead nation in the world to recognise, with an almost reactionary frankness the debt of modern civilisation to ancient learning.'

" The Archdeacon continued to refer to the pleasure it gave him to be present on that occasion. He concluded by saying that he found Kandy this time, in his rather infrequent visits to Kandy, more beautiful than it ever was.

" The prizes were then awarded by the chairman, the following being

THE PRIZE LIST

SCRIPTURE PRIZES

Special	Herath, T. B.
Given in memory of Advocate J. T. Blazé	
Upper School	Keegel, N. W. H.
Middle School	Razak, Z. A.
Lower School	Keegel, A. E.

FORM PRIZES

Form V (Senior)	(not awarded)
Form V (A) (Junior)	Keegel, N. W. H.
Form IV (B)	Van Sanden, L.
Form III	1—De Sylva, H.
	2—De Silva, O. K.
Form II	Fernando, D. W.
Form I	Arifeen, A. R.
4th Standard (A)	1—Brantha, M. C.
(B)	1—Herat, K. B.
3rd Standard	1—Smith, A. K.
	2—Keegel, A. E.
2nd Standard	1—Yatigammana, P. B.
	2—Lantra, M. A. R.

1st Standard	1—Saldin, T. Y.
	2—Hannan, B. U.
Infant Class	1—Fernando, G.
	2—Ranasinghe, K.

SPECIAL PRIZES

Cadets Shooting Prize	—
Mathematics	Mendis, J. O
General Knowledge, Upper . .	De Saram, Francis
General Knowledge, Middle . .	Fernando, D. W.
General Knowledge, Lower . .	Palavandrem, K.
Eaton Memorial	Melder, S. W.
Crowther Cup—Best All-round Boy	Herath, T. B.
Hill Memorial	Dissanaike, T. B.
Denham English Prize, Senior . .	Herath, T. B.
Denham English Prize, Junior . .	De Saram, Francis
Dornhorst Prize	Razak, M. A.

Continuing, *The Ceylon Observer* proceeds:—

ALI TOULBA BEY'S SPEECH

"The distinguished Old Boy from Egypt said:—

"Ladies and gentlemen:—Far more would I have preferred to be amidst my comrades of Kingswood than here on this platform; but Mr. Blazé has asked me here, and to an old headmaster we still always owe a certain degree of duty and obedience, as loyalty is due to Country, King and School.

"From a speaker on this platform one generally expects advice and words of wisdom, but it is only those adapted for such by their rare attainments, their high distinction, and their long experience, as our distinguished and venerable chairman, who are best fitted for such an onerous task; and to such qualifications I can lay no claim. But I am expected to say something, so, I hope you will not take my few words amiss.

"The first thing I should like to say is how glad I am to be back once more in this charming land after an absence of twenty-four years—a pleasure doubly enhanced by the delight of visiting my dear old school, and assisting at this function I have yearned for these many years past; but need I say that the greatest joy of all is to find the Grand Old Man of Kingswood still at its helm? If Kingswood is fortunate in Mr. Blazé still being at its head, equally fortunate is she in the possession of such a fine motto as *Fide et Virtute*.

"People speak of the loyalty of Old Kingswoodians, and it was only the other day that the distinguished Principal of Trinity, the Rev. Fraser, so graciously alluded to it. But why wonder when it is the very motto of our school. To us it must be something real and living, not a mere sham or alloy, else it would be a shame and blot on us. Moreover, have we not the familiar saying "Example is better than precept"? By doing our duty to our school, which, after all, is but a small world in miniature, we learn to play the game fairly and squarely, and develop those qualities that help to build a fine character and prove so useful in the long run, so that when the day of trial comes, and the sterner voice of duty calls, we are prepared and well equipped for the task, and play the game in a finer and nobler manner. It is this very loyalty therefore, the bedrock on which the prestige of Kingswood stands, that enabled her, with a touch of pardonable vanity I beg to say, to faithfully and dutifully answer the country's call and send seventy-nine of her sons to the Great War, a record, in spite of her modest position, equalled only by her bigger and older sister Royal College.

"But loyalty of itself would be of little value were it not based on a really clean, manly and irreproachable character, and though it does not fall to the lot of every man to gain distinction in public life, still, we can be worthy citizens of the land to which we belong; and happy is he who can end his days in peace, with the self-satisfaction that he enjoys the esteem and affection of his fellowmen, as he is sure to reap the reward of a God-fearing, virtuous and conscientious life in the Hereafter.

"It is for you, therefore, young gentlemen of Kingswood to take to heart the motto of your school, and emulate the example of your predecessors. As they have held aloft untarnished the banner of your school, so do your duty in your turn, and, imbued with such a fine spirit, and inspired by such a lofty ideal, Kingswood cannot but always flourish, and you be a credit to your country and your school. And, in this connection, with what singular aptness might the words of another school appropriately apply to us:—

"Ours is no carven belfry tower,
No cloisters hoar with age,
To be of far-off centuries
A dream, an heritage.

But on our little chapel wall
Are names we mark with pride,
Men who for England and for God
Have done their work and died.

But what in size or fame we lack
Our loyalty supplies,
From hand to hand we pass the torch
Whose brightness never dies."

. . . . .

"To those who, like myself, have seen Kingswood in her infancy, and see her to-day, is given the privilege of better appreciating her present position; and though comparisons are, as a rule, odious, still they are at times instructive, and, happily, the present instance might be approached in a favourable light.

"A quarter of a century ago she was a small school in her infancy, toddling along with barely a hundred pupils. She had no buildings of her own—not that the present premises are in any way suitable or in keeping with her dignity as a leading school—no, not even a name in the proper sense of the word. Our playground was the public highway, and what sports we indulged in suffered for the lack of proper organisation; and so on was she handicapped in several other ways.

"But one invaluable asset she had, ladies and gentlemen, and that she treasured and prized as a priceless gem. Need I say who it was? Certainly you can guess to whom I refer, and though he may object very much to my allusion to him and taking him unawares, still, with me, it is a case of now or never. Mr. Blazé is that priceless gem that has lit the path of Kingswood so brightly, and raised her from the weak, toddling infant of yesterday, to the hefty, strapping institution of to-day.

"For thirty years he has guided her destinies with a paternal solicitude and a conscientious hand, and during these thirty years she has advanced further and further ahead. A man of less courage and tenacity, and with not so pronounced a determination and so high a sense of duty might have quailed before the task. But with him it has been otherwise, and in his quiet, modest way—too modest, indeed, at times to a fault—he has carefully but unostentatiously steered Kingswood through the many shoals that have beset her path into the haven of safety she now reposes in. All the more credit, therefore, to Blazé of Kingswood, as he must for ever live in the annals of this country, even as Arnold of Rugby, Thring of Uppingham, Hawtrey of Eton, and many another schoolmaster live in the annals of their own land.

"For thirty years Mr. Blazé guided the fortunes of his school, and if for such a long period he had served the Government, he would certainly, when the time came, have retired with the thanks of a grateful State and a well-earned pension. Not that we shall part with him. No, a thousand times no. But why not in some tangible form give expression to our deep sense of gratitude? Why not let him realise in his lifetime how great and beneficial has been his influence, and how imperishably he has carved for himself a name in our affections? To

[By courtesy of Mrs. I. M. Del Tufo

A Corner of Gregory Lake, Nuwara Eliya

Facing page 264]

[By courtesy of Mrs. I. M. Del Tufo

SCRUBS TEA ESTATE, NUWARA ELIYA

Facing page 265]

such end, therefore, I now propose to make the following suggestion.

"In the ordinary course of circumstances one might have offered him a testimonial of the usual conventional type; but what testimonial more enduring and more welcome and dearer to his heart could there be than one devoted to the welfare and prosperity of the school to which he has consecrated his life, and in whose service he has grown old? With such an end in view, therefore, I propose the creation of a scholarship, to be called the 'Blazé Scholarship'. It shall be given to the best all-round boy of Kingswood, entitling him to finish his studies at Oxford or Cambridge, according as he deems fit. By such a step we shall be serving a two-fold purpose: we shall be serving the sacred cause of learning and enabling Kingswood to give her quota to the higher venues of education, as we shall at the same time be fittingly perpetuating a name dear to the hearts of all.

"To you, therefore, ladies and gentlemen, I now appeal, and in appealing, I do so, not so much with the object of getting your donations, as that you will serve thereby to show and prove in what high esteem and regard you hold the honoured name that is now to adorn the scholarship under review.

"And to the Old Boys of Kingswood in particular I turn; from us, more than from anybody else, must help come to make this project a success, if for anything, at least that our hearty and ready response betokens our lasting gratitude to our *alma mater*, as it will serve to show the world at large that in deed, as in word, we are worthy of the tribute that is paid us as being amongst the most loyal of all Old Boys. Let us all pull together, and even though it take as hard and strenuous a pull as once when Kingswood pulled over St. Benedict's on a memorable occasion, still let us all ably rise to the occasion.

"And, if in this project I can be assured of success, and of such I trust I can rely upon, for as *The Ceylon Independent* so aptly and nicely put it some days ago:

'When we speak of the friends of Kingswood, who are not?' then surely all and sundry will certainly give, and give with no unstinted hand, then, ladies and gentlemen, I shall feel all the more gratified that I have had something to say, and turned it to good account, even as I now feel doubly overjoyed that the Kingswood Cadets, in spite of several newcomers to their ranks, have none the less pluckily and gallantly responded to the call of their school, and brought back for the third time in succession the Hermann Loos Cup.

"And now, ladies and gentlemen, forgive me for having encroached on your indulgence and patience so long. In a couple of days I go back to my beloved country, and it is a crowning pleasure to me that a most enjoyable holiday has been capped by so fitting and welcome an event as the 'Kingswood Week'. I go back with the pleasantest of recollections and feelings of the deepest gratitude. To all who have helped to brighten my stay here I offer my most heartfelt thanks; and in thanking all I might avail myself of the present occasion to publicly offer my thanks to the British Government for the kindness shown my father during his residence here, which helped to soften the bitterness of exile, as for the courtesy and facilities rendered me, thus enabling me to spend a most delightful holiday here.

"Good-bye, ladies and gentlemen. After three or four years I expect to come back, but let me hope when I return that I shall come as a happier man—happier with the feeling that the good old school is at last worthily and suitably accommodated, with her Grand Old Man, hale and hearty as ever, still at her helm; as happily also that the scholarship that is to bear his honoured name has materialised and is definitely established on a firm and lasting basis; but happiest of all, ladies and gentlemen, that I come from good old Egypt as the citizen of a free, independent, and sovereign State to the shores of a mighty, yet none the less magnanimous and chivalrous, allied Empire.

. . . . .

The Chief Justice's Remarks

"Sir Anton Bertram said:—I have only a very few words to say. I have come here with no special message to give you, but I come on an invitation which I could not refuse—the invitation of the Principal—and what I feel, and what all feel, who come here on these occasions, it that we cannot resist the opportunity given us to pay homage to so distinguished a character as you have in Mr. Blazé.

"I know that these occasions must make him exceedingly uncomfortable. He is an extraordinarily modest man, and nothing pains him more, I am sure, than to hear such lavish praise of his merit. But the fact remains that no speaker can stand upon the platform in 'Kingswood Week' without expending his soul in sincere and genuine panegyrics on Mr. Blazé, and he has to listen to them.

"There is another reason why I am proud to come here, and that is for the sake of the School. The Archdeacon remarked that the Headmaster Thring, of Uppingham, said that the chief object of his school was in turning out men. Well, now, ladies and gentlemen, we have seen an example to-day that Kingswood can turn out people who are emphatically men, such as the speaker who has just preceded me. I feel sure you are all proud of that Old Kingswoodian, and that you wish him an honourable and distinguished career in the great country to which he belongs. It will be a feather in the cap of Kingswood that she has produced and been responsible for the education of an Egyptian statesman; and I am sure that we all wish him all possible honour and the most effective career that his country can afford him.

"And again, ladies and gentlemen, as to the production of men, I still remember when I last spoke here. It was in the middle of the Great War. I remember how anxious our hearts were, though none of us had any doubts as to the end. One thing we were proud of was the splendid contribution Kingswood made, and was making to the War. Many of them have paid the great sacrifice. Many of them have come back to serve their country in every walk of life. These occasions of the prize-givings of our Public Schools are perhaps the most important functions in the life of Ceylon, particularly at this period of the history of Ceylon. We are on the brink of a time when the past is having its reward, when the long years of labour in schools like these have turned out men, men qualified to exercise a greater responsibility, and the future of Ceylon lies in schools like these. Institutions that provide men, who fill the professions, who take part in Government service, who are now, more and more, taking part in the great industry of the country—the industry of agriculture—who will take part in its public life of the future, who will carry out that work of marked progress, which has taken place during the past generation in all spheres of life.

" Ladies and gentlemen, it is easy to say these things. But those who are watching the principal schools to-day, those who are seeing the men they are turning out, those who are seeing the boys who come year after year for their prizes, know that in schools like Kingswood, Trinity, Royal, St. Joseph's and others, that there are being moulded the young men of the future, who are going to be responsible for the national life in the years that are coming. It is always, therefore, with very great pleasure that I come to a school, where I feel in the audience, in the boys, and in the old boys, there is a spirit of real life, which no one can fail to recognise in the audience to-day. There is vitality, there is robustness, there is manliness which comes of character, of application to work, of application to manly games, of the habit of facing life with the true ideal, that tradition which you have in the school of Kingswood, fostered by those who preceded you, fostered more particularly by your Principal, to whom, as I said, it is impossible to come to these prize-givings without paying a tribute of honour—I heartily wish both him and you a successful ' Kingswood Week'.

. . . . .

Rev. Cornish's Speech

" The Rev. H. R. Cornish, of the Wesleyan Mission, Hatton, next addressed the gathering. He spoke of the good work being quietly done by Kingswood. He anticipated a bright future for the school, and likened the influence of the institution to a spring from which went out a benefit, the importance and greatness of which cannot easily be realised. The young people of Kingswood were learning more than to merely pass examinations; they were learning by example and precept what life is. To live was to receive and accept, in the full responsibility of life with a public and unselfish spirit; also to take part in the burden the world presents so as to make for the commonwealth of humanity, looking forward to the better day which all knew must dawn one day.

Vote of Thanks

" The Rev. John Eagle rose to propose votes of thanks to the Archdeacon for having presided at the proceedings, and to the Chief Justice for the words he had spoken, and the interest Sir Anton Bertram had evinced in the welfare of Kingswood. The speaker went on to say he rejoiced with all in the presence among them of so many old boys of the school. He was sure they were particularly glad and proud to have with them their friend from Egypt. They keenly appreciated the interest Ali Toulba Bey has shown in his old school by his special visit and his inspiring address. The speaker thanked Rev. Mr. Cornish for his presence and his kind words;

also for consenting to preach at Sunday morning's special service.

"Rev. Eagle had also a few words to say about Kingswood and its interests. The school was confronted with the problem of providing better premises for itself. He assured the authorities and all interested in Kingswood that the church officials had the concerns of the school well in their minds, and he read an extract from a letter confirming this assurance. Mr. Blazé's health, he said, was far from what it had been. They were much more concerned about this, and they hoped to relieve him of some of his onerous duties. He trusted they would soon be in a position to enter upon a definite scheme of general improvement, and when that scheme is settled they would want the help both of Old Boys and friends.

"The following song was heartily joined in at the end of the proceedings:—

THE KINGSWOOD SONG

Hill-throned, where Nature is gracious and kind,
Home of our early youth, grant us the love of truth,
Health for the body, and light for the mind,
Kingswood, O may we be loyal and true to thee,
Holding what'er betide, Virtue and Faith our guide.

Loyally, manfully,
All of us true to thee,
No room for trimmer, coward, or fool;
Word and will true and clean,
Work and play strong and keen,
None for himself, but all for the School!
School! School! None for himself, but all, all for the School!
All for the School!

Nor shall the world destroy our love and pride,
For both, we know, the stronger shall grow,
And whatever thy fortunes, we stand at thy side,
Present and Past shall be one in heart, all for thee,
Holding what'er betide, Virtue and Faith our guide.

Then in all things, whatever Duty's voice may call,
Ready we follow, and spring to our work!
Country or School, may call, play the game,
Forward all!
Shoulder to shoulder, disdaining to shirk
Duty we dare not flee, heavy the cost may be,
Holding what'er may betide, Virtue and Faith our guide.

. . . . .

The School Sports

"The sports took place on Saturday afternoon, the 17th, on Bogambara Green, specially roped in and appropriately appointed for the purpose. A few of the events had been worked off on the Thursday before. The lengthy programme of Saturday's sports was taken up at 2 p.m. in the presence of a few spectators—few compared with the crowd that thronged the grounds as the evening wore on. The gathering presented many aspects, from the well-dressed to the motley; but the whole was significant of the popularity of Kingswood in the scholastic way as on the field of sport. A comfortable pressure provided 'loop-holes of retreat', as the Prologue had it.

The Officials of the Sports,

who guided the operations were:

Stewards of the Course: Members of the Union.

Starters: C. S. M. R. Newell, Dr. H. Ludovici, and Mr. V. M. A. Ludowyke.

Time-Keepers: Rev. Fr. H. Hyde, O.S.B.; Mr. W. J. L. Rogerson, C.C.S.; and Mr. M. S. Samarasinghe.

Judges: Mr. E. H. Davis, C.C.S.; Rev. J. Eagle, Mr. W. Barber, Mr. H. R. Pilcher, and Dr. V. H. L. Anthonisz.

The Prizes

"The Prizes, consisting of cups and other presents, were given away by Mrs. W. J. L. Rogerson, wife of the Kandy Police Magistrate. The darkness of the evening from banked-up clouds and the late hour, precipitated proceedings, but did not rob them of anything in interest or spirit. One, or perhaps two, of the programmed events were not entered upon; and Mrs. Rogerson pulled off the prize for the uncompleted 'Rickshaw Musical Race event, by a concensus of donation, voiced by Mr. Edwin Boulton, who announced the winners.

ST. CECELIA'S BAND PROGRAMME

March ...	Pomposo	*J. Ord Hume*
Overture ...	Thousand and One Nights ...	*K. Svoboda*
Valse ...	Roses of Picardy	*H. Wood*
Selection ...	Best of the Bunch	*W. Williams*
Valse ...	I'm for ever Blowing Bubbles	*Etherinton*
Fox-Trot ...	Dardanella	*F. Bernard*
Valse ...	Wyoming	*Gene Williams*
Two-Step ...	Lilac Blossoms	*P. Wenrich*

God Save the King

THE RESULTS

E.—CLASS EVENTS

80 Yards Race:—1, Izadeen; 2, T. Samhion; 3, T. P. Saldin.
All Fours Race:—1, M. Izadeen; 2, T. P. Saldin; 3, Samhion.

D.—CLASS EVENTS

Blindfold Race:—1, H. B. Hannen; 2, Dennegama; 3, G. Pereira.

[Photo by Platé, Ltd., Colombo

PLUCKING TEA

Facing page 272]

[Photo by the Author

THE KANDY-MATALE ROAD—A ROUTE OF SYLVAN BEAUTY

Facing page 273]

100 Yards Race:—1, M. S. Yoosoof; 2, K. Vanderwall; 3, B. S. Hannen.

C.—CLASS EVENTS

Three-Legged Race:—1, T. S. Saldin and T. Salley; 2, E. Atwell and E. Keegel.

120 Yards Race:—1, B. Sally; 2, D. L. Wendt; 3, T. S. Saldin.

B.—CLASS EVENTS

220 Yards Race:—1, C. de Silva; 2, B. C. Sariffodin; 3, A. M. Pereira.

120 Yards Race:—1, C. de Silva; 2, A. M. Pereira; 3, T. Samsudeen.

Three-Legged Race:—1, A. M. Pereira and C. de Silva; 2, Lionel de Silva and B. N. Sally.

A.—CLASS EVENTS

High Jump:—1, E. L. de Kretser; 2, T. B. Dissanayake; 3, S. K. Amith.

120 Yards Race:—1, S. K. Amith; 2, M. C. Brantha; 3, M. Haniffa.

Girls' Race:—1, Matilda Wijesinghe; 2, Marshy de Silva; 3, Lilian de Silva.

OPEN EVENTS

Cigarette Race:—1, Miss Lockhart and Aelian Goonewardene.

Bicycle Bending Race:—1, L. G. de la Motte.

Mixed Shooting Competition:—Miss E. Wells and G. Wells.

OLD BOYS' EVENTS

220 Yards Race:—1, M. C. Brantha; 2, A. de Silva; 3, P. B. Abeykoon.

120 Yards Race:—1, M. K. Brantha; 2, A. de Silva; 3, P. B. Aveykoon.

One Mile Race:—L. G. de la Motte.

PRESENT BOYS' EVENTS

Throwing the Cricket Ball:—1, R. Cranleigh; 2, K. W. D. Soyza; 3, T. H. Gibson.

LONG JUMP:—1, K. W. D. Soyza; 2, T. H. Gibson; 3, S. Baie.
PUTTING THE SHOT (16 lbs.):—1, H. A. Perusinghe; 2, K. W. D. Soyza; 3, R. Cranleigh.
HIGH JUMP:—1, H. A. Perusinghe (5-ft. 1-in.); 2, F. de Saram; 3, T. H. Gibson.
KICKING THE FOOTBALL:—1, R. Cranleigh; 2, T. H. Gibson; 3, F. de Saram.
120 YARDS FLAT RACE:—1, H. A. Perusinghe; 2, K. W. D. Soyza; 3, T. H. Gibson.
HURDLES RACE:—1, K. W. D. Soyza; 2, H. K. Mylvaganam; 3, F. de Saram.
QUARTER MILE RACE:—1, K. W. D. Soyza; 2, T. H. Gibson; 3, M. Haniffa.
ONE MILE FLAT RACE:—1, K. W. D. Soyza; 2, T. H. Gibson; 3, Z. A. Razak.
SPENCER CHALLENGE CUP:—K. W. D. Soyza.

. . . . .

THE CONCERT

"The Kingswood School Hall was packed to overflowing at the concert held on Saturday night. The proceedings were of a homely nature, and hilarity and vivacity were predominant features. Most of the items were encored and re-encored, a motor-horn introduced by some naughty person being most assertive in the demands. It was well-night 11.30 p.m. when the varied programme (the items of which were announced by Major Guy Sansoni in their incidence) came to an end. The contributors were as follows:—

PROGRAMME

PIANOFORTE SOLO	Mr. C. Drieberg
SONG	The School Choir
RECITATION	Master Ivor de Kretser
SONG	Miss Green

PROGRAMME (*contd.*)

PIANOFORTE SOLO	Miss Grace Nell
SONG	Miss F. de Vos
DANCE	Miss M. Jonklaas
SONG	Mr. E. A. de Kretser
VIOLIN SOLO	Miss Dorothy Martinus
SONG	The School Choir

INTERVAL

PIANOFORTE SOLO	Mr. C. Drieberg
SONG	The School Choir
SONG	Mr. A. N. Keegel
RECITATION	Master Shirley Meynert
SONG	Mrs. St. J. Jonklaas
VIOLIN SOLO	Miss Dorothy Martinus
SONG	M. C. Robinson
SONG	The School Choir

. . . . .

SPECIAL SERVICE

" Divine service of the nature of a thanksgiving was held on Sunday at 9.30 a.m. in the Wesleyan Church in Brownrigg Street, and was largely attended and deeply devotional. It also took the form of a church parade, attended by the Cadets and Scouts of Kingswood. The Rev. R. H. Cornish, of Hatton, conducted the service, and preached a stirring sermon, a feature of the service being the singing of a hymn written by the Principal of Kingswood. This service proved a fitting finale to a crowded programme of celebration."

. . . . .

Such a commanding personality as is that of the great Principal of Kingswood, as also the outstanding position he holds in the educational world of Ceylon, that hardly does there seem reason for mentioning Kingswood than his honoured and esteemed name is as sure as ever to crop up and line itself side by side with Kingswood, so inseparably bound up has his name become with the school he has so long been associated with, and which as a matter of fact is his own creation and handiwork. In the fitting nature of things, therefore, I might add just one more tribute to the many that have so meritoriously been lavished on Kingswood's great Headmaster.

Thus, in a leading article of the 19th of September, 1921, commenting on the "Kingswood Week" which had just closed, *The Ceylon Independent* writes:—

Kingswood College

"We cannot think of any educational institution in this country that is so saturated with the personality of its Principal, as Kingswood College. It is hard to dissociate St. Thomas's and Warden Stone, Wesley and Mr. Highfield, St. Benedict's and Brother Bolcan, St. Joseph's and Rev. Father le Goc, or Trinity and Mr. Fraser. It is impossible to think of Kingswood without Mr. Blazé. The school is of his creation; he has watched over its growth with paternal care and solicitude; fashioned its career with infinite tenderness, from its anxious infant years, through its early youth, and now when it has reached full development every part of the country and several parts of the world are evidencing the success of his efforts in the shape of fine manly men, clean-limbed and clear-brained—men who are as much a pride to the country and the general community, as they are to the great Headmaster responsible for their training.

"For many years—more than we care to recall—we have looked forward to the annual prize-givings at Kingswood College with delight and interest, having grown to associate them with the brilliant and scholarly production of the learned Principal, the Prize Day Prologue, the clever chronicle of the school year, epitomising the chief events of the previous twelve months in the educational world of Ceylon, and bringing together an assembly of learning and culture such as few school platforms succeed in attracting. All these characteristics were noticeable at the prize-giving last week. That an old boy of Kingswood, and not one of this country either, who left it twenty-four years ago, should have made the long journey from his home in Egypt to be present at the prize-giving tells its own tale of unswerving loyalty to the old school and devotion to its great-hearted Principal. Discriminating critics, difficult of pleasing, but whose wide experience invests their judgment with the utmost value have, after close personal contact with Kingswood, pronounced it to be of the finest type of the English public school, where boys and masters work together for the good of the school and not that of their individual selves.

" Sir Anton Bertram paid a great tribute to Mr. Blazé with every word of which the public will associate themselves. The Chief Justice, with the culture and traditions of the great University of Cambridge behind him, said that what he felt, and what all those who attended Kingswood prize-giving felt, was that they could not resist the opportunity to pay homage to so distinguished a character as Mr. Blazé. No truer words have been spoken of any one. Like Thring, of Uppingham, Mr. Blazé's life-work has been the turning out of men, and Mr. Ali Toulba Bey, who spoke last week from the platform of his old school, furnished both the Chief Justice and the Archdeacon with living evidence of how well Mr. Blazé has succeeded, and there are many Ali Toulba Beys—products of Kingswood—scattered throughout the country.

" We are profoundly impressed by what fell from the Chief Justice when he said, in reference to the men turned out by Kingswood, that the future of Ceylon lies in schools such as Kingswood. The responsibilities on the men of this country are greater to-day than ever, and the ideals Kingswood has set before her, and is living up to are the fashioning of men who will shoulder such responsibilities in the true and proper spirit. This should make those who have not given thought to it before realize what a great force for good Kingswood is."

CHAPTER XXXII

FAREWELL CEYLON!

RARELY have I spent a couple of busier days than September 18th and 19th. From the moment I reached Colombo about noon of the 18th, to the time I embarked on the following day, I had not a moment's rest, so deeply absorbed was I with the things I had to attend to personally, and even in my last night in Colombo I had to sit up into the small hours of the morning to finish the packing, etc., and retired to bed finally for a couple of hours or so only through sheer exhaustion. And all this owing to my having so unwisely left so many things till the end on the assumption that the *Naldera* would not leave Ceylon before the 22nd, as I had originally anticipated.

During this period I was constantly flitting here and there, sometimes buying this; at other times getting delivery of things ordered or sent, and paying for them and their transport; on a third occasion settling the hotel's accounts or some other bill, or arranging with the baggage master for the safe shipment of my effects; but constantly, as ever, having to cope with the tipping nuisance—which simply aggravated matters amidst my hundred other pre-occupations—if only to get rid of the importunities of the fellows who would keep waylaying me and scurrying after me in and out exactly as Mr. H. G. Milner has so graphically portrayed. Funnily, also, during my last two days at the G.O.H. there were

Vide, Chapter vi, p. 27.

five waiters in turn serving me at table instead of the usual table "boy"! But what is worse, even some who had done me no service at all whatever, and thus had not the slightest pretension to a tip in any way, would accost me and sometimes even badger me quite unexpectedly right up to my room, and say unctuously with an air of smugness, "Master leaving to-morrow?" or "Master leaving to-day?" as the case might be, and keep staring and gaping vacantly at me! In such a situation this could not but jar on one's worn nerves, and be the last straw to one's burdens.

Of course I knew perfectly well what they were driving at, and had perforce to yield to the remedy of a few rupees for each in turn, if only to send him away and attend to my work; and a few rupees here, or a note there to those who merited such is only natural in such circumstances; but to be constantly called to dole out rupees indiscriminately all round was simply intolerable, inasmuch as these tips were bound in due course to multiply into a quite considerable sum subsequently. Yes, "Take care of the pence, and the pounds will take care of themselves."

. . . . .

And then the shop people, what an annoyance they were in some instances. Some, of course, were very considerate, as Mr. Louis Siedle for instance, who, in spite of the 18th being the Sabbath, still most generously offered to meet me at his establishment directly after my arrival to settle our business and square up accounts; whereas, take the reverse, another firm from whom I had ordered some walking sticks for which I had already paid, in spite of their being aware of my impending departure, and my actually having communicated with them by telegraph, still did absolutely nothing to give me satisfaction, with the result that I had to leave without the sticks, and without the money being returned, of course, but with the hope that some friends who had kindly volunteered to see the matter through on my

[*By courtesy of Mr. H. F. Macmillan*

THE COCOA TREE

Facing page 280]

THE PICTURESQUE TERRACED PADDY FIELDS OF URUGELA

From " A Handbook of Tropical Gardening and Planting " (Colombo : Cave & Co.). *By courtesy of the Author, Mr. H. F. Macmillan*

Facing page 281]

behalf, might eventually take these people severely to task for such outrageous behaviour.

. . . . .

Then again, I had to make the usual round of farewell calls on all my friends, and this also took up no mean share of my already limited time. One good friend in particular, Mr. F. L. Daniel, I was deeply grieved to miss seeing though I called on him at his house, owing to his having just before left for Up-Country, and it saddened me indeed to quit Ceylon without having met him just once more to thank him again most cordially for all his kindness and goodness towards me.

But there is an end even to one's worries. With my approaching departure Mr. Aldo Diacono adds yet another kindness to the many for which I was already indebted to him. In addition to the excellent bedstead cabin Nos. 379—80 I had booked on the hurricane deck of the *Naldera*, thanks to his good offices and intervention with Mr. T. H. Tatham,[1] of Messrs. Mackinnon, Mackenzie & Co., the Agents of the P. & O. S. N. Co. in Colombo, Mr. Diacono accompanied me there again, and obtained a letter of introduction from the Hon. Mr. R. S. Philpott, of the same Company, to the Purser who, on receipt of it, rendered me every facility in regard to

[1] Nor did my 1924 trip pass off without laying me under as deep and lasting an obligation to another gentleman of the P. & O. Agency in Colombo. To Mr. Tatham I had written from Egypt before leaving, begging for a renewal of his former courtesy and kindness in reserving for me a fine cabin on the promenade deck of the *Mongolia* for our homeward voyage, especially that now I was accompanied by my wife, who was making her first trip overseas, and was, moreover, in delicate health.

Notwithstanding Mr. Tatham's absence in England at the time, Mr. A. R. Quarme, who was in control, nevertheless most courteously, and of his own accord, very kindly offers me the splendid bedstead cabin Nos. 195–6 on the promenade deck, having even gone to the length of cabling to Australia to have it reserved for me. As long as I live I shall certainly never forget this kindness of his, as also his extreme courtesy in several other ways, none the least in personally introducing me to Commander Asbury of the *Mongolia*, and recommending us to his care. And the acme and quintessence of comfort and joy proved this trip, thanks to Mr. Quarme. Commander Asbury, the Purser, and the Staff of the ship, for never indeed did I enjoy a voyage more than I did my homecoming on the good and stout *Mongolia*.

the plants and mangosteens I was taking with me to Egypt.

. . . . .

If my time during the day proved trying still night brought its compensations, my last dinner at the good G.O.H. being indeed one after my own seeking and quite to my taste. To our last meal together we sat, a small, jolly circle of friends, and that they should have been the very friends who had been most kind and generous to me only served to enhance the conviviality of this pleasant function. And the meeting of such delightful company made me forget the fatigue of the daytime, though it could not help driving home the sadness of impending separation.

. . . . .

The morrow brought a continual stream of friends, who kindly called to return my farewell visits of the previous day and to say good-bye to me, including the Hon. Mr. W. M. Abdul Rahiman, who must add yet another kindness in the shape of a substantial present of jaggery and cashew-nuts to take back home, and, needless to say, I was deeply touched by this mark of courtesy and kindness on their part.

. . . . .

Finally, at 2 o'clock, after having had my last tiffin in the magnificent dining-hall of the G.O.H., including a most enjoyable curry and rice, and some most delicious iced papaw, the like of which I knew I would not taste for many a long day till fortune brought me back once more to this picturesque land, I say good-bye to Mr. Frank Winfield, the manager, thanking him for the fine and comfortable time I passed at this splendid hostelry, as also such members of the staff, who had been most attentive and dutiful in their ministrations to my needs.

Finished with this, I leave for the jetty accompanied

by a small band of true friends who had considerately stayed behind to the last moment to see me off. I next step on to the steam-tender which the P. & O. agency very thoughtfully provide for their passengers, accompanied by Mr. Aldo Diacono and Mr. W. T. Samaraweera who insist on going aboard with me in spite of all my efforts to dissuade them from so doing, overwhelmed as I was by all their unfailing kindness.

In the *Naldera's* smoking-room we sit, this small party of ours, round some soft drinks, and join in a short, friendly, valedictory chat; but there was no mistaking the atmosphere of gloom that pervaded this scene in the thought of impending separation.

The ship's bell then sounds for visitors to go ashore, but its ringing at that moment seemed even more raucous, jarring, and painful than it unwittingly meant to convey, sounding as it seemed to me the knell of those dear associations with Ceylon, which had been thinning little by little during the last few days until now, with the ringing of this bell, they had dwindled to vanishing point with the departure of these two good friends.

And as Mr. Aldo Diacono was the first to greet me on deck in Colombo, so was he the last to say good-bye, Mr. Samaraweera just preceding him down the gangway, and it was only fit that such a rôle should have fallen to him, so close were the ties of intimate, lifelong friendship that bound our two families.

. . . . .

Glad as I was to be returning home, still at the moment I could not help a certain sadness at parting from my second home, loved and many as were my fond associations with it already, which my recent trip had only too readily re-kindled afresh and augmented. Besides, living as I did, far away from Ceylon, the mere thought that the distance and expense militated against a frequent repetition of such visit, was enough to intensify the bitterness of parting.

At last, at three o'clock sharp, the big, stately *Naldera* weighs anchor and steers towards the open sea, past the fine breakwater that was doing such yeoman service to the harbour of Colombo. More and more as the panorama of Colombo had unfurled itself to me as nearer and nearer we drew to it on my arrival, farther and farther it now receded as more and more we outdistanced it, the heart growing sadder and sadder to lose touch with its pleasant associations for many a long day, as faster and faster it beat with joy when we were approaching it.

A couple of hours more, a few last sorrowful glimpses, and the diminishing speck that stands for the beautiful land far, far beyond then suddenly vanishes, swallowed up as it were, by the broad expanse of waters. We are now on the wide, wide ocean sailing towards the great Indian Peninsula, and Ceylon has vanished except in so far as it still fondly lingers in my troubled imagination.

CHAPTER XXXIII

HOMEWARD BOUND!

THE *Naldera* is now on the high seas, and naturally I have to settle down as resignedly as possible to an ocean run of nearly a fortnight. The first thing, of course, that occurs to me is to make a careful scrutiny of my cabin, and take stock, so to speak, or rather make a cursory survey of this floating hotel *de luxe*. A fine steamer indeed was this 16,000 leviathan, the largest and most up-to-date of the P. & O. fleet, together with her sister ship the *Narkunda*. As a matter of fact, I was told on returning to Cairo, by an English friend of mine, anent my complaint of the high fares ruling, that these fine vessels had cost £3,500,000 apiece, they also having been requisitioned by the British Government during the Great War, and having rendered yeoman service as Auxiliary cruisers. Moreover, considering the high cost of living and production still ruling, it was only to be expected that the P. & O. Company would still continue, for some further time at least, to demand high fares, if only to cover such items and provide for gradual depreciation of the vessels from increasing wear and tear.[1]

[1] Up to the time I wrote this, these liners were actually the biggest ships plying on the Eastern Seas, and with their graceful proportions, three funnels, and high decks, they looked like veritable leviathans, and appeared even larger than those which were commissioned later on and supplanted them in size. Thus, with the advent of the *Maloja* and the *Mooltan*, each of 21,000 tons, the *Naldera* and the *Narkunda* had to yield premier honours to them—but in size only. For, though in my 1924 trip to Ceylon I sailed on board the *Maloja*, still, notwithstanding that I booked my passage as early as the beginning of April, the very limited number of the fine bedstead cabins on the promenade deck left me no alternative but to accept a cabin just below, all of which, as those still further below, were the obsolete, portholed ones on the tandem principle, not abutting on and overlooking

The *Naldera* certainly looked larger and more commodious than the equally fine *Mantua;* but, as a matter of fact, there was little to choose between the two vessels in their general outline, as also in their fine Public and State Rooms, they differing only very slightly in their construction internally. Thus, the smoking-room of the First Saloon of the *Naldera* was on the promenade deck, unlike that of the other ship, which was just below on the hurricane deck. Again, the dining-hall of the *Naldera* was deep down below on the main deck, whereas that of the *Mantua* was one story up on the spar deck. Besides, the *Naldera* seemed to enjoy a little extra turn of speed, steaming usually between 15 and 16 knots on an average, though it could be brought up to 18½ knots if necessary.

From the personal point of view also I seemed to enjoy my voyage on the *Naldera* far more than I did on the *Mantua*, though this could in no way be the direct fault of the latter. The fact is that I was favoured with the excellent bedstead cabin Nos. 379180 on board the *Naldera*, as I have already stated, thanks to Mr. T. H. Tatham. A commodious and airy cabin it proved, with a cool, fresh breeze always blowing through its large window, and with a copious supply of light which did not necessitate the switching on of the electric lamp to dress.

. . . . .

And speaking of this cabin, I really cannot understand why, in these days when shipping companies seem to be only too eager to add to the comfort and amenities of sea travelling, a good many, including such a popular and leading line as the P. & O. will still show such a predilection for cabins on the tandem principle. There is no doubt that in favouring this class they stand to gain more in profits by the increased accommodation. But

a spacious deck, as in the *Naldera* and *Mantua* classes, but each connected with the sea by a long channel, each proportionately longer as each cabin was placed farther back from the sea. Need I therefore add what a trying experience this proved, especially with the Monsoon and the hot season on ?

then, how can we reconcile this policy to their very laudable desire to minister to the needs of the travelling public? Of course they cannot expect to run their ships at a loss; but then, has not the public also a claim on their consideration, even to a greater degree than what obtains at the moment—at any rate, those who, on paying the highest fare, naturally expect a corresponding high ratio of comfort in return. I believe that shipping companies can successfully strike the golden mean without either they or the public being any the worse for it.

Thus they could provide for a larger number of *cool, roomy, comfortable bedstead cabins, abutting on and overlooking the spacious upper decks*, such as are already provided for on board the *Naldera* and *Mantua* classes, where on both the promenade and hurricane decks there are practically two whole rows of such cabins; nor, of course, should they forget to provide for a larger quota of single-berth cabins as well, which happily, now seems to be on the increase. And since a passenger travelling First Saloon has to choose between three grades of rate "A", rate "B", and rate "C", according to the position and nature of the cabin, it is only fair, therefore, that those plumping for rate "A" of the First Saloon on the strength of greater convenience, and, therefore, correspondingly paying a higher fare, should accordingly be assigned the spacious, comfortable bedstead cabins on the promenade and hurricane decks, instead of being relegated to the dingy, stuffy, and rather dark cabins of the tandem class further below—as so unfortunately fell to me on board the *Mantua*—unless, of course, at the time of booking all accommodation of this nature has been already snapped up, and there is no alternative for the would-be voyager but to accept a cabin further below, or postpone his voyage. And, of course, what I have said here in regard to the First Saloon I mean shall apply to the Second Saloon as well, apart from such variations as may be necessary to meet the exigencies of the situation here and the distribution of cabins in this class.

. . . . .

But then, after all has been said and done, is this question of bedstead cabins *versus* tandem cabins one that really justifies so much grousing about? As a matter of fact, in airing our grievances, we are not inspired by any lack of acknowledgment of the share of the shipping companies in the evolution of the liner of to-day, and the correspondingly high ratio of comfort resultant upon such; nor are we prompted by any attempt to belittle or ungratefully under-rate their splendid record and fine achievements, or their equally laudable and sincere desire to keep pace with the march of progress, and constantly and unremittingly to strive to cater more and more substantially to the needs of the public. In reality, we are unconsciously being spurred on by that hard yet inevitable law of the insatiability of human nature; and though, on the surface of it, we may at first be liable to be taken to task for a sufficeint lack of appreciation of the efforts and labours of others toiling for the good of the human race as a whole, yet what does science and human progress not owe to this law, and when was fair and sincere criticism ever said not to serve its purpose?

Thus, were we to compare conditions prevailing to-day, to what obtained, say thirty years ago, why, we cannot but marvel at the wonderful strides that human progress has made within the last three decades, even as we cannot help being proportionately grateful that we are so far better off than those who sailed the seas years ago. Thus, one has but to quote the innumerable uses to which electricity has been put, and note how it has revolutionised our everyday life, to be all the more thankful for the world and the age we now live in.

If electric fans, for instance, and electric fans in four graduated degrees of currents of air to meet the convenience of passengers, now seem rather commonplace on board, still who, of our ancestors, could have dreamt of lifts actually being in vogue on board ocean-going liners to-day? As a matter of fact, I came across this pleasant innovation on board the *Naldera*, and though circum-

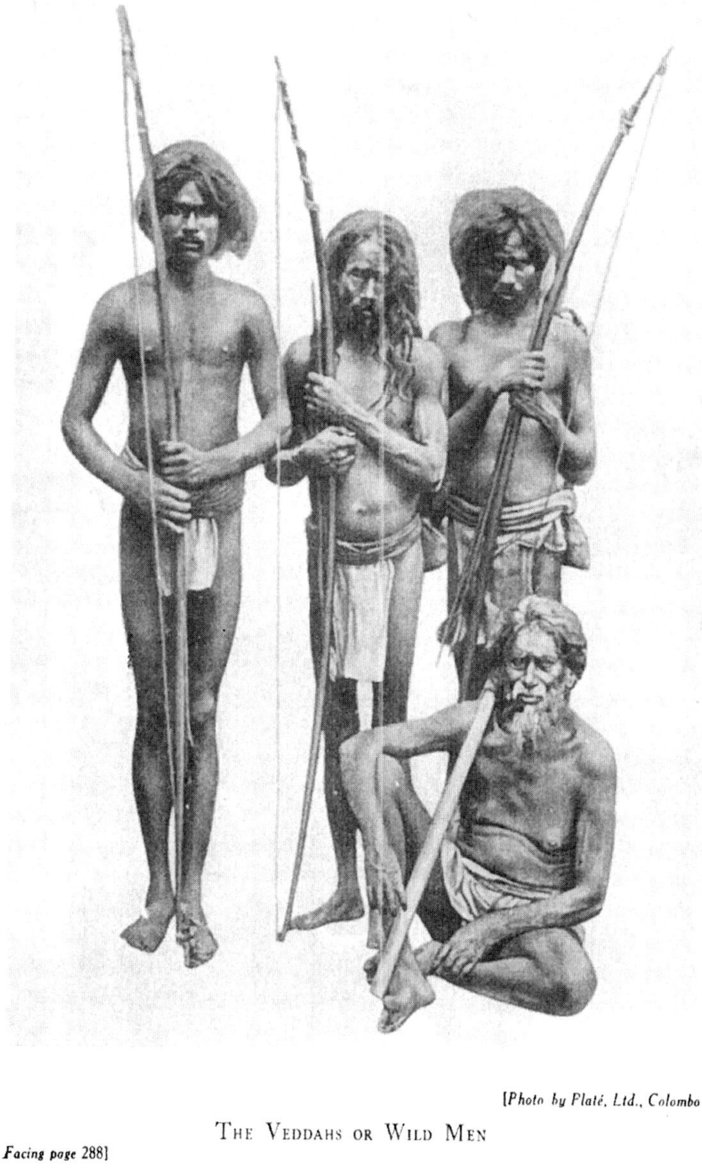

[Photo by Platé, Ltd., Colombo

THE VEDDAHS OR WILD MEN

Facing page 288]

A GLIMPSE OF TRINCOMALEE'S FAMED NATURAL HARBOUR

From "Golden Tips," by H. W. Cave (London: Sampson Low, Marston & Co.). *By courtesy of Mrs. L. B. Moore*

Facing page 289]

stances may not have warranted their existence so much as an indispensable necessity here, nor would voyagers have missed them so much either, were they non-existent, still they were welcome enough as a pleasant novelty and surprise, if only to drive home more forcibly than ever the great strides in science to-day.

Take also another welcome innovation on liners of to-day. Apart from the gymnasium which was fitted up on board the *Naldera*, although this vessel could not boast a permanent swimming bath in the real sense of the word, as are usually installed on several of the largest Trans-Atlantic liners, still who could not be grateful for an early morning "dip", or an afternoon swim, in this semblance of an improvised swimming-bath, of a huge canvas provisionally rigged up nearly every day between the First class and the Second class, to hold the water which was pumped in from the sea, and then emptied again after a fixed period, the canvas then being taken down and tucked up in its usual place?

Thus, though here it may have looked as if there was nothing that a passenger could desire but that he would get, still, it is on the Atlantic seaboard as a rule that travelling on the high seas attains its quintessence, and it is here, more than anywhere else, and especially in the northern Trans-Atlantic service, that one encounters all those devices and appliances and amenities which human ingenuity has devised to make sea travelling a real pleasure and delight.

To quote one instance by way of example where the Trans-Atlantic have forestalled their sisters of the Eastern routes, I wonder whether in any of the liners habitually sailing to and from the Orient one has already come across the ubiquitous cinematograph! Nevertheless, if this institution has not made its appearance as yet in these waters, still who is there who has not welcomed the Marconigrams on board supplying the latest world news in tabloid form, so to say?

After all, the world continues to advance apace, and hardly a year passes without fresh delights being added to the already numerous amenities of sea travelling. May these Marconigrams but prove the forerunners of unhidden delights to come, but above all, let us hope for an accelerated service that may tend to bring distant lands nearer to each other in a corresponding shorter space of time, especially in these days, when the keen and strenuous struggle for life renders even the slightest relaxation or the shortest holiday quite welcome to our jagged nerves, and when now, more than at any other time before, the truth of the old tag, "Time is money," is driven home to us with greater force than it ever was before. Moreover, the advent of the aeroplane bids fair to seriously challenge ocean-going traffic in the near future, and one hardly needs be a prophet to point out to shipping concerns that they will have to consider this menace quite seriously if they do not want to be left behind in the race.

CHAPTER XXXIV

EN ROUTE FOR BOMBAY

The run to Bombay, which took us two days and a half over a distance of 883 miles from Colombo, did not manifest anything out of the ordinary. Uneventful, however, as proved these days, still we were only too glad to get a chance, not only of seeing Bombay, the "Gateway of India", as it has been appropriately called, but also the possibility of breaking the tedium of a long voyage between Colombo and Aden. And when it is a mere speck of a ship on the distant horizon that sometimes causes such a flutter on board, especially when one has been out of sight of land for days, how much more does one, therefore, relish the chance of going ashore at some big town. And Bombay is not only a big town in the ordinary sense of the word, but it is a city and port enjoying a world-wide repute.

As a matter of fact, I passed this period in settling down again to the pleasures and amenities of "Life on the Ocean Wave," and accommodating myself to novel surroundings. Nor did these days pass without my striking up the customary acquaintanceships usual on such occasions; and in the present instance I was fortunate enough to have as genial a company of friends as on my outward voyage.

I shall certainly be grateful always to Mr. H. H. Hendry for the snapshot of the *Naldera* in Colombo harbour he so kindly gave me, as also that of myself which he took on deck: hardly any as I had of this trip to remind me in later years of the pleasant times long since gone.

However, it was Mr. and Mrs. J. Liddon Simpson's warm friendship in particular that I was glad to make on this voyage, and the courteous and sympathetic way this gentleman talked with me about my country will make me think gratefully of the pleasant times we had together on board. We are even now in touch by correspondence, and I do hope some day in the near future we shall meet again.

But there is one other little point which makes me remember this gentleman. With two nice children was he blessed, and any father would be glad to have such charming sons; and the way these two little lads romped and played and amused us all by their juvenile antics endeared them to all on board. May God bless them, and may they grow up within the wholesome influence of such good parents to be the pride of their home and their country.

CHAPTER XXXV

BOMBAY

THE morning of the 22nd September saw us anchored in the magnificent harbour of Bombay, which the *Naldera* had reached in the early dawn. The steamer was not moored alongside the pier, as is the case in Alexandria, but rode at anchor in the open roadstead some distance from the landing-stage at Ballard Pier, and this we eventually came to know was due to her sister ship, the *Narkunda*, having forestalled us there.

. . . . .

The harbour of Bombay is certainly one of the finest in the world, the verdure-clad, palm-fringed islets dotting it here and there, like those of Trincomalee, serving to heighten the effect of the beauty of the scene around, and the island of Bombay itself uniting with the mainland to transform this port into a practically landlocked harbour, and acting also as a natural barrier in keeping out the onrushing waves. The result is that this commodious harbour, far bigger even than Alexandria or Colombo, can afford safe anchorage to any number of vessels, thus dispensing with the necessity of a breakwater.

VIEW OF BOMBAY FROM AFAR

The view of Bombay from the sea gives a quite favourable impression. Right in front of us, dominating the whole picture, towers that imposing edifice the Taj Mahal Hotel, which I was recommended in Colombo to visit, behind it rising the domes and pinnacles of the splendid buildings for which this great port is so famous. Towards the left rose a verdure-clad eminence, which I subsequently came to know as Malabar Hill. Indeed, a most beautiful view did the great city present to us from where we lay, and no stranger approaching it from afar to answer the call of the East, can feel disappointed in the splendid sight that greets him.

. . . . .

Forewarned is Forearmed

On my outward voyage, owing to the delays consequent upon the Coal Strike in England at the time, the *Mantua* cut out Bombay from her itinerary, and sailed straight to Colombo from Aden; so I was somewhat disappointed to have missed seeing India's first seaport. On this occasion, the fates were kinder, in fact too kind, for one, or even two, instead of the three days we spent here, would have sufficed for Bombay, the rest having been spared for Colombo, instead of the sailing having been antedated so unexpectedly.

It was a happy foresight that made me not take things for granted, and feel cocksure of spending a ripping time in Bombay, on the strength of the likelihood of meeting a friend there. I took the wise course of none the less culling some information beforehand from my fellow-passengers of the sights of this large city, and right glad I was that I followed this course.

As a matter of fact, I had bargained on meeting an old classmate of mine, Mr. W. E. Schokman, who was the sub-editor of a Bombay newspaper called *The Advocate of India*,[1] to whom also our mutual friend, Mr. W. T. Samaraweera, had written just before I left Colombo,

[1] He has since joined the staff of the *Times of India*.

notifying him of my approaching visit, so that he might show me round as far as possible, else I would have made a better study of the place, or at least bought a guide-book.

As it turned out, this gentleman, whom I ran to earth after a good deal of inquiry, proved to be too busy with his multifarious duties, and thus enable to spare any time before five o'clock—which, of course, might afford some minutes for a friendly chat over a teacup, but would certainly not admit of the possibility of knocking about the town owing to the lateness of the hour, and my desire to return to the steamer and spend the night aboard and not in the city. It is for these reasons that I most unfortunately saw very little of this place, and, therefore, did not have the enjoyable time I had anticipated and eagerly looked forward to, nor in my rapid and speedy sightseeing could I catch the names of most of the streets and quarters and buildings I passed by.

First Impressions of Bombay

The first thing that strikes a visitor, particularly one fresh from Colombo, is that he can go his way without being pestered or even molested by a whole army of touts, and tourist-baiters such as await him in Colombo. Here also, of course, there are vehicles of every description, from the fast disappearing gharry, to the more ubiquitous and up-to-date motor car; but there they wait quietly and politely by the wayside near the landing-stage for their "fares", and you are at liberty to make your choice without any hindrance, or bother, or being unnecessarily hustled.

From the moment of landing also one sees evidences of the fine blocks of buildings, five and six storeys high, that grace this great Oriental city, such as that of the Port Trust, the Customs House, and the premises of Messrs. Mackinnon, Mackenzie & Co., the agents of the P. & O. S. N. Co.

But cheek by jowl with them is a sight which is a veritable eyesore to the traveller. True, here we do not find the spick and span, spotlessly clean, open square on to which the passenger steps on landing in Colombo; but then, it is not every city that is blessed with its like. Still, this is no reason why a person should not thread his way through a comparatively clean and undefiled street, instead of such an awful sight as the halt, the lame, the maimed, the leper, the diseased, and what not, confronting you at every step, as if this quarter, of all others, should be their trysting place, and every beggar and afflicted individual should parade his unwelcome self before your pained gaze! Yes, though one could not help pitying the emaciated forms as they held out their hands most piteously asking for alms, still the ungainly sight of the diseased and the afflicted was so repulsive as to make one almost beat a hasty retreat to his boat rather than run the gauntlet of a whole array of them for some considerable distance.

Contrasts of Weather in Bombay

How muddy did I find the streets as I was trying to seek the way to Mr. W. E. Schokman; indeed, one had actually to—well, not exactly wade—but cut through the slush and mire, and one felt that he had been literally "mutayyined" (mudded), as we say in Arabic, or, translated into English, been badly let down. And so Egypt was not the only place where a slight drizzle or shower would immediately make the streets uncomfortable, unlike beautiful Ceylon, which here again scored. Indeed, what a wonderful land is Ceylon, and yet how few in Egypt or Europe seem to have heard of its picturesqueness!

But now take the reverse the following day. The blazing, scorching, Indian sun seemed to have actually dried up the whole place; it might as well have baked it, instead of leaving the dust so loose that it flew up on

SAAMI ROCK, TRINCOMALEE

From "The Book of Ceylon," by H. W. Cave (London: Cassell & Co.). *By courtesy of Mrs. L. B. Moore.*
Facing page 296]

[Photo by Platé. Ltd., Colombo

SOLE REMAINS OF THE ONCE WONDERFUL BRAZEN PALACE, ANURADHAPURA

Facing page 297]

the slightest disturbance, and caused us no little annoyance. So dusty, indeed, did I find the streets, far dustier than the dustiest of Egypt's dusty roads, that I wondered where was the oil I once read of somewhere which was said to be used to sprinkle the streets to keep down the dust! Perhaps the War had used up the whole supply, and even water seemed to be too precious to squander indiscriminately! Still, a few drops of the precious oil might have been spared to pour on the troubled waters of our ruffled tempers which the dust could not help causing.

Malabar Hill

The drive up Malabar Hill and its Towers of Silence seems as inseparable as ever from Bombay, as are the Gizeh Pyramids and the Sphinx from Cairo. No wonder, therefore, that I made these places my first object. Thanks to Mr. Schokman, I succeeded in engaging a quite decent taxi, and the chauffeur kept pointing out and explaining the various places of interest we passed by, as if he were both chauffeur and guide rolled into one; and such a genus, needless to say, is a veritable boon of which any tourist would be only too glad.

The magnificent, open square, where I engaged the taxi, might easily run Trafalgar Square, or the Place de la Concorde very close, and to my own countrymen who have not seen either I might convey some idea of it by likening it to the Opera Square of Cairo, or the Mohammed Ali Square of Alexandria, but on a much larger and grander scale, so many and different were the fine, lofty buildings which graced this magnificent square.

Splendid edifices there were here galore, but if of such we can boast dozens in Cairo or Alexandria, in Bombay they existed by the hundred! So numerous indeed were they that I could hardly commit all to memory; yet even now I can recall a few, such as the Clock Tower with its beautiful steeple, a well-known landmark from afar; the University and its library; Elphinstone College, the leading school in the Presidency; the domed Library of the city, far grander even than our own splendid Arabesque State Library. Again, magnificent as is our Cairo Bab El-Hadid station, I wonder whether it can hold its own against Bombay's far-famed Victoria terminus, reputed to be the finest in the world. And Shepheard's Hotel or the Grand Continental Hotel, first class in every way, still it is to the Heliopolis Palace Hotel that we must go to and the nearest approach in beauty of design and external majesty to the famous Taj Mahal Hotel, the pride of Bombay.

But if in public buildings Bombay is so rich, in fine private residences it is not lacking, and as I drove along the sea front past Hornby Road, up Malabar Hill, what a galaxy of lovely villas and mansions, for the most part belonging to the rich and influential Parsee community, burst upon my view. Along this route we pass one or two railway stations, for Bombay is the starting-point of many railway lines, linking it up with the different parts of the vast Peninsula; but unprepossessing as was the external appearance of the carriages, and in particular those of the Third Class, which seemed to be choked full with their complement of suffering humanity, still I wondered whether the interior of the compartments kept in line with their outside.

Not so the tramways, some even two-decked, which looked very decent outwardly. But, curiously, they were not divided into two classes, and coupled with the snail-like pace at which they crawled along, one had but to see the dirtiness of some of the occupants to realise what a trial it must have been to travel in these cars.

Along the route a somewhat singular spectacle met our gaze. There in the distance, at the end of a causeway, was a small island which had been transformed into a domed mausoleum, from the top of which fluttered a green flag with the crescent emblazoned on it. This, I was told, had been selected by some rich Mohammedan as his last resting place, why, the chauffeur could not say. But even as I gazed on the sight I could not help reflecting on another palpable evidence of man's eternal vanity, even as it at the same time reminded me of some such similar craving on the part of the late Cecil Rhodes, who expressed a desire that he should be laid to rest on the crest of the Matoppos, as if in this sepulchre he could still be in the presence of the land where he spent so many of the years of his life!

The Towers of Silence

The famous Towers of Silence, five in number, and on the top of Malabar Hill, and called *Dakmas* in India, as inevitable an attraction as ever to the tourist, I also passed by, and had I a license with me I might have gained admittance to the grounds. In the circumstances I had to be satisfied with a glimpse of them from the car, and sure as ever I spied some of those voracious vultures which hover so ominously hard by, forming as these towers did the *raison d'être* for the existence of these huge carrion birds in their vicinity, and even in their very precincts. Perhaps not many of my countrymen are aware of the existence of these Towers, and the use to which they are put.

As a matter of fact they are used by the Parsees for the disposal of their dead. Descendants as the Parsees are of the Persians who migrated from their country at the time of the Mohammedan conquest, they take after the religion of Zoroaster, being commonly known as Magians, or fire-worshippers, to which, however, they take exception.

Since the worshipping of the four elements—earth, water, air, and fire—are among the tenets of their religion, and they dare not defile it by the so-called pollution resulting from burying the dead, they expose the corpses naked, but invisible to the public eye, within these towers, whereupon the beastly vultures come and peck these bodies, devouring the flesh, thus reducing them to a mass of bones in a comparatively very short time, the skeletons being then left exposed to be bleached by the sun, and time doing the rest.

That such a custom could be tolerated in these times speaks in a most illuminating manner to the tolerance of the British in matters of religion; but that a highly cultured community like the Parsees, in so big and modern a city as Bombay should not devise some more appropriate method for the disposal of their dead more in keeping with the character of these times is a wonder.

From the Towers of Silence we descended to the Victoria Gardens, in which are the Museum and Bombay's Zoo. The former we found closed; but the latter I entered through a fine archway without paying anything for admittance as here in Cairo, and gently brushed past some of the bystanders who scented me for a tourist, and were crowding round me, telling them that I did not need their services.

The Bombay Zoo

The Zoo I found a quite decent place, but I do not think it is on a par with ours in Egypt. But then, the Gizeh Zoo near Cairo, on the road to the Pyramids, can bear comparison with any of the finest in the world, not only for its grand assortment of animals, birds, and reptiles, but the very grounds are so exquisitely laid out, and so beautiful in the extreme that, minus the animals, they might be another Peradeniya Gardens, if not actually more lovely.

And no wonder, for these grounds are the sole relic of the once magnificent Gizeh Palace of the celebrated Khedive Ismail, and their very beauty to-day can amply testify to the splendour of the Court of this famous sovereign. Yes, a vandal hand may not have spared several of his works and palaces; but in the keeping of history safely reposes his ideal of a great and mighty Egypt; and more and more as the years roll by will time faithfully vindicate his illustrious name, and his noble-hearted efforts for the welfare and glory of his country. Indeed, if still not widely recognised as such, nevertheless history is sure some day to do him full justice as Ismail the Magnificent.

But to return. The animals in the Bombay Zoo, however, seemed to score off their brethren in captivity here by the banks of the Nile in one respect. There, in India, they seemed to have more elbow room and were allowed more moving space, in fact their cages were constructed in such a way that they seemed to exist in a semi-wild state, and it looked as if they relished this concession of greater freedom, and thus did not take to their captivity badly.

But, of course, it is the famous Hagenbeck Menagerie at Hamburg in pre-war days that excelled in this method of maintaining and running a Zoo, for in this case the animals seemed actually at large out in the open, and were only separated from one another, as also from the public, by large and broad moats filled with water; and even wild beasts have enough sagacity to look before they leap.

The Bombay Zoo I found fairly patronised by the inhabitants of the city; but it seemed that most of the people who came here did so more with the object of an airing out in the open in these pretty gardens, than with any great desire to cultivate the acquaintance of the wild beasts.

One singular exhibit in particular attracted my attention in these gardens. It is a far cry from Bombay to Egypt, but curiously I was not a little interested to find here the one pontoon boat—heavily riddled with bullets—which actually did succeed in crossing the Suez Canal to the Western bank at the time of the Turkish attempt on Egypt, only, however, to be immediately captured.

The Busy Indian Quarters

Through the busy Indian quarters we then motor, past the Racecourse, which I think is not so pretty as that of Colombo. Quite interested as I was to see the inhabitants in their everyday occupations, going about their work freely and unburdened with the trammels of convention—reminiscent of the Pettah in Colombo, or the Mousky in Cairo—I could not help observing how dirty they and their homes were.

Indeed, even in these comparatively poor quarters—not the slums—as against the statelier structures near the harbour, the dwellings though fairly big and well built, a good number of two and three stories high, still found their comeliness lost in the filth, the squalor, the dangling rags, the blackened walls, the what not, that gave even the most originally decent building ultimately such a sordid and repellent look; and no wonder when a good proportion of their very occupants were no less squalid and dirty. Indeed, one had but to look at the colour and nature of their attire to realise the truth of my statement.

I should like, however, to make it quite plain, and say quite frankly that I in no way want to wound the susceptibilities of the Indians, who have so many good points about them otherwise. Besides, where in the world does one ever find the lower classes above reproach in this respect—to a certain extent at any rate—unless, of course, peoples elsewhere can claim to be a band of saints or angels living in Paradise! Still, however, if poverty may, in a sense, be responsible for such a sorry state of affairs, and the climate and ignorance as well to a certain extent, is it not up to the educated classes and those more fortuitously placed up the social ladder, whether by reason of wealth, or position, to stoop to ameliorate their less fortunate brethren? I fear that unless we take warning of the ominous rumblings of a social upheaval in time, those who seem to be living in a fool's paradise, oblivious of these ominous portents, or callously regardless of the writing on the wall, will one day receive such a rude awakening as to rue the day they did not heed these signs.

The Crawford Fruit Market

But every cloud has its silver lining, and the depressing and repellent air I just passed through, now gives place to the welcome, clean atmosphere of the Crawford Market where I went to buy some fruit. This market situated in a central spot of the city, and comfortably accessible to tourists and passengers, surpasses even Cairo's chief market, " Souk El-Khodar ".

How neat, trim, and prim looked Bombay's Covent Garden Market, and the dainty and tantalising manner the fruits were so carefully stacked in their rows on their various stalls, or suspended, made them appear all the more appetising, and a would-be purchaser who perhaps hesitated owing to the high prices asked could not but finally yield to the temptation of securing even a few.

As a matter of fact, the fruits here, most surprisingly, were not a bit as cheap as I had anticipated, and to one who had just left Ceylon it sounded ridiculous to have to pay Rs. 4 for a dozen of mangoes, when one could have got them for less than a rupee per dozen in Colombo —and this in India, the land of mangoes *par excellence!*

Trying ever so hard to bargain, and even remonstrating quite vehemently at their preposterous prices, the dealers continued adamant in their demands, and would not budge an inch. Although I even offered Rs.3 per dozen, on the assumption that I was in Egypt, and might, therefore, consider myself not very badly let down on comparing the prices ruling here to what obtained in my country, still the dealers refused to lessen their charges of four rupees! And every next one I went to seemed as if he were the echo or mouthpiece of his neighbour, as if some Freemasonic undercurrent seemed to have made all act in league and in unison—whilst competition, why, it did not seem to exist here, and for all we know, it might on the present occasion have been a word that existed only in the dictionaries!

Out of pique, therefore, I, in turn, refused to increase my offer, and satisfied myself with nearly as good a quality of mangoes at the rate of Rs. 2 per dozen, also custard apples at the same rate, buying two dozens of each from a fruiterer some way down who very obligingly closed in with my offer, as distinct from the rather indifferent and uncivil air the others seemed to wear. I bought also half a bunch of bananas, or plantains, as they are called out East, nearly at the same rate they are sold in Colombo, and quite delicious did I find these fruits.

The Taj Mahal Hotel

To the Taj Mahal Hotel I finally go, and the wonderful thing is that this long and interesting drive called for a payment of only Rs. 12! The chauffeur, however, I gave Rs. 15, the three extra as a well-merited tip for him and his welcome aid as an impromptu guide as well, and a decent fellow he proved all the way. It was still gratifying to find him in turn as polite at the end of our journey, in the civil way he thanks me for his fare and small tip with a touch of his cap and a polite "Thank you, sir." Yes, I found the people of Bombay quite polite and courteous, and one or two occasions when I seemed to be lost in this vast city, and asked some of the passers-by for my way, how politely they pointed it out to me, some even considerately accompanying me for some distance until I got on to the right track.

A grand and imposing edifice certainly is the Taj Mahal Hotel—worthy namesake of Shah Jehan's famed mausoleum at Agra. On the Apollo Bunder facing the sea it lies; and long after many of Bombay's noted buildings have vanished from our gaze still, as a distant landmark, this palatial building looms afar. But alas! how its interior belies its magnificent exterior! Not to be too critical or captious, one wonders why its catering and its internal arrangements are not on a par with the edifice which is the pride of Bombay. Why, the Grand Oriental

[*Photo by Platé, Ltd., Colombo*

THE SACRED BO-TREE, ANURADHAPURA—THE OLDEST TREE IN THE WORLD

Facing page 304]

[*By courtesy of Mrs. W. F. Diacono and Mrs. I. M. Del Tufo*

A Group Photograph of the Diacono Family

Facing page 305]

Hotel, even when it shines forth in all the splendour of the new structure, or the Galle Face Hotel, though it may fall short of the Taj Mahal Hotel in beauty of outline and design and external magnificence, still is far superior in every other way. What a pity, therefore, that this stately hostelry, so grand externally that it compels universal admiration, should not see its way to cater more worthily, and in keeping with its repute and unique beauty, to the needs of those who pass into its portals.

How Bombay Lost her Galle Face

What a pity it is that the dockyard and the arsenal just after the Ballard Pier, and near the splendid Town Hall in Elphinstone Circle, should preclude the posibility of having one fine, long, continuous promenade along the sea front, running past the Taj Mahal Hotel onwards, like Colombo's famous Galle Face. Their very presence spoils the effect of this beautiful frontage; but, of course, it does not seem likely, nor an easy thing now to remove them elsewhere, and have this spot filled in and banked up to be on an alignment with the whole sea front.

The Elephanta Caves—Missed!

On returning to Cairo, and looking up one of the books I had on India, how many things it transpired I had missed seeing in this great city, including the famous Elephanta Caves, renowned for their sculptures connected with the Brahmin religion, and lying in an island opposite the Apollo Bunder, six miles away, and which I had heard of previously, but never knew to be so wonderful. The more was my regret, therefore, that they should have been within such easy reach, and yet I fail to visit them!

BOMBAY—A CITY OF CONTRASTS

To me Bombay seemed in more ways than one a city of contrasts! On landing, if handsome structures meet your gaze on one side, why, there just opposite to them lay the disgusting sight of as many Lazaruses! If it is very dusty to-day, it is pretty sure to be muddy to-morrow! Splendid buildings you may come across, six and seven storeys high, and " flat " life may seem very popular and very much in vogue; but as sure as ever, there, by the seaside, along Hornby Road and up Malabar Hill, were the lovely and pretty villas and mansions standing in their own grounds. A magnificent and immense harbour has Bombay, but what a lack of piers, even far less than at Alexandria.

In the city the people may seem to be rolling in wealth, but further afield there is no lack of evidence of the poverty of the less fortunate classes! The costliest and gaudiest of *saris*, of the finest texture and the loveliest embroidered silks and brocades, may be gracing the comely shoulders of some local *belle;* but only look at the apparel of the lower classes to see what a contrast they present. There, at Bombay, is the famous and wonderful Pinjrapole Hospital, where sick and old and decrepit animals and birds may be nursed back to health, or tended in their old age; would it not be only meet therefore to commiserate likewise with the poor stricken folks who dot the pavements near the Ballard Pier, and found as generous a home or asylum for them as well—not that Bombay is lacking in any amount of hospitals, but a little more zeal in the right direction would relieve this fair city of a veritable eyesore?

But most curious of all, where the British Raj holds such sway—and unlike my own country where, unfortunately, the bulk of the people hardly ever take the initiative in enterprises of public utility, but invariably wait for the Government to take the lead, still it is to the very generosity and munificence of the city's local philanthropists themselves in the main that Bombay glories in its magnificent buildings and public institutions! Which, in turn, gives rise to another paradox incidentally. In a population numbering 315,000,000 souls, India possesses only about 100,000 Parsees scattered about the whole country, the major part of them, however, being in Bombay; and yet it is to these very people, of all others, that Bombay is most indebted.

Wealthy they are, and as enterprising and influential; yet nobly and munificently have they made use of their wealth and affluence to promote the interests and prosperity of this great city. All the more credit, therefore, to them. Indeed, even *Punch* has chronicled such laudable behaviour on their part, and sung their praises in as pretty a pun in regard to one of India's greatest philanthropists called Sir Cowasji Jehangir Readmoney, who once offered, amongst his many donations far and wide, a sum of £200 for charities in London on the occasion of the recovery of the then Prince of Wales: "Is Mr. Readymoney a Parsee? At any rate, he is not parsimonious."[1]

The Long Arm of Coincidence!

At Bombay we had the rather unusual occurrence of two sister ships meeting at the same time! By a curious yet happy coincidence the *Naldera* and the *Narkunda* met there, the incoming *Naldera*, on the second day of our stay, moving towards evening from her moorings on to the berth of her sister ship just alongside the Ballard Pier, as the outgoing *Narkunda* vacated it to proceed on her voyage to Colombo and Australia. It was a pretty sight indeed this meeting of the two "ocean greyhounds," and one never appreciated the huge and immense proportions of these leviathans as when we observed them so close from the quay!

[1] *Picturesque India*, by W. S. Caine, p. 16.

Farewell Bombay!

At Bombay we received a quite large batch of passengers, including T.H. the Maharajah and Maharanee of Porebunder and a large suite, several of whom, quite affable and courteous, also heartily entered into the games on board, and showed to great advantage in deck cricket in particular.

Pages indeed might be written of Bombay, as it would need days to see this big place properly; still I hope this brief and scanty account of mine will not be out of place in this little volume, endeavouring as I have done to jot down at random a few impressions of things just as I saw them in this important city.

At five o'clock in the afternoon of the 24th the *Naldera* weighs anchor, and steams slowly away from Bombay and her splendid buildings. Gradually we move out of her handsome harbour, and one by one her domes and spires melt away in the distance, until at last it is only her magnificent domed Taj Mahal Hotel, outlined against the horizon, that looms afar, the one conspicuous landmark of this city of domes and spires, resplendent as ever in the golden rays of the setting sun.

A few minutes more, and even the Taj Mahal Hotel dips in the distant horizon, and then vanishes. Another moment, and we are on the open sea, *en route* for Aden, Bombay and all that it stands for far, far behind.

CHAPTER XXXVI

ADEN

THE run of 1,660 miles from Bombay to Aden was a very enjoyable part of my voyage. The weather conditions were almost perfect, and the large complement of newcomers served to enliven matters to no inconsiderable degree, games being entered into with a great zest, and all-round merriment and jollity prevailing. Of course not all the newcomers were sociable and affable in their manner, for here and there, unfortunately, one would come across one of that stiff, stand-offish genus who seemed to be afflicted with "colonial fever" in its most virulent form; still, as a matter of fact, no one missed him at all.

Curiously, there were one or two Indians who were prone to ape these airs, and went to the extent, as I was told, of adapting their names to smack of an English accent and nomenclature, as if their own names were too low to be used! The folly of such action is so obvious as not to need any comment. Indeed, one had but to hear the outspoken views of their own compatriots in no measured terms, and to observe the natural grace, charm, and urbanity of the Maharajah of Porebunder and his relatives, which made them so popular with all, to realise how such action was deprecated. It could in no way raise the misguided individuals in the estimation of others.

. . . . .

Aden we reach just before midnight of the 28th, and it is a pity that on this occasion again we should have arrived at so late an hour as to preclude the possibility of a short trip ashore.[1] Our disappointment was aggravated by the fact that it was pitch dark, unlike when the *Mantua* steamed in, when the lovely moonlight shone forth in all its brilliancy, and served to dispel to some extent the gloom that might have otherwise pervaded the scene around.

Leaving as we had to only four hours later, that is to say, in the small hours of the morning, there was no question of landing to the majority of the passengers. However, there were some adventurous souls who could not let such an occasion slip by without "stretching their legs a bit" on shore, and I for one availed myself of the kind invitation of a leading merchant and notable of the place, Mr. Mohammed Abdul Kadir Mackawee, who had come on board at Bombay after leaving his son at the famous Mohammedan College of Aligarh, and was now disembarking at Aden.

Seeing that some of my companions on board were also bent on landing, this gentleman, with his wonted generosity, kindly extends the invitation to them as well, and together we all go ashore. At the jetty we find two fine, large motor cars awaiting him, and in them we drive from Steamer Point—as the part about the landing-stage is called—through Aden Camp, the marine quarter by the sea, on to the Old Town some distance away behind the volcanic hills where the majority of the inhabitants live. It stands on the site of the crater of Aden's extinct volcano, as geologists say.

In spite of the lateness of the hour, and the brief spell

[1] During my 1924 trip however, I fared better in regard to Aden, for both on my outward trip to Colombo on board the *Maloja*, and on my homeward trip on board the *Mongolia*, I was able to go ashore on both occasions owing to these vessels reaching port in the daytime.

Though on these occasions I found Mr. Mackawee away at Lahej—a small sultanate twenty-five miles away in the hinterland of Aden, under British protection—still, fortunately for us, Mr. Abdel Kerim Hassanally, whom I got the pleasure of knowing during my last trip when he came to meet Mr. Mackawee, kindly steps into the breach.

Together we all go ashore, and certainly we would not have enjoyed our time half so well but for the generous way he kindly places his motor cars at our disposal, and most courteously personally conducting us round the sights of Aden, including the famous Tanks, and the rather poor attempt at a botanical garden at Sheikh Osman, eight miles away from Aden.

we spent ashore, we still appreciated our joy-ride immensely, and were exceedingly grateful for the kindness of this warm-hearted gentleman and his equally cordial relatives and friends who were very obliging, with the traditional courtesy and hospitality of the Arabs from whom they were descended. It was indeed a welcome change from the tedium and humdrum routine of a long sea voyage, and though there was nothing much to see at Aden, especially at this late hour, still it was a novel experience. To me in particular it afforded an additional pleasure to be once more amongst people who could speak my own tongue; and one has but to take the case of an Englishman, say, wandering in the heart of Africa suddenly stumbling across another Britisher in these remote, impenetrable regions, to realise the joy he must feel at such good luck, and to appreciate my sentiments and emotions on the present occasion.

The weather was warm enough, and even sultry to some extent. One missed the cool northerly breezes of Egypt, which, at night in particular, compensate for the discomfort resultant upon the heat of the daytime. Though the night was very dark, still the dim-lit streets enabled us to perceive what a depressing, arid and desolate countryside this district presented, with hardly any of the refreshing greenery and foliage that help so much to soften and beautify a landscape. And this very fact drove home to me nearer than ever what Egypt might have been but for the life-giving, bounteous waters of Father Nile which made what otherwise might have been a lifeless, waterless wilderness to blossom as the rose, and pulsate with the life and energy of a hardy, vigorous, and industrious race.

No wonder, therefore, that a considerable portion of the inhabitants of Aden, especially the labouring classes, were of such poor physique, and looked so spare, pallid and sallow, the dark, frail, semi-emaciated forms of the coaling coolies, Somalis from the African coast opposite, I think, who could hardly abate their chattering before getting to work, forming a striking contrast to the sturdy, fine, muscular, bronzed forms of their counterparts in the Egyptian ports or fields.

The houses and shops in the marine quarter at Steamer Point as it is locally known, were quite fair and passable specimens of their kind; not so the dwellings in the Old Town, which were of an inferior character, and had not much about them to commend, as they lay one straggling, indiscriminate mass. Here and there one did find a building which looked bigger and trimmer, such as those of my host, Mr. Mackawee, or his friend Mr. Ābdul Kerim Hassanally, who met us on board, and now formed one of our party, but these were few and far between. Besides, this quarter was conspicuous by an entire lack of anything in the nature of a pretty villa or bungalow nestling in as lovely a garden. Yes, though it was for the brief spell of an hour or so that we drove through these quarters, still we could not help remarking on this lack of comfortable and pleasing dwellings.

These two quarters of Āden are connected by roadways bored through the volcanic rocky ridges to link up the two localities, the most notable being Main Pass; and at times these paths are more in the nature of mountain defiles flanked with steep and scowling rocky acclivities, the giddy heights on either side of some ravine being even in some places bridged overhead to facilitate intercourse.

One quaint sight attracted our attention here: the hubble-bubble, or *nargilah*, or *shishah*, as it is called in Egypt. The wonderful thing about those at Aden is that they were not the small, dainty glass receptacles with the long, neat serpentine coils one can enjoy his smoke through, but huge vessels as tall as a man; and as the smoker inhaled the seemingly enjoyable breath through the long coils to the gurgling and bubbling of the waters inside the glass bottle, with eyebrows upraised, and the air of one who had realised the apotheosis of all that is worldly, one wondered whether it was he

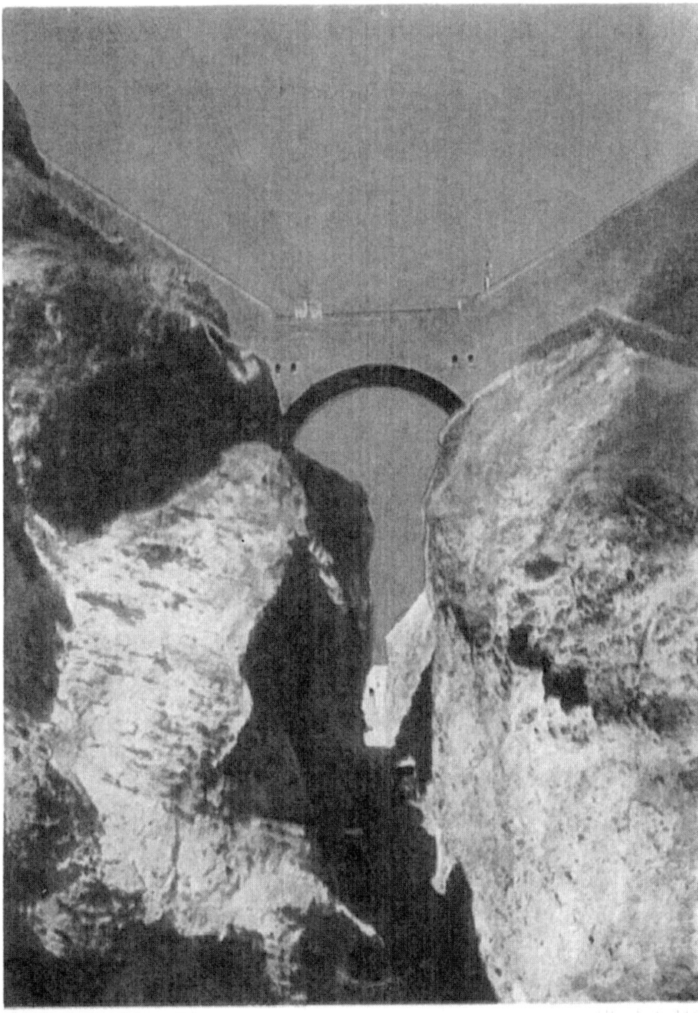

Photo by] [Benghiat, Aden.

Main Pass, Aden.

p. 312

who enjoyed his smoke the more, or de Quincey his opium.

It is a wonder how people can eke out an existence on this barren, cheerless rock standing on the site of an extinct volcano; and but for the excitement consequent upon the arrival and departure of the big liners Aden might, for all we know, be a woebegone, God-forsaken town. Still, nothing daunted, nor their ardour and business acumen damped by such drawbacks, its inhabitants industriously and enterprisingly do their best to make the best of a bad situation, and succeed very cleverly in driving a brisk trade in ostrich feathers from the African coast opposite, and in amber necklaces, and fancy baskets with the passengers of the ships calling here, at the same time exporting hides and skins, and the famous Mocha or Yemen coffee, and frankincense from the outlying districts. All the more credit, therefore, to these hardy Arabs who thereby prove themselves worthy descendants of their great predecessors.

Moreover, Aden is not without its own local attraction, incidentally furnishing an inducement for supplying a livelihood to a good number of people. No passenger going ashore for sightseeing fails to visit the well-known Tanks famous all the world over, and lying in a mountain gorge somewhere near the Old Town. Dating back to 1000 B.C., though erroneously attributed by some to Solomon, these Tanks were neglected for many centuries, and lay buried beneath the accumulating sand, being ultimately unearthed only in 1854 by Sir Lambert Playfair, who accidentally stumbled across them.

Hollowed out of solid rock, supplemented by dams of masonry and cement, these marvels have wonderfully stood the test of time; and though the rainfall is so meagre as hardly to admit of their being filled often, still the little water these gigantic cisterns collect, though unfit for drinking, is nevertheless turned to some use in being utilised for domestic purposes, the drinking water being obtained by condensation. These Tanks of course we could not visit this time; but in November 1897, when I was going to Egypt from Ceylon on board the *Sachsen* of the Norddeutscher Lloyd, I had the pleasure of seeing them in the company of a party of passengers who kindly took me ashore with them, and most wonderful indeed they looked, though they were empty at the time.

Of course it was neither the temperature nor the climate that first attracted Englishmen to this barren rock. The story of the occupation is a characteristic episode of the expansion of the British Empire. In the year 1837, a ship flying the British colours was wrecked near the rock, and those on board were barbarously maltreated by the natives. Reparation was demanded by the Government, and solemnly promised; but before the agreement had been carried out the Sultan died, and his son refused to fulfil his father's promise. Force, therefore, had to be used, and the place was taken by storm. So far, the incident is simple enough; but why did our troops remain there permanently? Having accidentally come into possession of the place, the authorities began to perceive dimly the advantage of having somewhere in that region a bit of British territory. It was the time when the Mediterranean and Red Sea route to India was beginning to attract the serious attention of far-seeing energetic men. Only a few months before the occupation of Aden a monthly service had been established for carrying the mails across Egypt, and it seemed tolerably certain that the trade by this route would annually increase. In these circumstances it was convenient to have a half-way house between Suez and Bombay; and with the rapid development of trade caused by the opening of the Alexandria-Suez railway in 1858, and of the Suez Canal in 1869, what was only a convenience became a commercial and strategical necessity of the first order. Aden was, therefore, not only retained, but also strongly fortified, and other precautions had to be taken. To prevent the French Government from carrying out its intention of seizing Perim, which completely commands the mouth of the Red Sea, we had to hoist the British Flag on the island in 1857. The French replied by obtaining in 1862 the cession of Obock on the African mainland, and in 1882 it showed a tendency to extend its borders in the direction of Somaliland. This was a serious danger for Aden. Under British protection the population had increased more than twenty-fold, whilst the production of the necessaries of life had remained almost stationary. Consequently provisions had to be drawn in large quantities from the Somali coast on the African side of the Gulf, and it was of the utmost importance that this granary of the fortress should be protected against foreign annexation. To prevent annexation by France, Somaliland was declared a British Protectorate, and so it remains even unto the present day.[1]

It is as a coaling and military station, therefore, that Aden has since developed, and now bulks large in Britain's Red Line; and commanding as it does the approaches to the Red Sea and the routes to the East, blessed also with a fine harbour, no wonder that the British, notwithstanding its climatic, residential, and other shortcomings, have none the less made the most of its possibilities to fortify it strongly, and transform it into something of a Gibraltar of the Indian Ocean. Standing as it does on a peninsula connected by a low-lying isthmus with the mainland, at the gateway of which stands the small Sultanate of Lahej, over which Great Britain, as a measure of precaution declared a protectorate, and coupled with its powerful fortifications, Aden is practically invulnerable by both land and sea.

As a sentry to the Red Sea, therefore, this impregnable rock-fortress mounts guard, even as its counterpart Gibraltar dominates the approaches of the Western Mediterranean; and how remarkable it is that along the chain of Britain's world-wide dominions these naval stations at strategic points act like links in her far-flung empire.

[1] *The Web of Empire*, by Sir Donald Mackenzie Wallace, pp. 55–6.

Speaking of the Aden Hinterland, perhaps there are some who still remember the late Sultan of Lahej, who came to Cairo about a dozen years ago, and was in the limelight for some time.

Not the least interesting point about this petty Arab potentate was the decoration he conferred on the late Lord Kitchener at the time, and one wonders how this distinguished soldier took to this mark of distinction, and whether it found an honoured place by the side of, say, the insignia of the Garter.[1]

[1] During May 1924, H.H. Sultan Abdel Kerim Fadl, the present ruler of Lahej, accompanied by my friend, Mr. Mohammed Abdel Kadir Mackawee, paid Cairo a visit on his way to England. How glad indeed I was to meet my friend again, and this time in my own country, and though it was for a short time only that he stayed, still I was none the less delighted to have had the chance of seeing him again.

Thanks to Mr. Mackawee, I had the honour of being presented to H.H. the Sultan, and notwithstanding his exalted position, I could not but be deeply touched by the condescension he invariably displayed towards me whenever I had occasion to call to see Mr. Mackawee at the Grand Continental Hotel, where they were sojourning at the time.

Indeed, such graciousness on the part of the Sultan serves but to reflect his broadminded and democratic spirit. Happy therefore must Lahej be to have in his person a ruler so democratically imbued with the spirit of the age, and one who, as I gathered from what little I saw of him, was only too eager to keep pace with modern conditions, and uplift his people and add to their prosperity and welfare.

CHAPTER XXXVII

HOME!

SOON after quitting Aden we enter the Red Sea through the famous Strait of Bab El-Mandab (Gate of Tears), once so notorious for the number of shipwrecks here before the days of careful charting and wireless telegraphy. The Island of Perim, right in the middle of the Strait, as if it were a sentinel, we then pass, as also several other small volcanic islands.

As a matter of fact, whereas during the six days' voyage between Aden and Colombo one hardly ever sees any land after the Island of Socotra, and rarely ever encounters a sail either, still, on the four days' run through the Red Sea between Aden and Suez, especially in the opening and closing stages of this phase, one is scarcely out of sight of land, and often as not one does espy some sail in the distance. In these waters shoals of flying fish also keep us company, though it is in the Indian Ocean just before Aden where they seemed to me to be more numerous. Now and then also, a porpoise or two, and sometimes even several at a time, racing to keep pace with the steamer, dart through the waters just above the surface.

Moreover, I have never seen the Red Sea rough; and though at the time we were giving Socotra a wide berth, owing to its lying out of our route between Bombay and Aden, still, somehow about these regions one did get a bit of a swell now and then, as if Socotra was still bent on not letting us pass without making her unwelcome presence felt.

. . . . .

The first day in the Red Sea was abnormally hot, and I was beginning to fear that there would be a recurrence of the uncomfortable time we had on our outward voyage. Happily, owing to the season of the year, and our heading northwards, the weather cooled day by day, and it kept blowing a stiffer and stiffer breeze the more we proceeded northwards, until in the Gulf of Suez the wind actually whistled, and we literally had to cut our way forward on our early morning strolls round the deck.

As we enter the Gulf of Suez on either side lie ranges of mountains, but how barren and repellent they looked, devoid as they were of every vestige of foliage and vegetation. If only the lovely hills of Ceylon could but transplant some of their luxuriant verdure here, less dismal and barren would these ridges look, inasmuch as they could have given a foretaste of the wealth of cultivation and incomparable fertility of the valley of the Nile that lay beyond.

. . . . .

Even as the majestic *Naldera* threads her way through these desolate and parched ridges I keep asking myself whether this, perchance, might not be the spot where the Israelites crossed the Red Sea in their flight from Egypt. This reflection could not help reminding me of a funny story I once read which Booker Washington, the noted American negro publicist, related of a negro missionary.

The story goes that this priest was preaching a sermon about the flight of the Israelites across the Red Sea, and desiring to impress his congregation with an ostentatious display of his learning and rhetoric, he starts:

"Of course you would like to know how the Israelites crossed the Red Sea?"

"Yes, certainly," cry out many in unison.

"Well, you see," he proceeds, waxing even more eloquent at the encouragement received, and the eagerness he evidently saw depicted on the faces of his audience, "when the Israelites arrived in the morning at the shores of the Red Sea, it was frozen at the time, so they were able to cross over the ice; but by the time the pursuing Egyptians, with Pharaoh at their head, arrived, the sun had risen in the heavens, and even as they were crossing the Red Sea the sun grew hotter and hotter, finally melting the ice, Pharaoh and his hosts being thus engulfed in the waters and drowned."

Then follows a pause, and he comes to a dead stop, with dramatic demeanour smugly reflecting on the favourable effect he seemed to have produced by what he believed to be his admirable and hitherto unheard-of explanation of this mystery which had baffled so many before him.

But as surely as ever there must be the inevitable fly in the ointment—at any rate, so it must have seemed to him.

Up stands one of the congregation. "But, your worship, we have learnt in geography that Egypt lies near the Equator, and therefore has a warm climate; so how could the Red Sea freeze?"

Here was a poser indeed! The catechism was producing some commotion. Ah! here was something interesting indeed, thought some of the congregation. Had the would-be erudite priest caught a tartar? No. Nothing flabbergasted, he rises admirably to the occasion, and with brazen effrontery coolly seeks to scotch his unforeseen heckler:

"Yes, I was sure I would encounter one of these priggish upstarts like the person who has just asked me such a silly (*sic*) question! Doesn't he know that I was speaking of a time when there was no geography, nor any such thing as the Equator?"

. . . . .

Gradually Suez draws near, and closer as I approach my native land, the faster beats my heart with joy. How could I resist the sensation of gladness of being back home once more? How truly and beautifully has Scott interpreted these emotions in words when he says:

> "Breathes there a man with soul so dead
> Who never to himself has said,
> 'This is my own, my native land'?
> Whose heart hath ne'er within him burned,
> As homewards his footsteps he hath turned,
> From wandering on a foreign strand?"

. . . . .

At last, in the Suez roadstead the *Naldera* anchors in the afternoon of October 2nd, at 2 p.m., first, to take on the pilot; second, for the passengers to be medically examined by a doctor from ashore; and third, till our turn comes to enter the Canal, a Dutch steamer and the P. & O. *Kashmir* having already forestalled us in this respect.

The funny thing about the medical inspection was that it was conducted by an English lady doctor! But why it should have been a lady instead of a gentleman, as is usual in such cases, I cannot comprehend! Was it that there existed a dearth of men doctors consequent upon the Great War, or lady doctors had proved more efficient? Perhaps, next time it will be a lady pilot who will lead us in!

Yes, the fair sex have come on greatly, and are running us pretty close in everything, and the sterner sex will have to look to their laurels if they don't want to go under and play second fiddle.

And reasoning on these lines, does it not sound rather equitable that since the fair sex have left their own lovely world, which suited them so finely, and entered the arena to compete against us in vocations which at one time might have been considered the rightful preserves of

[Photo by John & Co., Kandy

THE BOGAMBARA RECREATION GROUND, KANDY

Facing page 320]

[*By courtesy of Mr. H. H. Hendry*

THE R.M.S. "NALDERA" IN COLOMBO HARBOUR

Facing page 321]

their sterner brethren, it is only fair that they in turn should be prepared to shoulder the obligations and responsibilities which appertain to the fields of action they have embarked upon?

Thus, if any of the sterner sex should superficially appear to be ungallant now and then, it is not that this is inherent in their character, or that they have not the decency to treat the fair sex with all the courtesy and consideration due to them, but it is more with a desire to bring home to the female mind the onerous duties of their new position, and their duty accordingly to stand the strain of what is of their own seeking; or, possibly also, that in some cases, several of them seem to be so shorn of that decorum, charm, and ladylike grace, which are such priceless assets to the fair sex, that they could no more be entitled to the appellation of a lady, than a man to that of a gentleman, unless each party comports itself as such.

. . . . .

Another remark I would like to make is why shipping companies do not do something to provide such facilities as could enable passengers to land at Suez, dash on to Cairo, see some of its wonderful sights, such as the famous Pyramids of Gizeh and the Sphinx, and then catch the boat at Port Said—and for doing which I think there is ample time if the arrangements could be carefully made to admit of such a possibility, even with the extension of the stay of the ship at Port Said slightly.

Besides, in response to the proposal and good offices of the various shipping companies, the Egyptian Government might possibly see its way to accelerate the railway service, and have some of the trains timed to synchronise with the arrival and departure of the various big liners; or, in such cases where the railway service may not be available at the time, or a sufficient inducement exists, a special train might be engaged, as some of the navigation companies do for home-going passengers.

Thus, in spite of the rather prolonged stay of four hours at Suez, none of the passengers were able to land, and how many wished they could have gone on to Cairo, so near it lay to them, and yet so far, owing to the rather hard regulations of the steamers.

When the modern suburb of Cairo, the new Heliopolis, was built there was some talk of a very fast railway service between Cairo and Suez right across the desert, which could cover the distance in a couple of hours only. Had such a project materialised, what a boon it would have been, and a strong inducement for the shipping companies to reconsider and even relax the present prohibition of landing.[1]

. . . . .

Through the Suez Canal we sail all night, the huge wide beam of the *Naldera* at times seeming as if it actually filled up the whole breadth of the Canal. Morning dawns, but even as on the eve of my approach to Colombo I tasted not of sleep, here again sleep was out of the question.

Slowly and slowly the distant white walls of Port Said glistening in the golden morning sunshine come into view, and nearer draws the magnificent domed building of the Suez Canal Headquarters, as if it were another Taj Mahal Hotel. A little while more, and Port Said is right in front of us, the *Naldera* casting anchor right opposite the Marina Palace Hotel, from where three months and a half ago, eagerly and often I scanned the horizon in the direction of the far-famed, gigantic statue of de Lesseps to descry the long-awaited *Mantua* as

[1] I am glad to be able to record here that since these lines were penned I have had not long to wait for such hope to materialise—in a rather modified form though it may be. In the present instance it is the motor car that comes to our rescue; for the Egyptian Government seeing the feasibility and great possibilities of such a project, accordingly tackled this problem in grim earnest, finally in April 1925 granting a credit of £22,000 for the construction of a fine motor road between Cairo and Suez, *via* Heliopolis. Needless to say, this road when finished, will have met a long needed want, and with the distance covered only in a couple of hours, passengers landing at Suez can save a good deal of time by dashing on to Cairo, instead of proceeding by the circuitous railway track *via* Ismalia, taking more than double this period. Besides, it will also incidentally prove a quite welcome outlet for week-enders who may wish to picnic by the silvery sea.

anxiously, as I now gazed landwards to return to my home.

. . . . .

Once more are enacted those very scenes that heralded my arrival in Colombo; handshakes all round; salutations of farewell, and hopes of meeting some day soon again; mutual promises to communicate with those with whom I was on closer terms of friendship; thanks to the genial captain, Commander H. G. H. Lewellin, R.N.R., also to the kind and obliging purser, the very obliging steward, and the equally polite and attentive old baggage master who had kindly tended my plants on board.

Then Hassanein Effendy Hilmy—a notable of Port Said—once more I meet, the first to board the steamer to meet me here, as he was the last to see me off on the *Mantua* on my outward voyage. And then at last, after as enjoyable a voyage as one could wish for, I set foot once more on Egypt's hoary soil, thankful to the Almighty that I had lived to return to my native land.

. . . . .

The noon train I then take for Cairo, and as gay and as beautiful I find Egypt's metropolis and Africa's greatest city. But even as I drive to my house it is with mixed feelings of joy and sorrow that I cross the threshold of my home; joy that I have lived to return, but sorrow in that how different was this homecoming to that of 1918, when I returned from a football trip with my club—the National Sporting Club—to Port Said.

Then, it was my beloved, invalid mother leaning on a stick, at the head of the staircase, who greeted me lovingly and fondly as only a devoted mother can; but now, alas! in spite of the hearty and loyal manner my faithful servants greeted me, still there was no one dear and near to welcome me back.

Never indeed, never did I feel the loss of my beloved mother so deeply and poignantly, and with so great an agony of bleeding sorrow, as at that moment when I entered my home with that feeling of choking in my throat which my readers can well understand.

But still withal to be back in one's home is a joy better felt than described, and in the words of Payne's famous song, "Home, Sweet Home!" which every *prima donna*, from Adelina Patti of another day to Dame Melba and Tettrazzini of our time has immortalised:

> "'Mid pleasures and palaces though we may roam,
> Be it ever so humble there's no place like home!"

CHAPTER XXXVIII

IMPRESSIONS

It would be perhaps appropriate to have concluded this book with the magic word "Home!" and all that it implies. But when I came to reflect on the point, I thought it might be worth while summing up the present work with a few supplementary remarks, if only to bring out more lucidly, and in a more connected form, any such points as may have escaped the attention of my readers, and also to give them some faint idea of my own personal impressions of the island in a final and general summing-up.

The Lovely View of Ceylon from Afar

I quite agree with Cave that the best time to approach Ceylon is the early dawn, as fortunately fell to me. "The scene which unfurls itself to us if we are early risers, and have the good fortune to approach the coast at break of day, is one of unique beauty.

"We behold first the mountain zone, sacred to tea production, rising in one mighty upheaval from the plains of Ceylon, and capped in the centre by the venerated peak named after our first parent. The mists are as yet lying in the valleys, and the cool blue tones above them give us the true contour of those fertile mountains upon which millions of tea bushes are flourishing. . . .

"As we approach nearer and nearer we see the mists arise, attracted above by the rays of the rising sun, and a scene of verdant loveliness is disclosed which stands in welcome contrast to the parched and barren shores we have left behind at Suez and Aden. The mountains are now lost to view, and the details of the beautiful palm-fringed shores gradually increase as we steam towards the harbour."[1]

Why Summer is the Best Time to Visit Ceylon

I cannot, however, concur with Cave in that what we usually term the winter months are the best season to visit Ceylon. A fairly equable climate has Ceylon throughout the year, unchangeable in the sense that we recognise the change of the seasons here in Egypt or Europe. It is therefore immaterial to the tourist what time he visits Ceylon. As a matter of fact, it is the north-east Monsoon blowing from October to April, and the south-west Monsoon blowing from May to September which affect its climatic conditions; so, when one district would be receiving the attentions of Jupiter Pluvius, elsewhere it would be King Sol who would be ruling paramount, and *vice versa*. Thus, when it is hot in Colombo, the jaded townsman can flee to the Kandyan Hills or the mountains of Nuwara Eliya, whereas when it is very rainy there the hillsmen can afford a change by the seaside.

Besides, blessed as Ceylon is with a salubrious and equable climate all the year round, there is the weather of each locality to suit every taste. Warm, and perhaps a little too damp it may be on the western coast, but amidst the Kandyan Hills is the ideal weather, as if to keep fit company with the incomparable beauty of these regions. A little farther up, and there at Nuwara Eliya is the cold, crisp, bracing atmosphere to remind one of Merrie England or Bonnie Scotland. Why bother then about the climate when the desired weather lies at one's disposal, as if it were at his simple beck and call?

[1] *The Book of Ceylon*, by H. W. Cave, p. 30.

If to this advantage the tourist can add several others, why then should he not choose the time best suited for such. It is generally in the months of July, August and September that one can find Ceylon brimful of events of all kinds and excitement of every shape—in other words, these are the months of Ceylon's "Season", and during this period can the tourist taste of almost everything that is his heart's desire.

Even Cave himself admits that August and September are quite delightful months, and if he more strongly advocates the claim of the winter months, it is in the main, I think, because it is during this period that a good number of the people of Europe flee from the rigours of their winter to seek warmth and sunshine in more hospitable climes, and to Ceylon, as a consequence, he might as well endeavour to attract them at this period.

It is during Ceylon's "Season" also, that is to say, during summer, that we have the biggest race meetings, culminating in the Governor's Cup—the Derby of Ceylon—and as if the social side also must assert itself, "August Week" attains the *clou* of the season in the State Ball at Queen's House—the Colombo residence of the Governor of the Island. Also, as if "August Week" were the one outstanding event of the year, and it were the most fitting time to make hay with the sun of seeming prosperity shining so brightly, even the shops take their cue from the prevailing vogue, and are never so lavish or assertive in the display of their goods as during these days.

Moreover, the biggest sporting events of the year claim their share of the limelight during this eventful period, and whether it is football (both codes), cricket, hockey, or tennis, each never fails to draw the greatest exponents of the game and evoke the highest enthusiasm amongst its numerous votaries.

Most probably also there is sure to be the lady or the gentleman with the sweet tooth. Could they really return from the East and say they did not taste of the wonderful mangosteen, or the luscious mango, or the delicious custard apple, and the numerous other sweet fruits which are never so abundant as during this season?

And the East, "The Gorgeous East" and all that it connotes of pageants of barbaric pomp and splendour, who does not wish to have some personal experience of the truth of this phrase? Happily, it is in these months that we do meet with them, in July there being the great Vel Festival of the Tamils in Colombo, with the silver car drawn by a pair of handsome bulls as the dominant figure; followed in August at Kandy by the even more famous and wonderful Perahera of the Sinhalese; and its wonderful phalanx of threescore richly caparisoned elephants in line, taken in a magnificent procession round the town to the sound of music, dancing, and the flare of a thousand torches, is a spectacle indeed that can never fade from one's memory. If there were no stronger inducement to visit Ceylon during these months, it were enough to come and see the far-famed Perahera and all that it represents of the grandeur of ancient Lanka.

What tourist then can resist the temptation of all these shows? He is out to enjoy himself, and it is such spectacles and attractions that can cater for his pleasures. Why then should he throw away such golden chances and come in December or January, when there is hardly anything out of the ordinary to assert its claim or arrest the attention of the traveller?

However, it is not every tourist who can choose his own time to fit in with "August Week" and the other attractions I have just enumerated; still, exclusive of these advantages, he can find Ceylon at all times as interesting and picturesque as ever. Here we have no annual exodus in the sense we meet with in other lands. Of course there will be those who will be going home on furlough, or on business bent, or in quest of pleasure; but here in Ceylon there is no winter exodus as in Europe, nor a wholesale rush abroad in summer as in Egypt. Come at what time he likes, the traveller will find Ceylon as attractive as ever; and if perchance he finds one district a bit too warm or rainy, why, in a few hours, whether

[Photo by Mitchell, Bombay

THE VICTORIA TERMINUS, WITH THE MUNICIPAL CORPORATION HALL ON THE LEFT, BOMBAY

Facing page 328]

THE PARSI TOWERS OF SILENCE

From " The Wonders of the World " (London : Hutchinson & Co.). *By courtesy of the Publisher*

Facing page 329]

by motor car along its splendid roads, or by rail through matchless scenery, he can be transferred, as if by Aladdin's magic lamp, to some more congenial sphere.

How Colombo Impresses a Stranger Favourably

And man being human, it is only natural that he would expect a reasonable allowance of creature comforts. What is his amazement, therefore, when, first in Egypt, and then in Ceylon, he can stumble across those amenities of life and the last word in comfort and luxury his wildest imagination could not have dared to picture! To him it comes as a revelation in some sense to find such an incredibly grand city as Cairo, or such a prosperous and flourishing seaport as Colombo rolling in all the wealth and luxury of London or Paris, and when once he moves about their business and shopping quarters why, it were as if that part of London known as the City with all its galaxy of shops and array of priceless goods had been transplanted, in less degree, perhaps, but still no matter, in the Opera Square of Cairo and its adjoining streets, or in the Fort of Colombo and its bye-streets.

No traveller, therefore, who has formed a favourable idea of the beauty of Ceylon by his first glimpse of it from afar, can have reason to be disappointed on landing when he comes to know it more intimately in the prosaic and mundane aspect of everyday life. No passenger indeed can ever fail to be as deeply impressed by the trimness of the open square leading to the jetty, and its spotlessly clean character; and the able way the traffic is manipulated here cannot but redound to the credit of this fair city.

With such an imposing pair of buildings as the Grand Oriental Hotel on the one side, and the Victoria Arcade on the other, as if they were a pair of sentinels guarding the gateway of modern Lanka's metropolis, the passenger immediately passes into such a bewildering eddy of stately shops, quaint scenes, divers races, deafening traffic, and what not, that it looks as if he were carried unconsciously, involuntarily along this kaleidoscopic show right into the heart of some magic wonderland, where East and West seem as if they merge, if only for a while, into some common blend for the good of this great city.

To passengers, in particular, who have barely a few hours to stay in port what a delightful experience must this stroll prove amidst such quaint scenes and interesting objects, and whether it is to replenish their stock of tobacco, or buy curios or souvenirs, or silk or wool for crochet work or knitting, or the most up-to-date novel, or even merely to go skylarking, it would still prove quite worth while landing, and the passengers would feel only too gratified that they ever did go ashore at Colombo.

But a grander and more palatial building indeed will greet the gaze of the passenger a few years hence, when the third wing of the Grand Oriental Hotel is added, and in consequence it blossoms forth in all its completeness into one of the most magnificent hostelries in the whole of the East. Perhaps it will be only meet then that the Victoria Arcade followed suit, and added another storey to its present structure, if only to keep worthy company of its grand sister opposite. Not that I am a lover of skyscrapers. No; but still there is the æsthetic aspect of the city to maintain, and in the present instance I think my remark is not without foundation.

But not only in the Grand Oriental Hotel is Colombo blessed, for, there by the sea, at the southern extremity of the famous promenade that gives it its name, is the equally fine Galle Face Hotel; and to those who may need greater quiet and rest, and would like to hear the roar of the waves and the moaning of the wind, this, indeed, is the ideal spot.

As a matter of fact, Ceylon can boast of a quite good number of hotels second to none in the world; and whether it is the two I have just mentioned, or the Queen's Hotel in Kandy, or the Grand Hotel and Maryhill Hotel at Nuwara Eliya, or the New Oriental Hotel at Galle, or the Mount Lavinia Hotel, to give a few only at random, they are all first rate in every sense. In this respect, therefore, Ceylon scores again, and fortunate indeed is the tourist who can enjoy the beauty of this wonderful land in such ideal conditions.

Yet, funnily, there are those, like my friend Dr. Abdel Rahman Gouda—a veritable Falstaff, and as hearty, bluff, and boisterous—who suppose Colombo and Ceylon all to be one, and hardly as large as Girga,[1] and who, curiously, have no idea what a wonderful and prosperous country Ceylon is, and one replete with all the modern conveniences and amenities of life!

Exit Messrs. "Touts, Tourist-baiters, & Co."

But one must not be too lavish with one's praises, else people might be led into believing that touring in Ceylon is an endless joyride or triumphal show, with the path strewn, as it were, with the roses of comfort and the fragrance and flavour of sweet things. I might as well once more impress upon the authorities concerned the necessity of devoting more attention to the importunities of the touts, the "sharks", the tourist-baiters, and their kindred species who hover and loaf about the jetty, and are such a curse to passengers; as also the tipping nuisance in the hotels. Of course one has to reckon with such annoyances everywhere, and Ceylon, accordingly, is no exception to the general rule all the world over. But still, would it not be to her advantage if she could tackle this problem effectively, or at any rate endeavour to reduce these annoyances to a minimum?

"Island Refuges" in the Streets—a Necessity

Most pluckily as the Ceylon "Bobby" carries out his duties, still this is no reason why he should carry his life

[1] Girga is a small provincial town on the Nile, far to the south of Cairo. Is it that Dr. Gouda, with his Falstaffian jocularity, was inclined to be facetious, or he had already forgotten the geography Mr. H. Swift hammered into him at Khedivieh, but as readily imbibed the medical lore Dr. H. P. Keatinge and his coadjutors poured down his throat?

in his hands. Would it not, therefore, be possible, as I have already pointed out, to erect small kerbed "islands" in the middle of dangerous corners or crossings, or at points where several streets intersect one another, as a safeguard against the perils of heavy traffic? The signposts are a welcome boon; they might prove even more serviceable and appreciable were their bases places of refuge to which the pedestrian who is still not tired of life can betake himself for the moment as a stepping-stone to a further span of life, and perhaps incidentally to happier days to come.

Motoring—How it can be Made more Pleasant

I know the day of the gharry is past, and it is Mr. "Taxi" who will henceforth fill the picture. But then, for Heaven's sake let the fares be more reasonable. The big hotels are to blame in a sense for this state of affairs. What is the use of supplying excellent accommodation and liberal and appetising fare, when they cannot provide you with the means of going about as well in a reasonably cheap and comfortable manner?

Yes, we have the public conveyances; but in the good old days, which the Queen's Hotel still thoughtfully adheres to in a minor degree, the big hotels did provide their clientèle with their own liveried equipages. Why not do the same now in regard to the motor car as well? Above all, why not give their patrons the benefit of their custom and goodwill by a corresponding concession in the shape of reduced fares compared to what obtains in public, instead of offering the cars when so available, at even higher rates than one obtains elsewhere?

If anything, the tourists, at any rate *bona-fide* residents of the hotel, should get them cheaper, and be afforded greater facilities for going about and even moving Up-Country, for, I understand, a certain solidarity exists between the leading hotels of Ceylon, and they are something like affiliated branches of some big hotel trust. It is not every tourist who is a millionaire, or every traveller who feels that he is justified in paying, even with a prolonged stay, treble what the ordinary resident usually does for putting up at the hotel! Is it that every tourist is assumed to be legitimate prey who may be fleeced with impunity, and even dignified and highly reputed hotels, usually so considerate and obliging, must, however, now and then depart from their highly commendable line, and stoop to join in the fray for a share of the spoils?

Poor Mr. "'Rickshaw"!

I am aware that there is a Society for the Prevention of Cruelty to Animals. But alas! there does not seem to be one for human beings! Perhaps it is that, following the reasoning of "a dog never bites a brother dog's ears", human beings are assumed to be loftier, and as a consequence more readily animated by the kindest feelings towards one another.

No, I am not a sentimentalist, but is it not a crying shame that human beings who sweat all day and toil for all they are worth with a rare hardihood in a harsh and cruel world, should do so for a mere pittance that can barely keep body and soul together, when animal-drawn vehicles should get more? If it were only some justification and reason for enabling them to obtain better sustenance, it were still worth while raising the charges of the 'rickshaw coolies a bit.

Indeed, how often had I to get down from one of them on seeing that the frail, emaciated, skeleton of a coolie could barely drag me along, and jump into another of a more robust fellow. I have always paid them double their usual fare out of sheer compassion for them and their degrading and humble work, and though not all of them seemed to be grateful, and would still crave for more just because he knew me for a tourist, still I have deemed it my solemn duty to pen these few remarks about them from a purely humanitarian point of view.

A Tramway between Colombo and Mount Lavinia

I also hope my proposals in connection with the linking up of Mount Lavinia and Colombo on the one hand, and Peradeniya and Kandy on the other, by electric tramways will not fall on deaf ears. I do not know what serious objections there may be for the carrying out of such schemes; but on the face of it, as I have already explained in their respective places, they sound quite feasible, and might even be embarked upon with the certainty of paying in the long run.

Tea—and how it can be "Boosted"

Much ink has already been spilt over the bad tea supplied in Ceylon, that I hardly have the courage to return to a subject that has already been thoroughly threshed out quite sufficiently in the Press.

Of course the black, watery concoction called coffee we drink in Ceylon is none too good—so much so that even Europe with all its vaunted superiority, nevertheless realises that in this one respect it has still to bow to the East, to such a degree indeed, that some of the biggest hotels have even gone to the length of engaging special Egyptians or Nubians for the sole task of brewing the coffee in the right, orthodox way, and vauntingly supplying it to their patrons. Not that the quality of the coffee in Ceylon is bad—and there are some who still remember the days when King Coffee held sway in the Island. No; but, as in Europe, the coffee suffers here from the same drawback of not being made properly, and Ceylon being a smaller and poorer country than the majority which form the great European Continent, it will not pay to engage a special *kahwagi* say, for £10 or £15 *per mensem.*

But this, of course, cannot hold good for the land where King Tea now rules supreme, nor can Ceylon on any pretext whatever find the shade of an excuse in extenuation of its failing in this direction. There are shops which specialise in a certain class of goods, and which in due course acquire a widespread reputation as the one place where the best can be obtained. Would it, therefore, not be possible for some enterprising shop or tea-room to blossom forth as *the* place where they do specialise in supplying a really good specimen of the cup that cheers?

I am sure such a concern will pay in the end, for once it acquires a reputation for the object with which it was started and is being run, such fame must in due course spread, and ere long those wishing for a really good cup of tea will be only too glad to find that they can be rewarded with it at this place. And if the manager can have the enterprise and taste to add all the other little niceties, say, delicious cakes, an orchestra if possible, good catering and service by a band of handy, clever, and polite waiters, and so on, all nicely set amidst ideal surroundings, why, his fortune is as sure as made. But, of course, all this must never make him lose sight of the *main object* of the *really good cup of tea*. This should be his *forte*.

Of course this is but one suggestion for the town in general; but though a hotel is certainly not run for the sole object and purpose of supplying tea—if anything, it might, as a matter of fact, be the least important of its many functions—still, there is nothing to lose by giving instructions for the tea to be better made, and then supplied, not with tinned or condensed milk, but with real, fresh cow's milk.

And speaking of tea, may I make one suggestion in the light of personal experience? Perhaps it is not everyone who has taken note of the fact that it is generally the first cup of tea that is usually more delicious than the others! Whatever may be assigned for the cause of this, still, the fact remains, that I have invariably enjoyed my first cup of tea more than I have the others; and, as if to make doubly sure of enjoying it even more, and a bigger quantity into the bargain, whenever I drink my tea at home I do so in an unusually big cup, about double the size of an ordinary one, and whatever people may say of other beverages, to me at any rate, when the tea is of such an excellent brand as that of " Scrubs ", and well brewed, and in my big cup, it is *the* drink of the gods. Of course, it may be rather difficult to adopt this course in public tea rooms, but let my readers essay this suggestion of a big cup of tea in their homes, and I am almost pretty sure they will be only too grateful that I ever proposed it to them.

The Inhabitants of Ceylon

Ceylon, unlike Egypt, does not seem to have one homogeneous people in the sense we come across in my country, or in England, nor does it enjoy one national tongue. Numerically preponderant as are the Sinhalese, yet it is the least populous community of the Island which is the most powerful and influential, namely the British. And closely wedged in between these two come the Tamils, the Moors and the Burghers, in their order of numbers.

It is not for me to go deeply into the ethnological history and characteristics of each, nor can I lay claim to any ability to deal with such a subject fairly well. Nevertheless, in the short time I spent in Ceylon I did observe certain distinctions between each. I may not be right in what I think; still however, so they appeared to me at the time at any rate.

The British

In the official world, supreme as the British rule there, especially in the higher venues of the public service, still, quite as cleverly and shrewdly have they not failed to benefit by the other openings awaiting talent and enterprise. Thus, what Englishman who has left his home to seek his fortune abroad, does not feel overjoyed to be

[Photo by Benghiat, Aden

STEAMER POINT, ADEN

Facing page 336]

[Photo by the Author

A Camel Drawing a Cart in Aden

Facing page 337]

installed as the superintendent of some flourishing estate? If anything, I am sure there is many a young Britisher who would by far prefer the free, open, unrestricted life of his domains to being a "big wig" of the Civil Service, or even the head of some department, and be thus saddled with all the worries and responsibilities appertaining to such a post, even though the emoluments and the so-called glitter and tinsel, and pomp and circumstance of such a high position may prove very alluring. There in his estate the planter roams and rules at will, as if he were a feudal lord in his ancestral fief, and the coolies his vassals. And to him in such a situation, more than to anyone else perhaps, might the well-known words of Alexander Selkirk apply quite aptly:

> "I am monarch of all I survey;
> My right there is none to dispute."

And to this sphere has England sent some of her bluest blood, and as loyally have they maintained the noblest traditions of Old England.

Again, the big emporiums and banks and business houses the British have, for the most part, monopolised; but to such a position they have attained to in the fair and open field of competition, to which all comers were welcome. If others have lagged behind, they alone are to blame. However, it seems that the Ceylonese are now awaking to the possibilities of flourishing business in this field, and are thus slowly nibbling at what once seemed to be the exclusive preserves of the European.

The Moors

But of all the indigenous inhabitants of Ceylon it is the Moor who shines most in this sphere. Imbued with a keen and rare acumen for business, he has never been slow to benefit by any openings of trade; and his very daring, his enterprise, and his pushfulness have helped him splendidly along! Such big establishments as those of Messrs. Macan Markar, or Abdul Caffoor, or Naina Marikar, or Cassie Lebbé (Kandy) might well testify to the prosperity of their community. But how many other shops are there scattered all over the Island which, if less pretentious, as a matter of fact, can, nevertheless, speak of wealthy merchants and prosperous tradesmen who are none the less unostentatiously accumulating money and pushing on business, though it be in the backwaters of this great city of Colombo, or in other parts of the country! Indeed, it did impress me no little during my motor trip across Ceylon to notice that even in the remotest and the most out-of-the-way villages, far from the beaten track, there, as sure as ever, was the local Tamby, and his very ubiquitousness reminded me most strikingly of the equally enterprising, and pushful Greek of my own country.

The Sinhalese

To all the five races I mentioned at the beginning of this theme though Ceylon may belong in more senses than one, still it is to the Sinhalese more essentially their home than to anybody else. Yet curiously and unfortunately the present generation of the Sinhalese do not seem to be doing much, in proportion to their preponderant numbers and the immense interests they have at stake, for the welfare of the Island. Not that they have failed to add their own share for the present developed and prosperous state of Ceylon, but owing to their special position they might have done better!

With such a grand past behind them, and traditions worthy of a great race, it is only natural that the more thinking, refined, and educated Sinhalese should aspire to revive their former grandeur. But one swallow will no more make a summer than a few of the leading families, inspired by the noblest sentiments, raise her even higher.

Must I reiterate that platitude that has so often been repeated that development and progress must come from the bottom, from the very root? Quite worthy citizens as these leading families are, and calling for the highest esteem and respect, why do they not extend more frequently to their less fortunate brethren the helping arm, the guiding hand; why not strive to permeate them more extensively, even in some slight degree to start with, with the benefits they have already tasted of and reaped? If they are misguided, lead them into the right path; if they are lazy, as so many of them are, spur them on to profitable work, and to prosperity perchance. This is the age of keen competition, and it is the most thrifty, the most industrious, and the most enterprising who generally succeed in the long run.

If to the cultured and resourceful Britisher, the ever helpful and painstaking Burgher, the businesslike and enterprising Moor, and the hardy and industrious Tamil, we can bring the full weight of the clever and intelligent Sinhalese to bear, why, there would be less idle fields, less deserted countrysides, less stagnant trade, and the spectre of hunger would be more of a chimera than a grim reality.

A fine race are the Sinhalese: quite clean in their habits, quite comely in their appearance and their attire, and quite hospitable and warmhearted to the stranger. It is not that this indolence, this apathy towards greater and more sustained effort for a correspondingly greater return, when they seem satisfied with a small profit with the minimum of effort, is irretrievably ingrained in them. No, certainly not. In whatever sphere of activity they have earnestly and keenly embarked upon they have splendidly acquitted themselves. It only calls for the better application of their talents, wiser and sounder guidance, and a more paternal solicitude on the part of their betters to bring out these latent good points.

Even now do they realise that their future lies on the land. If to this they can put their shoulder, as in arts and crafts they have so brilliantly excelled, why, a brighter and more auspicious day will ere long dawn on this fair land.

The Tamils

If anything, the Sinhalese might take their cue from their hardy and industrious brethren, the Tamils; and Ceylon indeed can never be too grateful for the invaluable part this community plays in the development of the Island in all spheres of activity, but notably in agriculture. To them I raise my cap, and may they ever set a splendid example of the dignity of labour, which others might do well to emulate.

The Burghers

There is another community who, notwithstanding the handicap of numbers, are none the less most gallantly carrying on. Descendants of the old Dutch settlers as a good number of the " Burghers " are, divested though they be of the privileges of a governing class, as also of the ancestral domains which many of the Sinhalese have the advantage of possessing, still, in all walks of life, notably in the liberal professions, have they made their mark; and it is as the nucleus of a powerful and influential higher middle class they have figured for the most part.

Closely wedged in on all sides, still most pluckily they have made their stand; and it is all the more creditable that amidst all such powerful and crushing influences they have been able to hold their own proudly and with dignity, so as to make their voice heard and their influence felt in the destinies of this land.

In the East the Governor's "Lot is not a Happy One" To-day.

And with such a diversity of races and tongues, and conflicting influences, what a stupendous task lies before

[Photo by Benghiat, Aden

THE FAMOUS TANKS OF ADEN

Facing page 340]

[Photo by the Author

THE ENTRANCE TO THE SUEZ CANAL—FROM THE RED SEA

Facing page 341]

the Governor. No wonder that he finds his job none too easy, especially in these days when the world is in a more unsettled state than ever.

Indeed, I wonder whether even such an important personage does not sometimes feel inclined to concur with the less important dignitary, the policeman, and say, with some modification, " In the East a Governor's lot is not a happy one! " Indeed, his position is often a very delicate one, and it calls for the exercise of the greatest skill and shrewdness, as for no little tact. In this connection how neatly does a writer of a book on India aptly paint some such picture:

" If a Viceroy or a Commander-in-Chief, for example, regrets that there has been a number of cases of assault upon natives, sometimes with fatal results, and suggests that coolies should be treated more kindly in future, the resident sahibs immediately suspect him of leanings towards the extravagant ideas of the National Congress, and he becomes unpopular with them. On the other hand, if a Viceroy lectures a lot of native schoolboys on the advantages of truthfulness, the natives read into his observations a lack of sympathy with their aspirations, and the Viceroy ceases to be popular with the natives. Perhaps the most popular Viceroy would be a good-natured figure-head content to draw his pay and leave things alone."[1]

Some Additional Attractions of Ceylon

I fear this chapter has far outgrown the few impressions with which I started writing it. Besides, I am afraid some of my readers may even deem me to have been at times too critical and even captious, though Heaven knows how sincerely I have been inspired with the best of intentions. Approaching my subject as I have done with a quite open and unprejudiced mind, it is with an equally clear conscience I now conclude it.

[1] *India of To-day*, Walter Del Mar, p. 5.

I started singing the praises of this beautiful land and it is only meet that I should close my few remarks in as laudatory terms—not that they are unjustified, but one sometimes leaves the tit-bit for the end.

Ceylon—a Favourite Haunt of the Big Game Hunter

To the attractions I have already mentioned there are still others which can prove just as welcome. Thus, the ardent hunter of the wilds can also have his needs catered for; and if there are other lands which can claim their own votaries of the chase, still very few are the regions, as here in Ceylon, which are so easily accessible, thanks to the splendid roads and chain of good resthouses; or furnish such a diversity of big game, from the mighty elephant or the ferocious leopard to the tusked boar and antlered stag, to sate the greediest appetite; or where the pursuit of the chase could be undertaken and enjoyed under such ideal conditions and surroundings.

Ceylon—an Arcadia for the Motorist

Or the fairyland that awaits the motorist, why, here is an Arcadia, a veritable paradise of sylvan beauty for him. Rarely can we come across finer roads than those we meet here in Ceylon, and to motor along the smooth, dustless, and magnificent highways and byways of this wonderful land, and through such bewitching scenery, is a veritable joyride, the quintessence of rural travel.

Sweet Ceylon: Land of Eternal Charm

But if to all these attractions we can add the one supreme point of her incomparable beauty, in which Ceylon stands unrivalled, the one unique factor of her surpassing loveliness in which she towers head and shoulders above the rest of the world, why, it were still enough to attract the traveller from the farthest corners of the world to this Eastern paradise.

Go wherever a person can, or ask those who have been right across the world, and as often as ever will all unanimously and unreservedly award the verdict to " The Eden of the Eastern Wave " without a moment's hesitation in regard to the exquisite beauty and infinite charm of her wonderful and incomparable scenery.

Says Sir Everard im Thurm, when Lieutenant Governor of Ceylon: " To me there is no place in the world so greatly endowed as Kandy. I have been in a good many parts of the world, and have seen many beautiful places, and I can honestly say I have never seen another place the natural beauty of which appeals to me like that of Kandy."

Or, again, has not Sir William Gregory—one of the greatest and most popular Governors of Ceylon—said that Kandy was " The loveliest town in the loveliest island of the world"? I could, indeed, quote chapter and verse, so to say, in corroboration of my assertion, but for the moment the testimony of these two will suffice; besides, there are many others better qualified for such a task and more justifiably entitled than myself.

If, indeed, as tradition says, the Almighty chose this wondrous isle for our first parents, as the best substitute and nearest approach to the Garden of Eden, from which they were driven out, how justly, therefore, it can rightfully revel in its claim to be the most beautiful country in the world! Of all the amenities and comforts of life, of most of the other attractions may other lands possess, and even excel in in some cases; but in the one outstanding feature of its natural beauty Ceylon stands unique, unchallenged by the rest of the world, though many would perhaps run it close.

And yet how few, too few alas! compared to the many who go elsewhere, do ever take the trouble to come this way! Let them but once give Ceylon the benefit of their experience, and I am sure they will be only too glad to repeat the visit. A picturesque country, with a fine and equable climate, wonderful scenery, and a generous and warm-hearted people, Ceylon certainly deserves better at the hands of the tourist.

But it is to her own people that she must look to bring home to the door of such tourist the unheard of wonders, the manifold attractions of such a land, and as sedulously evoke in him a craving, a corresponding eagerness to answer with alacrity the call of the East.

Some of Ceylon's Beauty Spots

How often does one customarily hear the traveller's query as to which are Ceylon's best sights worth visiting. Happily, in the present instance, *The Ceylon Observer* has come to my rescue.[1] I might, therefore, give its own version, which, needless to say, is the version of one on the spot, one experienced in and well conversant with the affairs and conditions and sights of the Island, and thus all the more entitled to command the respect due to an authority on the subject.

" What is Ceylon's best view? It is not such a simple question after all, for tastes in views are more catholic than tastes in religion, and they are diverse enough in all conscience. The question arose in this way. An Australian came into the office of this paper and, announcing that he was breaking his journey until the arrival of the next boat, asked which were the six best and representative views of Ceylon scenery. With limited time at his disposal he wanted to get as good a grip as possible in the shortest possible time.

" The first view that suggests itself is, of course, Adam's Peak, but its disadvantage is that it entails a long climb in the early hours of the morning in order to see the main effect of the rising sun casting the shadow of the peak below. It is an undertaking for enthusiasts

[1] The *Ceylon Observer*, March 5th, 1921.

just as is the sunrise seen from Pedro. The result is worth the trouble, but we live in an age which is not too fond of walking. The modern idea of touring a country is to secure a comfortable car, halt for a while when the correct spot is reached, Kodak it, and carry on.

" Adopting that method of progression, Adam's Peak can be seen very effectively; then there is also the famous view of the low country jungles seen from the top of Haputale Pass with its almost sheer drop to the plains, reminiscent of the famous views in the Nilgheries. The picture from Ella Resthouse on a clear day is one that will ever linger in the memories of the spectator. Creature comforts can here be obtained, and photography is simple from the verandah table. Ambawella likewise has its votaries, while the World's End is also a sight worth seeing. The passes of Ceylon provide exceptional examples of scenery. From the Ginegathena Pass there is a splendid view of a gorge between two rows of hills, the slopes covered with tea shrubs ending in the bright green terraces of paddy in the foothills. Rambodda has a fascination of its own; while from the Hakgalla Pass the rolling patnas of Uva are spread before one's eyes.

" These are but a few of the better known beauty spots of Ceylon, and it would be interesting to hear general opinions on what in the estimation of our readers are the six best views of either hill or low country scenery. Ceylon offers a wonderful diversity in this respect, and he would be a bold man who would say that the picture from Hakgalla, or that from Ambawella was in any way superior to that presented from the barracks overlooking Trincomalee harbour."

Hark! Ceylonese! the World's Wonderland's A-callin'!

But, one word more, please. Why, above all, why indeed, do none of the Ceylonese in their turn ever visit my own enchanting country? If anything, it is easier for them to do so, than it is for an Egyptian to go farther Eastwards, lying as Egypt does, on their track to and from Europe.

Is it sheer apathy, or thoughtlessness, or is it that they are dazzled by the glare of mighty Europe, and that Egypt hath no wonders, no beauty, no glamour of her own? When Americans and Canadians from the Far West will flock to old, hoary Egypt, when even mighty Europe, notwithstanding its much vaunted civilisation of to-day, will yet send its thousands to see the wonders of this wonderland of Egypt, is it not meet that the Ceylonese who actually pass right through the Land of the Pharaohs, should, in their own turn, come and see for themselves the glories and the marvels which attract so many towards it from far and near?

Or, are we to assume that they do not know Egypt as the cradle of the world's civilisation, nor have heard of her mighty ruins and monuments, second to none in the world, dating back to 7,500 years, or of her wonderful climate, or her innumerable other attractions?

Come, Ceylonese, come in all your hundreds, all your thousands, and you will find a race as generous and as warm-hearted as you will find a land as picturesque and as fascinating as your own. The refugee's home has Egypt been, as she has been even the penniless alien's dumping-ground. How much more gladly, therefore, would she welcome the stranger who comes to drink of her beauty and her lore, for, "Freedom at home, hospitality towards all," this is her sacred motto.

CHAPTER XXXIX

AU REVOIR

AND now my task is done. Here have I had my say, as in ancient Lanka my holiday; but it has been *the* holiday of my life. What I have said has flowed forth as the outpourings of an appreciative mind, the thankfulness of a grateful heart. Most thoroughly as I have enjoyed my time, as glad I have been likewise to have visited the haunts of my happy childhood.

To you, once more, ladies and gentlemen of Ceylon, I reiterate my lasting gratitude, and may the Almighty for ever bless your most beautiful Ceylon, as He my loved Egypt.

Farewell! Of God I ask that I may yet live to see your lovely Island once again, and meet you all as hale and hearty as ever; but would to the Almighty that this happy day dawn soon.

FINIS

[Photo by the Author

IN THE SUEZ CANAL—SOON AFTER ENTERING IT FROM THE RED SEA

Facing page 348]

[*By courtesy of The Colombo Hotels Co., Ltd.*

THE GRAND ORIENTAL HOTEL, COLOMBO—AS IT WILL LOOK WHEN ENTIRELY FINISHED

Facing page 349]

INDEX